# Sunset

## BEST HOME PLANS

# Indoor/ Outdoor Living

Open views and easy outdoor access are a result of this informal country home's generous front porch and back deck. See plan C-8645 on page 136.

**Sunset Publishing Corporation** ■ **Menlo Park, California**

**Photographers: Mark Englund/ HomeStyles:** 4, 5; **Philip Harvey:** 10 top, back cover; **Stephen Marley:** 11 top left and right; **Russ Widstrand:** 10 bottom; **Tom Wyatt:** 11 bottom.

**Cover:** Pictured is plan NW-464 on page 219. Cover design by Naganuma Design & Direction. Photography by Mark Englund/ HomeStyles.

Editor, Sunset Books: Elizabeth L. Hogan

First printing September 1993

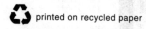 printed on recycled paper

# A Dream Come True

Planning and building a house is one of life's most creative and rewarding challenges. Whether you're seriously considering building a new home or you're just dreaming about it, this book offers a wealth of inspiration and information to help you get started.

On the following pages, you'll learn how to plan and manage a home-building project—and how to ensure its success. Then you'll discover more than 200 proven home plans, designed for families just like yours by architects and professional designers. Peruse the pages and study the floor plans; you're sure to find a home that's just right for you. When you're ready to order blueprints, you can simply call or mail in your order, and you'll receive the plans within days.

Enjoy the adventure!

Covered front porch creates a strong connection between this colonial-style home and its front garden. Large windows with fanlights open the rooms to light and views. See plan AHP-9020 on page 133.

# Contents

# Houses for Indoor/Outdoor Living

Looking for a home that allows you easy access to an inviting garden or pool area or one that takes advantage of a beautiful view? If so, you're sure to appreciate the home plans presented here. These proven designs, created by some of America's foremost architects and designers, pay special attention to the out-of-doors. Generous patios, porches, and decks provide natural transitions between interior and exterior spaces. Expanses of glass in windows, doors, and skylights welcome the sun's warmth and light and frame the view. Some of these houses work hand-in-hand with the sun for energy efficiency.

You'll discover a wide variety of styles, from traditional classics to striking contemporaries, and from country charmers to affordable starters.

The two keys to success in building are capable project management and good design. The next few pages will walk you through some of the most important aspects of project management: you'll find an overview of the building process, directions for selecting the right plan and getting the most from it, and methods for successfully working with a builder and other professionals.

The balance of the book presents professionally designed stock plans. Once you find a plan that will work for you—perhaps with a few modifications made later to personalize it for your family—you can order construction blueprints for a fraction of the cost of a custom design, a savings of many thousands of dollars (see pages 12–15 for information on how to order).

Covered patio with a summer kitchen lies just outside this elegant home's luxurious master bedroom and living room. A curved glass wall that overlooks the backyard brightens the breakfast area. See plan HDS-99-178 on page 185.

Roofed patio with a skylight offers year-round outdoor living just off the kitchen and family room. Behind a bay of glass, the dramatic living room features a sunken floor and vaulted ceiling. See plan CDG-4001 on page 123.

With its covered front porch and generous windows, this handsome tri-level home reaches out to the front yard. At the rear, the family room opens to a patio through sliding glass doors. See plan NW-450 on page 103.

Sunny deck welcomes the outdoors into this home's spacious family room, enhanced by a cathedral ceiling and large picture window. The bedrooms are separated from the living spaces by a vaulted entry. See plans P-7758-2A and -2D on page 54.

# The Art of Building

As you embark on your home-building project, think of it as a trip—clearly not a vacation but rather an interesting, adventurous, at times difficult expedition. Meticulous planning will make your journey not only far more enjoyable but also much more successful. By careful planning, you can avoid—or at least minimize—some of the pitfalls along the way.

Start with realistic expectations of the road ahead. To do this, you'll want to gain an understanding of the basic house-building process, settle on a design that will work for you and your family, and make sure your project is actually doable. By taking those initial steps, you can gain a clear idea of how much time, money, and energy you'll need to invest to make your dream come true.

## The Building Process

Your role in planning and managing a house-building project can be divided into two parts: prebuilding preparation and construction management.

■ **Prebuilding preparation.** This is where you should focus most of your attention. In the hands of a qualified contractor whose expertise you can rely on, the actual building process should go fairly smoothly. But during most of the prebuilding stage, you're generally on your own. Your job will be to launch the project and develop a talented team that can help you bring your new home to fruition.

When you work with stock plans, the prebuilding process usually goes as follows:

First, you research the general area where you want to live, selecting one or more possible home sites (unless you already own a suitable lot). Then you choose a basic house design, with the idea that it may require some modification. Finally, you analyze the site, the design, and your budget to determine if the project is actually attainable.

If you decide that it is, you purchase the land and order blue-prints. If you want to modify them, you consult an architect, designer, or contractor. Once the plans are finalized, you request bids from contractors and arrange any necessary construction financing.

After selecting a builder and signing a contract, you (or your contractor) then file the plans with the building department. When the plans are approved, often several weeks—or even months—later, you're ready to begin construction.

■ **Construction management.** Unless you intend to act as your own contractor, your role during the building process is mostly one of quality control and time management. Even so, it's important to know the sequence of events and something about construction methods so you can discuss progress with your builder and prepare for any important decisions you may need to make along the way.

Decision-making is critical. Once construction begins, the builder must usually plunge ahead, keeping his carpenters and subcontractors progressing steadily. If you haven't made a key decision—which model bathtub or sink to install, for example—it can bring construction to a frustrating and expensive halt.

Usually, you'll make such decisions before the onset of building, but, inevitably, some issue or another will arise during construction. Being knowledgeable about the building process will help you anticipate and circumvent potential logjams.

## Selecting a House Plan

Searching for the right plan can be a fun, interactive family experience—one of the most exciting parts of a house-building project. Gather the family around as you peruse the home plans in this book. Study the size, location, and configuration of each room; traffic patterns both inside the house and to the outdoors; exterior style; and how you'll use the available space. Discuss the pros and cons of the various plans.

Browse through pictures of homes in magazines to stimulate ideas. Clip the photos you like so you can think about your favorite options. When you visit the homes of friends, note special features that appeal to you. Also, look carefully at the homes in your neighborhood, noting their style and how they fit the site.

Mark those plans that most closely suit your ideals. Then, to narrow down your choices, critique each plan, using the following information as a guide.

■ **Overall size and budget.** How large a house do you want? Will the house you're considering fit your family's requirements? Look at the overall square footage and room sizes. If you have a hard time visualizing room sizes, measure some of the rooms in your present home and compare.

It's often better for the house to be a little too big than a little too small, but remember that every extra square foot will cost more money to build and maintain.

■ **Number and type of rooms.** Beyond thinking about the number of bedrooms and baths you want, consider your family's life-style and how you use space. Do you want both a family room and a living room? Do you need a formal dining space? Will you require some extra rooms, or "swing spaces," that can serve multiple purposes, such as a home office–guest room combination?

■ **Room placement and traffic patterns.** What are your preferences for locations of formal living areas, master bedroom, and children's rooms? Do you prefer a kitchen that's open to family areas or one that's private and out of the way? How much do you use exterior spaces and how should they relate to the interior?

Once you make those determinations, look carefully at the floor plan of the house you're considering to see if it meets your needs and if the traffic flow will be convenient for your family.

■ **Architectural style.** Have you always wanted to live in a Victorian farmhouse? Now is your chance to create a house that matches your idea of "home" (taking into account, of course, styles in your neighborhood). But don't let your preference for one particular architectural style dictate your home's floor plan. If the floor plan doesn't work for your family, keep looking.

■ **Site considerations.** Most people choose a site before selecting a plan—or at least they've zeroed in on the basic type of land where they'll situate their house. It sounds elementary, but choose a house that will fit the site.

When figuring the "footprint" of a house, you must know about any restrictions that will affect your home's height or proximity to the property lines. Call the local building department (look under city or county listings in the phone book) and get a very clear description of any restrictions, such as setbacks, height limits, and lot coverage, that will affect what you can build on the site (see "Working with City Hall," at right).

When you visit potential sites, note trees, rock outcroppings, slopes, views, winds, sun, neighboring homes, and other factors. All will impact on how your house works on a particular site.

Once you've narrowed down the choice of sites, consult an architect or building designer (see page 8) to help you evaluate how some potential houses will work on the sites you have in mind.

### Is Your Project Doable?

Before you purchase land, make sure your project is doable. Although it's too early at this stage to pinpoint costs, making a few phone calls will help you determine whether your project is realistic. You'll be able to learn if you can afford to build the house, how long it will take, and what obstacles may stand in your way.

To get a ballpark estimate of cost, multiply a house's total square footage (of livable space) by the local average cost per square foot for new construction. (To obtain local averages, call a contractor, an architect, a realtor, or the local chapter of the National Association of Home Builders.) Some contractors may even be willing to give you a preliminary bid. Once you know approximate costs, speak to your lender to explore financing.

## Working with City Hall

For any building project, even a minor one, it's essential to be familiar with building codes and other restrictions that can affect your project.

■ **Building codes,** generally implemented by the city or county building department, set the standards for safe, lasting construction. Codes specify minimum construction techniques and materials for foundations, framing, electrical wiring, plumbing, insulation, and all other aspects of a building. Although codes are adopted and enforced locally, most regional codes conform to the standards set by the national Uniform Building Code, Standard Building Code, or Basic Building Code. In some cases, local codes set more restrictive standards than national ones.

■ **Building permits** are required for home-building projects nearly everywhere. If you work with a contractor, the builder's firm should handle all necessary permits.

More than one permit may be needed; for example, one will cover the foundation, another the electrical wiring, and still another the heating equipment installation. Each will probably involve a fee and require inspections by building officials before work can proceed. (Inspections benefit *you*, as they ensure that the job is being done satisfactorily.) Permit fees are generally a percentage (1 to 1.5 percent) of the project's estimated value, often calculated on square footage.

It's important to file for the necessary permits. Failure to do so can result in fines or legal action against you. You can even be forced to undo the work performed. At the very least, your negligence may come back to haunt you later when you're ready to sell your house.

■ **Zoning ordinances,** particular to your community, restrict setbacks (how near to property lines you may build), your house's allowable height, lot coverage factors (how much of your property you can cover with structures), and other factors that impact design and building. If your plans don't conform to zoning ordinances, you can try to obtain a variance, an exception to the rules. But this legal work can be expensive and time-consuming. Even if you prove that your project won't negatively affect your neighbors, the building department can still refuse to grant the variance.

■ **Deeds and covenants** attach to the lot. Deeds set out property lines and easements; covenants may establish architectural standards in a neighborhood. Since both can seriously impact your project, make sure you have complete information on any deeds or covenants before you turn over a spadeful of soil.

It's a good idea to discuss your project with several contractors (see page 8). They may be aware of problems in your area that could limit your options—bedrock that makes digging basements difficult, for example. These conversations are actually the first step in developing a list of contractors from which you'll choose the one who will build your home.

# Recruiting Your Home Team

A home-building project will interject you and your family into the building business, an area that may be unfamiliar territory. Among the people you'll be working with are architects, designers, landscapers, contractors, and subcontractors.

## Design Help

A qualified architect or designer can help you modify and personalize your home plan, taking into account your family's needs and budget and the house's style. In fact, you may want to consider consulting such a person while you're selecting a plan to help you articulate your needs.

Design professionals are capable of handling any or all aspects of the design process. For example, they can review your house plans, suggest options, and then provide rough sketches of the options on tracing paper. Many architects will even secure needed permits and negotiate with contractors or subcontractors, as well as oversee the quality of the work.

Of course, you don't necessarily need an architect or designer to implement minor changes in a plan; although most contractors aren't trained in design, some can help you with modifications.

An open-ended, hourly-fee arrangement that you work out with your architect or designer allows for flexibility, but it often turns out to be more costly than working on a flat-fee basis. On a flat fee, you agree to pay a specific amount of money for a certain amount of work.

To find architects and designers, contact such trade associations as the American Institute of Architects (AIA), American Institute of Building Designers (AIBD), American Society of Landscape Architects (ASLA), and American Society of Interior Designers (ASID). Although many professionals choose not to belong to trade associations, those who do have met the standards of their respective associations. For phone numbers of local branches, check the Yellow Pages.

■ **Architects** are licensed by the state and have degrees. They're trained in all facets of building design and construction. Although some can handle interior design and structural engineering, others hire specialists for those tasks.

■ **Building designers** are generally unlicensed but may be accredited by the American Institute of Building Designers. Their backgrounds are varied: some may be unlicensed architects in apprenticeship; others are interior designers or contractors with design skills.

■ **Draftspersons** offer an economical route to making simple changes on your drawings. Like building designers, these people may be unlicensed architect apprentices, engineers, or members of related trades. Most are accomplished at drawing up plans.

■ **Interior designers,** as their job title suggests, design interiors. They work with you to choose room finishes, furnishings, appliances, and decorative elements. Part of their expertise is in arranging furnishings to create a workable space plan. Some interior designers are employed by architectural firms; others work independently. Financial arrangements vary, depending on the designer's preference.

Related professionals are kitchen and bathroom designers, who concentrate on fixtures, cabinetry, appliances, materials, and space planning for the kitchen and bath.

■ **Landscape architects, designers, and contractors** design outdoor areas. Landscape architects are state-licensed to practice landscape design. A landscape designer usually has a landscape architect's education and training but does not have a state license. Licensed landscape contractors specialize in garden construction, though some also have design skills and experience.

■ **Soils specialists and structural engineers** may be needed for projects where unstable soils or uncommon wind loads or seismic forces must be taken into account. Any

structural changes to a house require the expertise of a structural engineer to verify that the house won't fall down.

Services of these specialists can be expensive, but they're imperative in certain conditions to ensure a safe, sturdy structure. Your building department will probably let you know if their services are required.

## General Contractors

To build your house, hire a licensed general contractor. Most states require a contractor to be licensed and insured for worker's compensation in order to contract a building project and hire other subcontractors. State licensing ensures that contractors have met minimum training standards and have a specified level of experience. Licensing does not guarantee, however, that they're good at what they do.

When contractors hire subcontractors, they're responsible for overseeing the quality of work and materials of the subcontractors and for paying them.

■ **Finding a contractor.** How do you find a good contractor? Start by getting referrals from people you know who have built or remodeled their home. Nothing beats a personal recommendation. The best contractors are usually busily moving from one satisfied client to another prospect, advertised only by word of mouth.

You can also ask local real estate brokers and lenders or even your building inspector for names of qualified builders. Experienced lumber dealers are another good source of names.

In the Yellow Pages, look under "Contractors–Building, General"; or call the local chapter of the National Association of Home Builders.

■ **Choosing a contractor.** Once you have a list of names of prospective builders, call several of them. On the telephone, ask first whether they handle your type of job and can work within your schedule. If they can, arrange a meeting with each one and ask them to be prepared with references of former clients and photos of previous jobs. Better still, meet them at one of their current work sites so you can get a glimpse of the quality of their work and how organized and thorough they are.

Take your plan to the meeting and discuss it enough to request a rough estimate (some builders will comply, while others will be reluctant to offer a ballpark estimate, preferring to give you a hard bid based on complete drawings). Don't hesitate to probe for advice or suggestions that might make building your house less expensive.

Be especially aware of each contractor's personality and how well you communicate. Good chemistry between you and your builder is a key ingredient for success.

Narrow down the candidates to three or four. Ask each for a firm bid, based on the exact same set of plans and specifications. For the bids to be accurate, your plans need to be complete and the specifications as precise as possible, calling out particular appliances, fixtures, floorings, roofing material, and so forth. (Some of these are specified in a stock-plan set; others are not.)

Call the contractors' references and ask about the quality of their work, their relationship with their clients, their promptness, and their readiness to follow up on problems. Visit former clients to check the contractor's work firsthand.

Be sure your final candidates are licensed, bonded, and insured for worker's compensation, public liability, and property damage. Also, try to determine how financially solvent they are (you can call their bank and credit references). Avoid contractors who are operating hand-to-mouth.

Don't automatically hire the contractor with the lowest bid if you don't think you'll get along well or if you have any doubts about the quality of the person's work. Instead, look for both the most reasonable bid and the contractor with the best credentials, references, terms, and compatibility with your family.

A word about bonds: You can request a performance bond that guarantees that your job will be finished by your contractor. If the job isn't completed, the bonding company will cover the cost of hiring another contractor to finish it. Bonds cost from 2 to 6 percent of the value of the project.

## Your Building Contract

A building contract (see below) binds and protects both you and your contractor. It isn't just a legal document. It's also a list of the expectations of both parties. The best way to minimize the possibility of misunderstandings and costly changes later on is to write down every possible detail. Whether the contract is a standard form or one composed by you, have an attorney look it over before both you and the contractor sign it.

The contract should clearly specify all the work that needs to be done, including particular materials and work descriptions, the time schedule, and method of payment. It should be keyed to the working drawings.

## A Sample Building Contract

**Project and participants.** Give a general description of the project, its address, and the names and addresses of both you and the builder.

**Construction materials.** Identify all construction materials by brand name, quality markings (species, grades, etc.), and model numbers where applicable. Avoid the clause "or equal," which allows the builder to substitute other materials for your choices. For materials you can't specify now, set down a budget figure.

**Time schedule.** Include both start and completion dates and specify that work will be "continuous." Although a contractor cannot be responsible for delays caused by strikes and material shortages, your builder should assume responsibility for completing the project within a reasonable period of time.

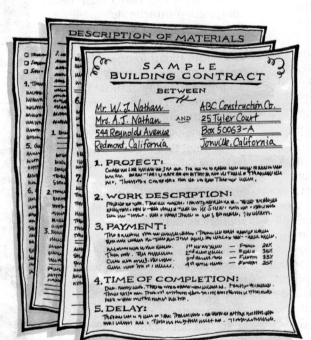

**Work to be performed.** State all work you expect the contractor to perform, from initial grading to finished painting.

**Method and schedule of payment.** Specify how and when payments are to be made. Typical agreements specify installment payments as particular phases of work are completed. Final payment is withheld until the job receives its final inspection and is cleared of all liens.

**Waiver of liens.** Protect yourself with a waiver of liens signed by the general contractor, the subcontractors, and all major suppliers. That way, subcontractors who are not paid for materials or services cannot place a lien on your property.

# Personalizing Stock Plans

The beauty of buying stock plans for your new home is that they offer tested, well-conceived design at an affordable price. And stock plans dramatically reduce the time it takes to design a house, since the plans are ready when you are.

Because they were not created specifically for your family, stock plans may not reflect your personal taste. But it's not difficult to make revisions in stock plans that will turn your home into an expression of your family's personality. You'll surely want to add personal touches and choose your own finishes.

Ideally, the modifications you implement will be fairly minor. The more extensive the changes, the more expensive the plans. Major changes take valuable design time, and those that affect a house's structure may require a structural engineer's approval.

If you anticipate wholesale changes, such as moving a number of bearing walls or changing the roofline significantly, you may be better off selecting another plan. On the other hand, reconfiguring or changing the sizes of some rooms can probably be handled fairly easily.

Some structural changes may even be necessary to comply with local codes. Your area may have specific requirements for snow loads, energy codes, seismic or wind resistance, and so forth. Those types of modifications are likely to require the services of an architect or structural engineer.

## Plan Modifications

Before you pencil in any changes, live with your plans for a while. Study them carefully—at your building site, if possible. Try to picture the finished house: how rooms will interrelate, where the sun will enter and at what angle, what the view will be from each window. Think about traffic patterns, access to rooms, room sizes, window and door locations, natural light, and kitchen and bathroom layouts.

Typical changes might involve adding windows or skylights to bring in natural light or capture a view. Or you may want to widen a hallway or doorway for roomier access, extend a room, eliminate doors, or change window and door sizes. Perhaps you'd like to shorten a room, stealing the gained space for a large closet. Look closely at the kitchen; it's not difficult to reconfigure the layout if it makes the space more convenient for you.

Above all, take your time—this is your home and it should reflect your taste and needs. Make your changes now, during the planning stage. Once construction begins, it will take crowbars, hammers, saws, new materials, and, most significantly, time to alter the plans. Because changes are not part of your building contract, you can count on them being expensive extras once construction begins.

## Specifying Finishes

One way to personalize a house without changing its structure is to substitute your favorite finishes for those specified on the plan.

Would you prefer a stuccoed exterior rather than the wood siding shown on the plan? In most cases, this is a relatively easy change. Do you like the look of a wood shingle roof rather than the composition shingles shown on the plan? This, too, is easy. Perhaps you would like to change the windows from sliders to casements, or upgrade to high-efficiency glazing. No problem. Many of those kinds of changes can be worked out with your contractor.

Inside, you may want hardwood where vinyl flooring is shown. In fact, you can—and should—choose types, colors, and styles of floorings, wall coverings, tile, plumbing fixtures, door hardware, cabinetry, appliances, lighting fixtures, and other interior details, for it's these materials that will personalize your home. For help in making selections, consult an architect or interior designer (see page 8).

Each material you select should be spelled out clearly and precisely in your building contract.

Finishing touches can transform a house built from stock plans into an expression of your family's taste and style. Clockwise, from far left: Colorful tilework and custom cabinetry enliven a bathroom (Design: Osburn Design); highly organized closet system maximizes storage space (Architect: David Jeremiah Hurley); low-level deck expands living space to outdoor areas (Landscape architects: The Runa Group, Inc.); built-ins convert the corner of a guest room into a home office (Design: Lynn Williams of The French Connection); French country cabinetry lends style and old-world charm to a kitchen (Design: Garry Bishop/Showcase Kitchens).

# What the Plans Include

Complete construction blueprints are available for every house shown in this book. Clear and concise, these detailed blueprints are designed by licensed architects or members of the American Institute of Building Designers (AIBD). Each plan is designed to meet standards set down by nationally recognized building codes (the Uniform Building Code, Standard Building Code, or Basic Building Code) at the time and for the area where they were drawn.

Remember, however, that every state, county, and municipality has its own codes, zoning requirements, ordinances, and building regulations. Modifications may be necessary to comply with such local requirements as snow loads, energy codes, seismic zones, and flood areas.

Although blueprint sets vary depending on the size and complexity of the house and on the individual designer's style, each set may include the elements described below and shown at right.

■ **Exterior elevations** show the front, rear, and sides of the house, including exterior materials, details, and measurements.

■ **Foundation plans** include drawings for a full, partial, or daylight basement, crawlspace, pole, pier, or slab foundation. All necessary notations and dimensions are included. (Foundation options will vary for each plan. If the plan you choose doesn't have the type of foundation you desire, a generic conversion diagram is available.)

■ **Detailed floor plans** show the placement of interior walls and the dimensions of rooms, doors, windows, stairways, and similar elements for each level of the house.

■ **Cross sections** show details of the house as though it were cut in slices from the roof to the foundation. The cross sections give the home's construction, insulation, flooring, and roofing details.

■ **Interior elevations** show the specific details of cabinets (kitchen, bathroom, and utility room), fireplaces, built-in units, and other special interior features.

■ **Roof details** give the layout of rafters, dormers, gables, and other roof elements, including clerestory windows and skylights. These details may be shown on the elevation sheet or on a separate diagram.

■ **Schematic electrical layouts** show the suggested locations for switches, fixtures, and outlets. These details may be shown on the floor plan or on a separate diagram.

■ **General specifications** provide instructions and information regarding excavation and grading, masonry and concrete work, carpentry and woodwork, thermal and moisture protection, drywall, tile, flooring, glazing, and caulking and sealants.

## Other Helpful Building Aids

In addition to the construction information on every set of plans, you can buy the following guides.

■ **Reproducible blueprints** are helpful if you'll be making changes to the stock plan you've chosen. These blueprints are original line drawings produced on erasable, reproducible paper for the purpose of modification. When alterations are complete, working copies can be made.

■ **Itemized materials list** details the quantity, type, and size of materials needed to build your home. (This list is extremely helpful in obtaining an accurate construction bid. It's not intended for use to order materials.)

■ **Mirror-reverse plans** are useful if you want to build your home in the reverse of the plan that's shown. Because the lettering and dimensions read backwards, be sure to buy at least one regular-reading set of blueprints.

■ **Description of materials** gives the type and quality of materials suggested for the home. This form may be required for obtaining FHA or VA financing.

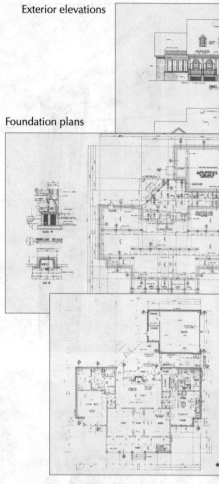

Exterior elevations

Foundation plans

Detailed floor plans

■ **How-to diagrams** for plumbing, wiring, solar heating, framing and foundation conversions show how to plumb, wire, install a solar heating system, convert plans with 2 by 4 exterior walls to 2 by 6 construction (or vice versa), and adapt a plan for a basement, crawlspace, or slab foundation. These diagrams are not specific to any one plan.

**NOTE:** Due to regional variations, local availability of materials, local codes, methods of installation, and individual preferences, detailed heating, plumbing, and electrical specifications are not included on plans. The duct work, venting, and other details will vary, depending on the heating and cooling system you use and the type of energy that operates it. These details and specifications are easily obtained from your builder or local supplier.

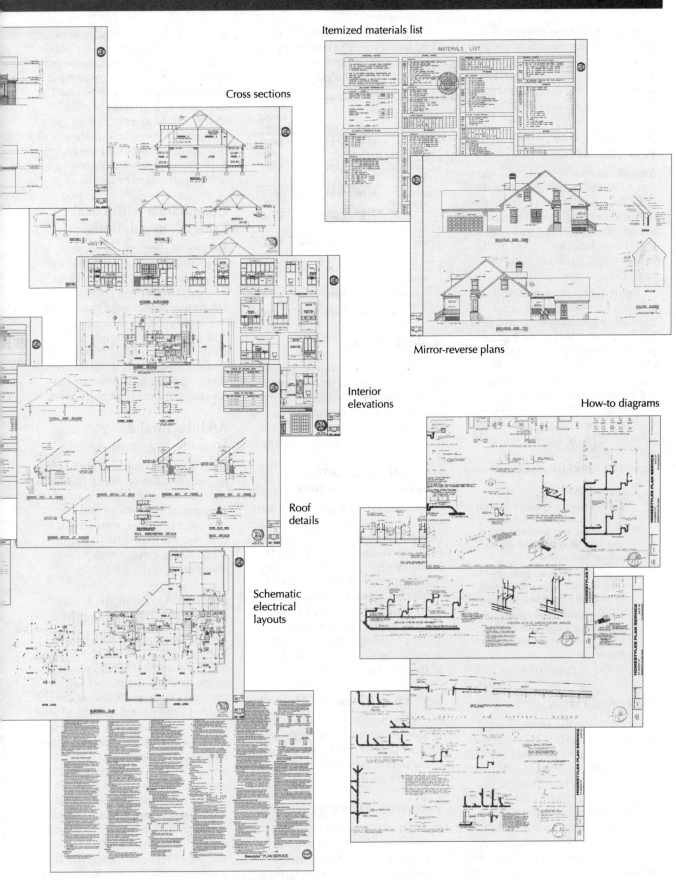

Itemized materials list

Cross sections

Mirror-reverse plans

Interior elevations

How-to diagrams

Roof details

Schematic electrical layouts

General specifications

# Before You Order

Once you've chosen the one or two house plans that work best for you, you're ready to order blueprints. Before filling in the form on the facing page, note the information that follows.

## How Many Blueprints Will You Need?

A single set of blueprints will allow you to study a home design in detail. You'll need more for obtaining bids and permits, as well as some to use as reference at the building site. If you'll be modifying your home plan, order a reproducible set (see page 12).

Figure you'll need at least one set each for yourself, your builder, the building department, and your lender. In addition, some subcontractors—foundation, plumber, electrician, and HVAC—may also need at least partial sets. If they do, ask them to return the sets when they're finished. The chart below can help you calculate how many sets you're likely to need.

### Blueprint Checklist

____ Owner's set(s)

____ Builder usually requires at least three sets: one for legal documentation, one for inspections, and a minimum of one set for subcontractors.

____ Building department requires at least one set. Check with your local department before ordering.

____ Lending institution usually needs one set for a conventional mortgage, three sets for FHA or VA loans.

____ TOTAL SETS NEEDED

## Blueprint Prices

The cost of having an architect design a new custom home typically runs from 5 to 15 percent of the building cost, or from $5,000 to $15,000 for a $100,000 home. A single set of blueprints for the plans in this book ranges from $250 to $535, depending on the house's size. Working with these drawings, you can save enough on design fees to add a deck, a swimming pool, or a luxurious kitchen.

Pricing is based on "total finished living space." Garages, porches, decks, and unfinished basements are not included.

| Price Code (Size) | 1 Set | 4 Sets | 7 Sets | Reproducible Set |
|---|---|---|---|---|
| A (under 1,500 sq. ft.) | $250 | $295 | $325 | $425 |
| B (1,500-1,999 sq. ft.) | $285 | $330 | $360 | $460 |
| C (2,000-2,499 sq. ft.) | $320 | $365 | $395 | $495 |
| D (2,500-2,999 sq. ft.) | $355 | $400 | $430 | $530 |
| E (3,000-3,499 sq. ft.) | $390 | $435 | $465 | $565 |
| F (3,500-3,999 sq. ft.) | $425 | $470 | $500 | $600 |
| G (4,000 sq. ft. and up) | $460 | $505 | $535 | $635 |

## Building Costs

Building costs vary widely, depending on a number of factors, including local material and labor costs and the finishing materials you select. For help estimating costs, see "Is Your Project Doable?" on page 7.

## Foundation Options & Exterior Construction

Depending on your site and climate, your home will be built with a slab, pier, pole, crawlspace, or basement foundation. Exterior walls will be framed with either 2 by 4s or 2 by 6s, determined by structural and insulation standards in your area. Most contractors can easily adapt a home to meet the foundation and/or wall requirements for your area. Or ask for a conversion how-to diagram (see page 12).

## Service & Blueprint Delivery

Service representatives are available to answer questions and assist you in placing your order. Every effort is made to process and ship orders within 48 hours.

## Returns & Exchanges

Each set of blueprints is specially printed and shipped to you in response to your specific order; consequently, requests for refunds cannot be honored. However, if the prints you order cannot be used, you may exchange them for another plan from any Sunset home plan book. For an exchange, you must return all sets of plans within 30 days. A nonrefundable service charge will be assessed for all exchanges; for more information, call the toll-free number on the facing page. Note: Reproducible sets cannot be exchanged or returned.

## Compliance with Local Codes & Regulations

Because of climatic, geographic, and political variations, building codes and regulations vary from one area to another. These plans are authorized for your use expressly conditioned on your obligation and agreement to comply strictly with all local building codes, ordinances, regulations, and requirements, including permits and inspections at time of construction.

## Architectural & Engineering Seals

With increased concern about energy costs and safety, many cities and states now require that an architect or engineer review and "seal" a blueprint prior to construction. To find out whether this is a requirement in your area, contact your local building department.

## License Agreement, Copy Restrictions & Copyright

When you purchase your blueprints, you are granted the right to use those documents to construct a single unit. All the plans in this publication are protected under the Federal Copyright Act, Title XVII of the United States Code and Chapter 37 of the Code of Federal Regulations. Each designer retains title and ownership of the original documents. The blueprints licensed to you cannot be used by or resold to any other person, copied, or reproduced by any means. The copying restrictions do not apply to reproducible blueprints. When you buy a reproducible set, you may modify and reproduce it for your own use.

# Blueprint Order Form

Complete this order form in just three easy steps. Then mail in your order or, for faster service, call toll-free.

## 1. Blueprints & Accessories

### BLUEPRINT CHART

| Price Code | 1 Set | 4 Sets | 7 Sets | Reproducible Set* |
|---|---|---|---|---|
| A | $250 | $295 | $325 | $425 |
| B | $285 | $330 | $360 | $460 |
| C | $320 | $365 | $395 | $495 |
| D | $355 | $400 | $430 | $530 |
| E | $390 | $435 | $465 | $565 |
| F | $425 | $470 | $500 | $600 |
| G | $460 | $505 | $535 | $635 |

Prices subject to change

*A reproducible set is produced on erasable paper for the purpose of modification. It is only available for plans with prefixes AG, AGH, AH, AHP, APS, AX, B, C, CAR, CPS, DD, DW, E, EOF, FB, GL, GML, GSA, H, HFL, J, K, KLF, LMB, LRD, M, NW, OH, PH, PI, PM, S, SDG, THD, UDG, V.

**Mirror-Reverse Sets:** $40 surcharge. From the total number of sets you ordered above, choose the number you want to be reversed. *Note: All writing on mirror-reverse plans is backwards. Order at least one regular-reading set.*

**Itemized Materials List:** One set $40; each additional set $10. Details the quantity, type, and size of materials needed to build your home.

**Description of Materials:** Sold in a set of two for $40 (for use in obtaining FHA or VA financing).

**Typical How-To Diagrams:** One set $12.50; two sets $23; three sets $30; four sets $35. General guides on plumbing, wiring, and solar heating, plus information on how to convert from one foundation or exterior framing to another. *Note: These diagrams are not specific to any one plan.*

## 2. Sales Tax & Shipping

Determine your subtotal and add appropriate local state sales tax, plus shipping and handling (see chart below).

### SHIPPING & HANDLING

| | 1–3 Sets | 4–6 Sets/ Reproducible Set | 7 or More Sets |
|---|---|---|---|
| U.S. Regular (4–6 working days) | $12.50 | $15.00 | $17.50 |
| U.S. Express (2 working days) | $25.00 | $27.50 | $30.00 |
| Canada Regular (2–3 weeks) | $12.50 | $15.00 | $17.50 |
| Canada Express (4–6 working days) | $25.00 | $30.00 | $35.00 |
| Overseas/Airmail (7–10 working days) | $50.00 | $60.00 | $70.00 |

## 3. Customer Information

Choose the method of payment you prefer. Include check, money order, or credit card information, complete name and address portion, and mail to:

Sunset/HomeStyles Plan Service
P.O. Box 50670
Minneapolis, MN 55405

## FOR FASTER SERVICE CALL 1-800-547-5570

SS07

---

## COMPLETE THIS FORM

**Plan Number** _____ **Price Code** _____

**Foundation** _____
(Review your plan carefully for foundation options—basement, pole, pier, crawlspace, or slab. Many plans offer several options; others offer only one.)

**Number of Sets:** $ _____
(See chart at left)
- ☐ One Set
- ☐ Four Sets
- ☐ Seven Sets
- ☐ One Reproducible Set

**Additional Sets** _____ $ _____
($35 each)

**Mirror-Reverse Sets** _____ $ _____
($40 surcharge)

**Itemized Materials List** $ _____
Only available for plans with prefixes AH, AHP, APS*, AX, B*, C, CAR, CDG*, CPS, DD*, DW, E, FB, GSA, H, HFL, I, J, K, LMB*, LRD, N, NW*, P, PH, R, S, SD*, THD, U, UDG, VL.*Not available on all plans. Please call before ordering.

**Description of Materials** $ _____
Only available for plans with prefixes AHP, C, DW, H, HFL, J, K, KY, LMB, N, P, PH, VL.

**Typical How-To Diagrams** $ _____
- ☐ Plumbing  ☐ Wiring  ☐ Solar Heating  ☐ Foundation & Framing Conversion

**SUBTOTAL** $ _____

**SALES TAX** $ _____

**SHIPPING & HANDLING** $ _____

**GRAND TOTAL** $ _____

☐ Check/money order enclosed (in U.S. funds)

☐ VISA  ☐ MasterCard  ☐ AmEx  ☐ Discover

**Credit Card #** _____ **Exp. Date** _____

**Signature** _____

**Name** _____

**Address** _____

**City** _____ **State** _____ **Country** _____

**Zip** _____ **Daytime Phone** (_____)_____

☐ Please check if you are a contractor.

**Mail form to:** Sunset/HomeStyles Plan Service
P.O. Box 50670
Minneapolis, MN 55405

**Or Fax to:** (612) 338-1626

## FOR FASTER SERVICE CALL 1-800-547-5570

SS07

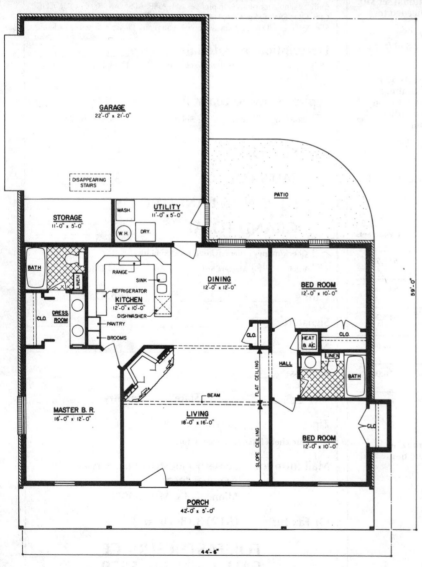

# Cozy, Rustic Country Home

- This cozy, rustic home offers a modern, open interior that makes it look much larger than it really is.
- Note the large, beamed living room with its massive fireplace, which flows into the dining area.
- The efficient U-shaped kitchen includes a handy pantry as well as a convenient broom closet.
- The master suite and master bath are especially roomy for a home of this compact size.
- Two other bedrooms share a full bath and offer good closet space.
- Also note the handy utility space in the garage entry area, and the storage space in the garage.

**Plan E-1109**

| Bedrooms: 3 | Baths: 2 |
|---|---|
| **Space:** | |
| **Total living area:** | 1,191 sq. ft. |
| Garage: | 462 sq. ft. |
| Storage & utility: | 55 sq. ft. |
| Porch: | 214 sq. ft. |
| **Exterior Wall Framing:** | 2x6 |

**Foundation options:**
Crawlspace.
Slab.
(Foundation & framing conversion diagram available — see order form.)

| **Blueprint Price Code:** | A |
|---|---|

*TO ORDER THIS BLUEPRINT, CALL TOLL-FREE 1-800-547-5570*

Plan E-1109

*PRICES AND DETAILS ON PAGES 12-15*

# Weekend Retreat

For those whose goal is a small, affordable retreat at the shore or in the mountains, this plan may be the answer. Although it measures less than 400 sq. ft. of living space on the main floor, it lacks nothing in comfort and convenience. A sizeable living room boasts a masonry hearth on which to mount your choice of a wood stove or a pre-fab fireplace. There is plenty of room for furniture, including a dining table.

The galley-type kitchen is a small marvel of compact convenience and utility, even boasting a dishwasher and space for a stackable washer and dryer. The wide open nature of the first floor guarantees that even the person working in the kitchen area will still be included in the party. On the floor plan, a dashed line across the living room indicates the limits of the balcony bedroom above. In front of this line, the A-frame shape of the living room soars from the floor boards to the ridge beam high above. Clerestory windows lend a further note of spaciousness and unity with nature's outdoors. A huge planked deck adds to the indoor-outdoor relationship.

A modest-sized bedroom on the second floor is approached by a standard stairway, not an awkward ladder or heavy pull-down stairway as is often the case in small A-frames. The view over the balcony rail to the living room below adds a note of distinction. The unique framing pattern allows a window at either end of the bedroom, improving both outlook and ventilation.

A compact bathroom serves both levels and enjoys natural daylight through a skylight window.

| | |
|---|---|
| First floor: | 391 sq. ft. |
| Upper level: | 144 sq. ft. |
| Total living area: | 535 sq. ft. |

FRONT VIEW

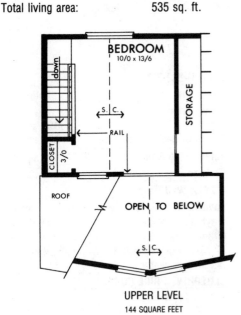

UPPER LEVEL
144 SQUARE FEET

(Exterior walls are 2x6 construction)

PLAN H-968-1A
WITHOUT BASEMENT
(CRAWLSPACE FOUNDATION)

FIRST FLOOR
391 SQUARE FEET

Blueprint Price Code A

## Plan H-968-1A

*TO ORDER THIS BLUEPRINT,* *CALL TOLL-FREE 1-800-547-5570*

*PRICES AND DETAILS* *ON PAGES 12-15*

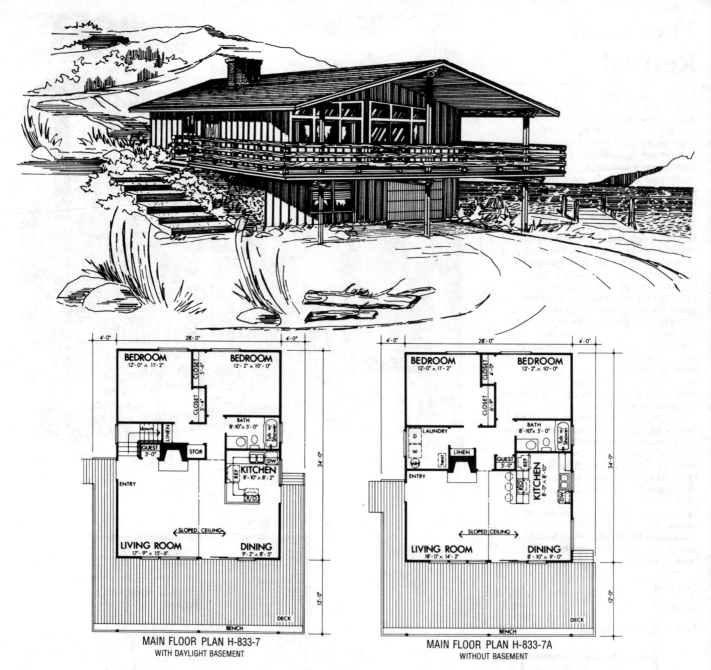

MAIN FLOOR PLAN H-833-7
WITH DAYLIGHT BASEMENT

MAIN FLOOR PLAN H-833-7A
WITHOUT BASEMENT

# An Owner-Builder Special

- Everything you need for a leisure or retirement retreat is neatly packaged in just 952 square feet.
- The basic rectangular design features a unique wraparound deck, which is entirely covered by the projecting roof-line.
- Vaulted ceilings and a central fireplace visually enhance the cozy living/dining room.
- The daylight-basement option is suitable for building on a sloping lot.

DAYLIGHT BASEMENT

| Plans H-833-7 & -7A | |
|---|---|
| **Bedrooms:** 2-3 | **Baths:** 1 |
| **Living Area:** | |
| Main floor | 952 sq. ft. |
| Optional daylight basement | 676 sq. ft. |
| **Total Living Area:** | **952/1,628 sq. ft.** |
| Garage | 276 sq. ft. |
| **Exterior Wall Framing:** | 2x6 |
| **Foundation Options:** | **Plan #** |
| Daylight basement | H-833-7 |
| Crawlspace | H-833-7A |
| (Typical foundation & framing conversion diagram available—see order form.) | |
| **BLUEPRINT PRICE CODE:** | A/B |

**TO ORDER THIS BLUEPRINT,**
**CALL TOLL-FREE 1-800-547-5570**

## Plan H-833-7 & -7A

**PRICES AND DETAILS**
**ON PAGES 12-15**

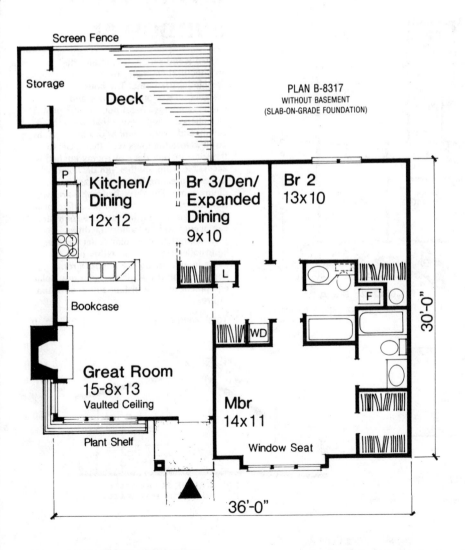

Screen Fence

Storage

Deck

PLAN B-8317
WITHOUT BASEMENT
(SLAB-ON-GRADE FOUNDATION)

P

Kitchen/
Dining
12x12

Br 3/Den/
Expanded
Dining
9x10

Br 2
13x10

Bookcase

L

WD

F

Great Room
15-8x13
Vaulted Ceiling

Mbr
14x11

Plant Shelf

Window Seat

30'-0"

36'-0"

# Design for Today's Lifestyle

- Compact and affordable, this home is designed for today's young families.
- The kitchen/dining room combination offers space for two people to share food preparation and clean-up chores.
- The master suite is impressive for a home of this size, and includes a cozy window seat, large walk-in closet and a private bath.
- The Great Room features an impressive fireplace and vaulted ceiling.
- The optional third bedroom could be used as a den or an expanded dining area.

**Plan B-8317**

| | |
|---|---|
| Bedrooms: 2-3 | Baths: 2 |
| Total living area: | 1,016 sq. ft. |
| Exterior Wall Framing: | 2x4 |

**Foundation options:**
Slab only.
(Foundation & framing conversion diagram available — see order form.)

**Blueprint Price Code:** A

# Living With Sunpower

Angled wood siding accentuates the architectural geometry of this flexible leisure home. The house is designed to exploit sun power and conserve energy. Focal point of the plan is an outsized living lounge that has pitched ceiling and overall dimensions of 18'-8" by 26'-0". Note the glass wall that leads to the spacious sun deck. A roomy kitchen is accessible from another sun deck and serves two eating bars as well as the dining room. The three bedrooms are well isolated from noise and traffic. Adjacent to the kitchen is the utility-storage room that can accommodate laundry facilities.

As an option, two solar collectors can be installed on the roof, either over the living lounge, or on the opposite roof, depending on the southern exposure. Solar equipment may be installed now or in the future.

Total living area:     1,077 sq. ft.

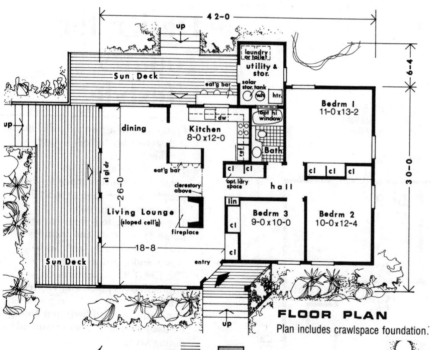

**FLOOR PLAN**
Plan includes crawlspace foundation.

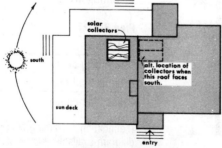

**ORIENTATION FEASIBILITY**
mirror plan also possible
home may be built without solar system

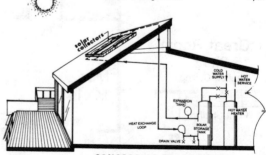

**CONCEPT OF SOLAR SYSTEM
FOR DOMESTIC HOT WATER**

Blueprint Price Code A

# Plan K-166-T

# Charming One-Story

- This charming one-story home has much to offer, despite its modest size and economical bent.
- The lovely full-width porch has old-fashioned detailing, such as the round columns, decorative railings and ornamental moulding.
- An open floor plan maximizes the home's square footage. The front door opens to the living room, where a railing creates a hallway effect while using very little space.
- Straight ahead is the dining area, which has sliding glass doors opening to a large rear patio. The dining area includes a compact laundry closet and adjoins the kitchen with center island.
- Focusing on quality rather than size, the home also offers deluxe features such as the tray ceiling in the living room and the stepped ceiling in the dining room.
- The three bedrooms are well proportioned. The master bedroom includes a private bathroom, while the two smaller bedrooms share another full bath. Note that the fixtures are arranged to reduce plumbing runs.

**Plan AX-91316**

| Bedrooms: 3 | Baths: 2 |
|---|---|
| **Living Area:** | |
| Main floor | 1,097 sq. ft. |
| **Total Living Area:** | **1,097 sq. ft.** |
| Standard basement | 1,097 sq. ft. |
| Garage | 461 sq. ft. |
| **Exterior Wall Framing:** | 2x4 |

**Foundation Options:**
Standard basement
Slab
(Typical foundation & framing conversion diagram available—see order form.)
**BLUEPRINT PRICE CODE:** A

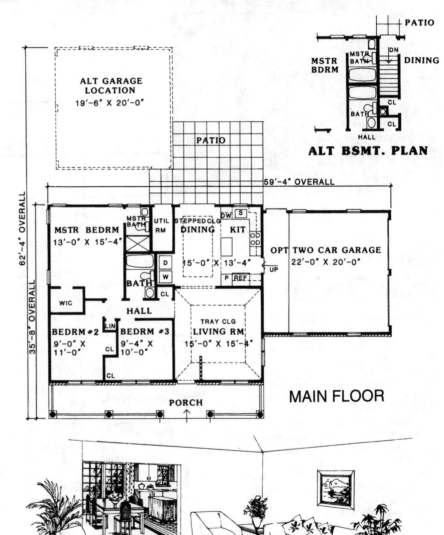

**ALT BSMT. PLAN**

**MAIN FLOOR**

**VIEW INTO LIVING ROOM, DINING ROOM AND KITCHEN.**

## Plans H-946-1A & -1B (Two Bedrooms)

| Bedrooms: 2 | Baths: 2 |
|---|---|
| **Living Area:** | |
| Upper floor | 381 sq. ft. |
| Main floor | 814 sq. ft. |
| **Total Living Area:** | **1,195 sq. ft.** |
| Basement | approx. 814 sq. ft. |
| Garage | 315 sq. ft. |
| **Exterior Wall Framing:** | 2x6 |

**Foundation Options:**
Daylight basement (Plan H-946-1B)
Crawlspace (Plan H-946-1A)
(Typical foundation & framing conversion diagram available—see order form.)

**BLUEPRINT PRICE CODE:**     A

CLERESTORY WDWS. ABOVE

BALCONY RAILING

down

LIN   Sh'wr

BATH

BEDROOM
17'0" x 11'6"

WALK-IN CLOSET
13'0" x 6'3"

UPPER FLOOR
PLANS H-946-1A & -1B

# Narrow-Lot Solar Design

- This design offers your choice of foundation and number of bedrooms, and it can be built on a narrow, sloping lot.
- The passive-solar dining room has windows on three sides and a slate floor for heat storage. A French door leads to a rear deck.
- The living room features a sloped ceiling, a woodstove in ceiling-high masonry, and sliding glass doors to the adjoining deck.
- The kitchen is open to the dining room but separated from the living room by a 7½-ft.-high wall.
- The upper-level variations include a choice of one or two bedrooms. Clerestory windows above the balcony railing add drama to both versions.

PASSIVE SUN ROOF

DECK

DINING
12'3" x 10'0"

WOOD STOVE

S. SLOPED CEILING

7'6" HIGH WALL

KITCHEN
8'0" x 8'0"

DW

RO

REF

LIVING ROOM
16'9" x 13'0"

up

BEDROOM
11'0" x 11'9"

CLOSET

down

LIN

D

BATH

W

GARAGE
13'3" x 23'9"

ENTRY

CLOSET

58'0"

28'0"

MAIN FLOOR

SUN ROOF

UPPER FLOOR

LIVING ROOM BELOW

CLERESTORY WINDOWS ABOVE

RAILING

down

SLOPED CEILING

CLOSET

BEDROOM
10'9" x 11'9"

BEDROOM
11'3" x 8'0"

PLANS H-946-2A & -2B

## Plans H-946-2A & -2B (Three Bedrooms)

| Bedrooms: 3 | Baths: 2 |
|---|---|
| **Living Area:** | |
| Upper floor | 290 sq. ft. |
| Main floor | 814 sq. ft. |
| **Total Living Area:** | **1,104 sq. ft.** |
| Basement | approx. 814 sq. ft. |
| Garage | 315 sq. ft. |
| **Exterior Wall Framing:** | 2x6 |

**Foundation Options:**
Daylight basement (Plan H-946-2B)
Crawlspace (Plan H-946-2A)
(Typical foundation & framing conversion diagram available—see order form.)

**BLUEPRINT PRICE CODE:**     A

# Build It on Weekends

- The basic design and use of truss roof framing promote easy and speedy erection.
- See-through kitchen allows a look into the living or dining rooms.
- Living room reveals the outdoors and surrounding deck through sliding glass doors.
- Separate bedroom/bathroom area eliminates cross-room traffic and wasted hall space.
- Plan H-921-2A utilizes the sealed crawlspace as an air distribution chamber for a Plen-Wood heating system.
- Plan H-921-1A has a standard crawlspace foundation and optional solar heating system.

**Plans H-921-1A & -2A**

| Bedrooms: 3 | Baths: 2 |
|---|---|

**Space:**

| | |
|---|---|
| Main floor: | 1,164 sq. ft. |
| Total living area: | 1,164 sq. ft. |

| Exterior Wall Framing: | 2x6 |
|---|---|

**Foundation options:**
Plen-Wood crawlspace system (Plan H-921-2A).
Standard crawlspace (Plan H-921-1A).
(Foundation & framing conversion diagram available — see order form.)

Blueprint Price Code: A

# Floating Sunspace

- Designed to take advantage of narrow or 'left-over' lots, this compact home is intended for the economy-minded small family. Even so, it still includes an entry hall and a spacious sun room, features not often found in plans of this size.
- Both the living and dining rooms are spacious and flow together to create a great space for parties or family gatherings.
- The optional daylight basement provides an additional bedroom as well as a garage and storage space.

### Plans H-951-1A & -1B

| Bedrooms: 2-3 | Baths: 1-2 |
|---|---|
| **Space:** | |
| Main floor | 1,075 sq. ft. |
| Sun room | 100 sq. ft. |
| **Total Living Area** | **1,175 sq. ft.** |
| Basement | 662 sq. ft. |
| Garage | 311 sq. ft. |
| **Exterior Wall Framing** | 2x6 |

**Foundation options:**
Daylight Basement
Crawlspace
(Foundation & framing conversion diagram available—see order form.)

**Blueprint Price Code:**

| | |
|---|---|
| Without Basement | A |
| With Basement | B |

PLAN H-951-1B
WITH BASEMENT

PASSIVE SUN ROOM
13'-5" x 7'-8"

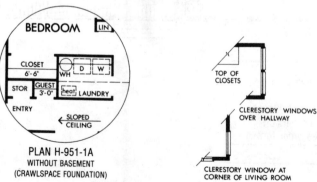

PLAN H-951-1A
WITHOUT BASEMENT
(CRAWLSPACE FOUNDATION)

TOP OF CLOSETS

CLERESTORY WINDOWS OVER HALLWAY

CLERESTORY WINDOW AT CORNER OF LIVING ROOM

BASEMENT

**TO ORDER THIS BLUEPRINT, CALL TOLL-FREE 1-800-547-5570**

# Plans H-951-1A & -1B

*PRICES AND DETAILS ON PAGES 12-15*

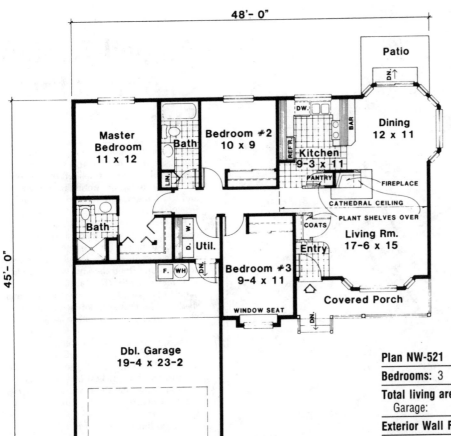

**Patio**

DN.↑

**Dining**
12 x 11

DW.

BAR

REF'R.

**Kitchen**
9-3 x 11

**Master
Bedroom**
11 x 12

**Bath**

**Bedroom #2**
10 x 9

LIN.

PANTRY

FIREPLACE

CATHEDRAL CEILING

PLANT SHELVES OVER

COATS

**Bath**

D. W.

**Util.**

F. WH

DN.

**Bedroom #3**
9-4 x 11

**Entry**

**Living Rm.**
17-6 x 15

WINDOW SEAT

DN.

**Covered Porch**

**Dbl. Garage**
19-4 x 23-2

48'- 0"

45'- 0"

# Classic
# One-Story
# Farmhouse

- This classic farmhouse design features a shady and inviting front porch.
- Inside, vaulted ceilings in the living and dining rooms make the home seem larger than it really is.
- An abundance of windows brightens up the living room and dining area.
- The functional kitchen includes a pantry and plenty of cabinet space.
- The master bedroom boasts a mirrored dressing area, private bath and abundant closet space.
- Bedroom 3 includes a cozy window seat.

**Plan NW-521**

| | |
|---|---|
| **Bedrooms:** 3 | **Baths:** 2 |
| **Total living area:** | 1,187 sq. ft. |
| Garage: | 448 sq. ft. |
| **Exterior Wall Framing:** | 2x6 |

**Foundation options:**
   Crawlspace only.
(Foundation & framing conversion
diagram available — see order form.)

**Blueprint Price Code:**  A

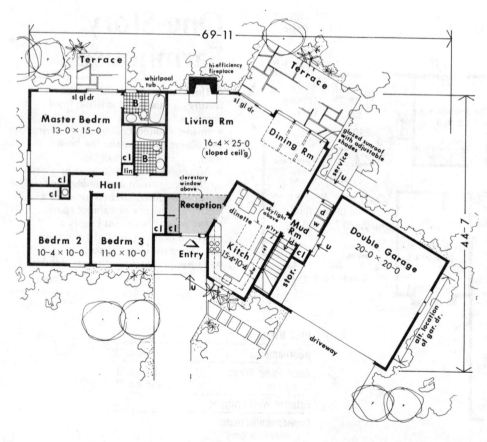

# Angled Design Captures the Sun

Finished in traditional clapboard siding and rustic roof shingles, this single-story passive solar design is deliberately angled at its core to capture optimum sunlight and to accommodate regular as well as irregular sites.

The living room is highlighted by a dramatic sloped ceiling and a wood-burning fireplace. The adjacent dining room is accentuated by the glazed ceiling and wall that flood the area with sunshine and solar warmth. The glazed ceiling panels have adjustable screens for summer shading. The U-shaped kitchen features a dinette area, crowned with a large skylight above.

Three bedrooms are isolated in a wing of their own. The master bedroom has a terrace and a private bath, equipped with a whirlpool tub. For best benefits, it is recommended that the rear of house faces south, or nearly south. Total living area is 1,237 sq. ft.; garage, mud room, etc., 525 sq. ft.; optional basement is 1,264 sq. ft.

| | |
|---|---|
| Total living area: (Not counting basement or garage) | 1,237 sq. ft. |
| Garage, mud room: | 525 sq. ft. |
| Basement (optional): | 1,264 sq. ft. |

Blueprint Price Code A

## Plan K-523-C

PRICES AND DETAILS ON PAGES 12-15

REAR VIEW

# Easy Living

- Large, beautiful living area with sloped ceiling and fireplace lies five steps below entry and sleeping areas.
- Attached dining room and kitchen separated by eating bar.
- Convenient main floor laundry near kitchen and side entrance.
- Secluded master suite includes personal bath and private access to sun deck.

## Plans H-925-1 & -1A

| Bedrooms: 3 | Baths: 2 |
|---|---|

| Space: | |
|---|---|
| Upper floor: | 288 sq. ft. |
| Main floor: | 951 sq. ft. |

| Total living area: | 1,239 sq. ft. |
|---|---|
| Basement: | approx. 951 sq. ft. |
| Garage: | 266 sq. ft. |

| Exterior Wall Framing: | 2x4 |
|---|---|

**Foundation options:**
Daylight basement (Plan H-925-1).
Crawlspace (Plan H-925-1A).
(Foundation & framing conversion diagram available — see order form.)

| Blueprint Price Code: | A |
|---|---|

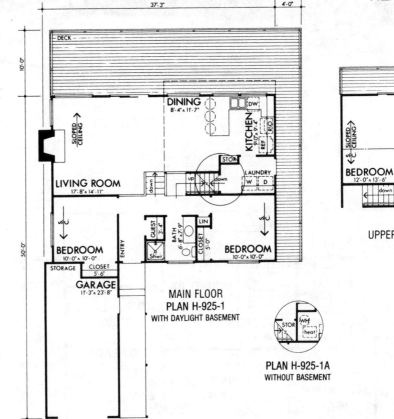

MAIN FLOOR
PLAN H-925-1
WITH DAYLIGHT BASEMENT

PLAN H-925-1A
WITHOUT BASEMENT

UPPER FLOOR

FRONT VIEW

# Affordable Country Charm

- A covered front porch, attached garage, and bay window add appeal to this efficient, affordable home.
- A spacious living room with fireplace and window seat offer plenty of family living space.
- The kitchen/dining room opens to a rear patio for indoor/outdoor living.
- The attached garage incorporates stairs for the optional basement.
- The plan includes three bedrooms and two baths on the same level, a plus for young families.

**Plan AX-98602**

| Bedrooms: 3 | Baths: 2 |
|---|---|
| **Space:** | |
| Total living area: | 1,253 sq. ft. |
| Basement: | 1,253 sq. ft. |
| Garage: | 368 sq. ft. |
| **Exterior Wall Framing:** | 2x4 |

**Foundation options:**
Standard basement.
Slab.
(Foundation & framing conversion diagram available — see order form.)

**Blueprint Price Code:** A

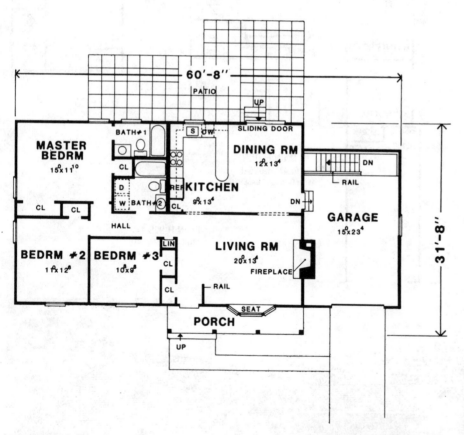

MASTER BEDRM 15x11¹⁰
BATH #1
DINING RM 12x13⁴
UP
SLIDING DOOR
KITCHEN 9x13⁴
DN
RAIL
GARAGE 15x23⁴
DN
BEDRM #2 12x12⁸
BEDRM #3 10x8⁸
LIVING RM 20x13⁴
FIREPLACE
RAIL
SEAT
PORCH
UP
60'-8''
31'-8''
PATIO

FRONT VIEW

# Sunshine Floods Rustic Design

- The main floor is virtually one huge room divided into areas for lounging, eating and cooking.
- A spacious deck, spanning the entire rear of the home, provides for outdoor living and entertaining.
- Upstairs, one large bedroom serves as a master suite, while the balcony room can be used for a variety of purposes, if not needed as a second bedroom.
- Five huge skylight windows across the rear slope of the roof flood the entire home with sunlight and solar heat, achieving a dramatic effect throughout the home.

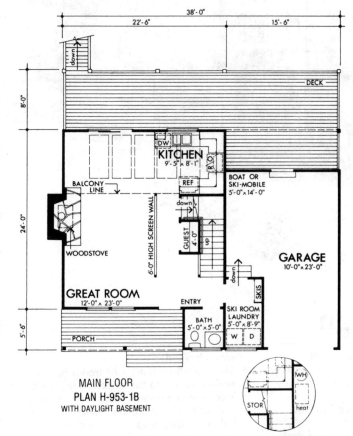

MAIN FLOOR
PLAN H-953-1B
WITH DAYLIGHT BASEMENT

PLAN H-953-1A
WITHOUT BASEMENT

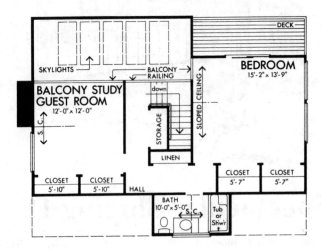

UPPER FLOOR

| Plans H-953-1A & -1B | |
|---|---|
| Bedrooms: 2 | Baths: 1½ |
| Space: | |
| Upper floor | 689 sq. ft. |
| Main floor | 623 sq. ft. |
| **Total Living Area** | **1,312 sq. ft.** |
| Basement | 540 sq. ft. |
| Garage | 319 sq. ft. |
| Storage | 70 sq. ft. |
| **Exterior Wall Framing** | **2x6** |
| **Foundation options:** | **Plan #** |
| Daylight Basement | H-953-1B |
| Crawlspace | H-953-1A |
| (Foundation & framing conversion diagram available—see order form.) | |
| **Blueprint Price Code** | **A** |

REAR VIEW

# Spectacular Sloping Design

- For the lake or mountain-view sloping lot, this spectacular design hugs the hill and takes full advantage of the views.
- A three-sided wrap-around deck makes indoor-outdoor living a pleasure.

- The sunken living room, with cathedral ceiling, skylight, fireplace, and glass galore, is the heart of the plan.
- The formal dining room and the kitchen/breakfast room both overlook the living room and deck

views beyond.
- The main-floor master bedroom has private access to the deck and the bath.
- Two more bedrooms upstairs share a skylit bath and flank a dramatic balcony sitting area overlooking the living room below.

### Plan AX-98607

| Bedrooms: 3 | Baths: 2 |
|---|---|

**Space:**

| | |
|---|---|
| Upper floor: | 531 sq. ft. |
| Main floor: | 1,098 sq. ft. |

| **Total living area:** | **1,629 sq. ft.** |
|---|---|
| Basement: | 894 sq. ft. |
| Garage: | 327 sq. ft. |

| **Exterior Wall Framing:** | 2x4 |
|---|---|

**Foundation options:**
Standard basement.
Slab.
(Foundation & framing conversion diagram available — see order form.)

| **Blueprint Price Code:** | B |
|---|---|

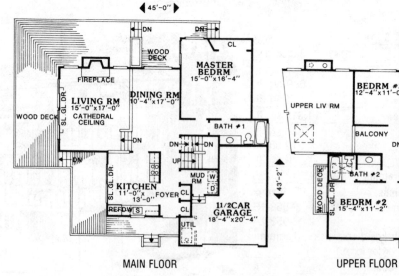

MAIN FLOOR

UPPER FLOOR

**TO ORDER THIS BLUEPRINT,**
*CALL TOLL-FREE 1-800-547-5570*

## Plan AX-98607

**PRICES AND DETAILS**
**ON PAGES 12-15**

FRONT VIEW

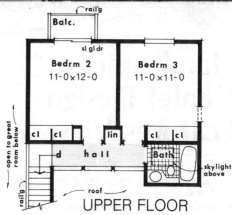

# More for Less

- Big in function but small in footage, this two-story passive solar plan puts every inch of space to efficient use, and is designed in such a way that it can be built as a free-standing unit or as part of a multiple unit complex.
- The plan flows visually from its entry, through its high-ceilinged Great Room, to a brilliant south-facing sun room.
- The master bedroom includes a deluxe private bath and two roomy closets.
- Upstairs, two more bedrooms share a second bath, and one bedroom offers a private balcony.

### Plan K-507-S

| Bedrooms: 3 | Baths: 2½ |
|---|---|
| **Space:** | |
| Upper floor | 397 sq. ft. |
| Main floor | 942 sq. ft. |
| **Total Living Area** | **1,339 sq. ft.** |
| Basement | 915 sq. ft. |
| Garage | 400 sq. ft. |
| **Exterior Wall Framing** | 2x4/2x6 |

**Foundation options:**

Standard Basement

Slab

(Foundation & framing conversion diagram available—see order form.)

| **Blueprint Price Code** | **A** |
|---|---|

REAR VIEW

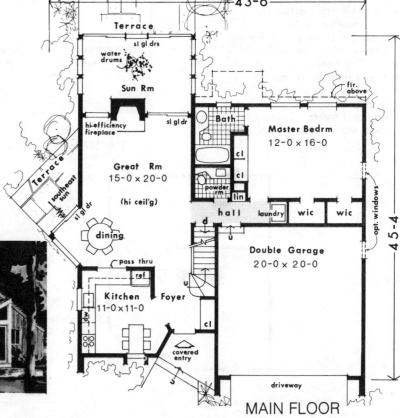

UPPER FLOOR

MAIN FLOOR

# Handsome Chalet Design Features View

- Roomy floor plan will make this chalet something you'll yearn for all year long.
- Massive fireplace in living room is a pleasant welcome after a day in the cold outdoors.
- Open kitchen has two entrances for smoother traffic.
- Generous laundry facilities and large bath are unexpected frills you'll appreciate.
- Upper floor bedrooms feature sloped ceilings and plenty of storage space.
- Optional basement plan affords more storage and general use space.

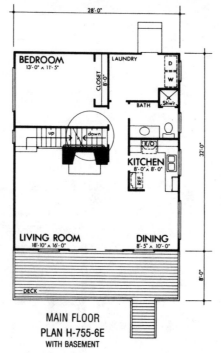

MAIN FLOOR
PLAN H-755-6E
WITH BASEMENT

UPPER FLOOR

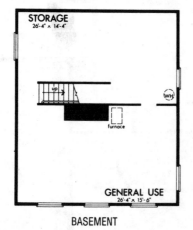

BASEMENT

PLAN H-755-5E
WITHOUT BASEMENT

WATER HEATER & FURNACE
LOCATED IN LAUNDRY RM.

## Plans H-755-5E & -6E

| Bedrooms: 3 | Baths: 2 |
|---|---|
| **Space:** | |
| Upper floor: | 454 sq. ft. |
| Main floor: | 896 sq. ft. |
| **Total without basement:** | 1,350 sq. ft. |
| Basement: | 896 sq. ft. |
| **Total with basement:** | 2,246 sq. ft. |
| **Exterior Wall Framing:** | 2x4 |

**Foundation options:**
Daylight basement (Plan H-755-6E).
Crawlspace (Plan H-755-5E).
(Foundation & framing conversion diagram available — see order form.)

**Blueprint Price Code:**

| | |
|---|---|
| Without basement: | A |
| With basement: | C |

*TO ORDER THIS BLUEPRINT,*
*CALL TOLL-FREE 1-800-547-5570*

## Plans H-755-5E & -6E

*PRICES AND DETAILS*
*ON PAGES 12-15*

# Vaulted Design for Narrow Lot

- Vaulted living spaces add to the spacious feel of this narrow-lot home.
- The focal point is a large fireplace flanked by windows that give views of a lovely patio and the yard beyond.
- The dining room offers access to a secluded courtyard, while the bayed kitchen overlooks a front garden.
- The master suite features a sitting room with sliders to the patio. The master bath leads to a large walk-in closet.
- The two remaining bedrooms share the hall bath.

### Plans P-6588-2A & -2D

| Bedrooms: 3 | Baths: 2 |
|---|---|

**Living Area:**

| | |
|---|---|
| Main floor (non-basement version) | 1,362 sq. ft. |
| Main floor (basement version) | 1,403 sq. ft. |
| **Total Living Area:** | **1,362/1,403 sq. ft.** |
| Daylight basement | 1,303 sq. ft. |
| Garage | 427 sq. ft. |
| **Exterior Wall Framing:** | 2x6 |

| **Foundation Options:** | **Plan #** |
|---|---|
| Daylight basement | P-6588-2D |
| Crawlspace | P-6588-2A |

(Typical foundation & framing conversion diagram available—see order form.)

**BLUEPRINT PRICE CODE:** **A**

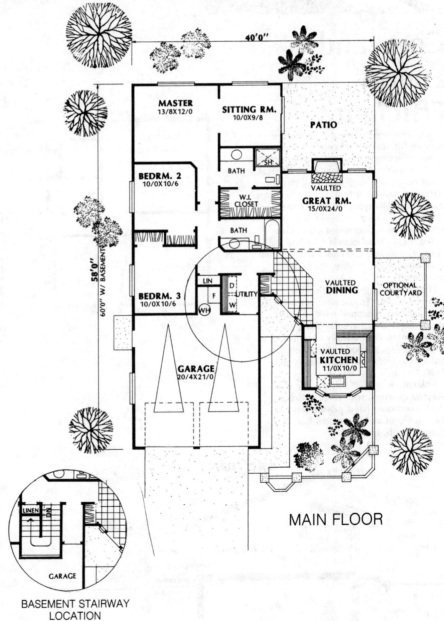

**MAIN FLOOR**

BASEMENT STAIRWAY LOCATION

# Cozy and Energy-Efficient

Planned for year-round comfort and energy efficiency, this passive solar design boasts a highly livable floor plan. Vertical wood siding and deep overhang give the exterior a natural appeal. Inside, the open plan is carefully designed to provide ample natural light with a minimum heat loss; windows and sliding doors are double-paned; heavy insulation is specified. In summer, operable clerestory windows aid in air circulation, cooling the house by convection.

The high-ceilinged reception hall neatly channels traffic. To the right is the family room/kitchen, equipped with an eating bar. Straight ahead are the living and dining rooms, dramatically accented by a sloped ceiling, a wood-burning fireplace and a light-filled sunroom. Sliding glass doors lead to a rear terrace.

Isolated on the left side are the quiet sleeping quarters, with three bedrooms. Master bedroom has a private terrace, a walk-in closet and a personal bath that features a whirlpool tub.

PLAN K-511-BA
WITH OPTIONAL BASEMENT

Total living area:     1,363 sq. ft.
(Not counting basement or garage)
Garage, mud room, etc.:     500 sq. ft.
Optional basement:     1,392 sq. ft.

**SECTION**
PASSIVE SOLAR AT WORK

Blueprint Price Code A

## Plan K-511-BA

# Warm Porch Welcomes Guests

● This cozy home provides adequate space for family life and for entertaining guests as well.
● Living and dining rooms are separate, yet flow together when the need for entertaining large gatherings arises.
● The large master suite includes a private bath and large closet.
● Kitchen is good sized and offers abundant counter space.
● A handy utility room is located in the entry area, and a large storage area is also positioned off the carport (there is optional storage space above the garage, also).

| Plan E-1308 | |
|---|---|
| **Bedrooms:** 3 | **Baths:** 2 |
| **Total living area:** | 1,375 sq. ft. |
| Porch: | 102 sq. ft. |
| Carport: | 430 sq. ft. |
| Storage: | 95 sq. ft. |
| **Exterior Wall Framing:** | 2x4 |
| **Foundation options:** | |
| Crawlspace. | |
| Slab. | |
| (Foundation & framing conversion diagram available — see order form.) | |
| **Blueprint Price Code:** | A |

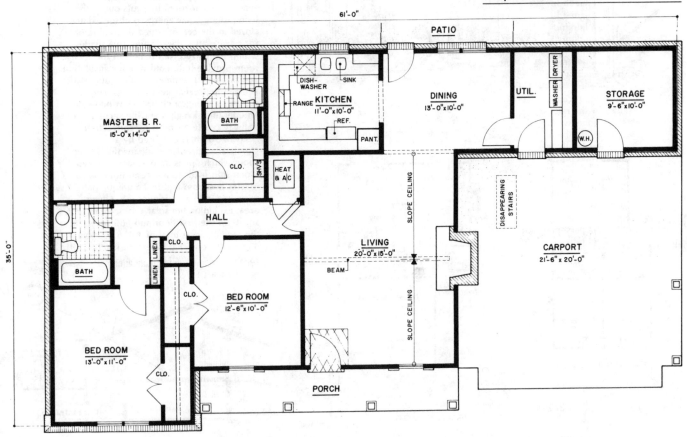

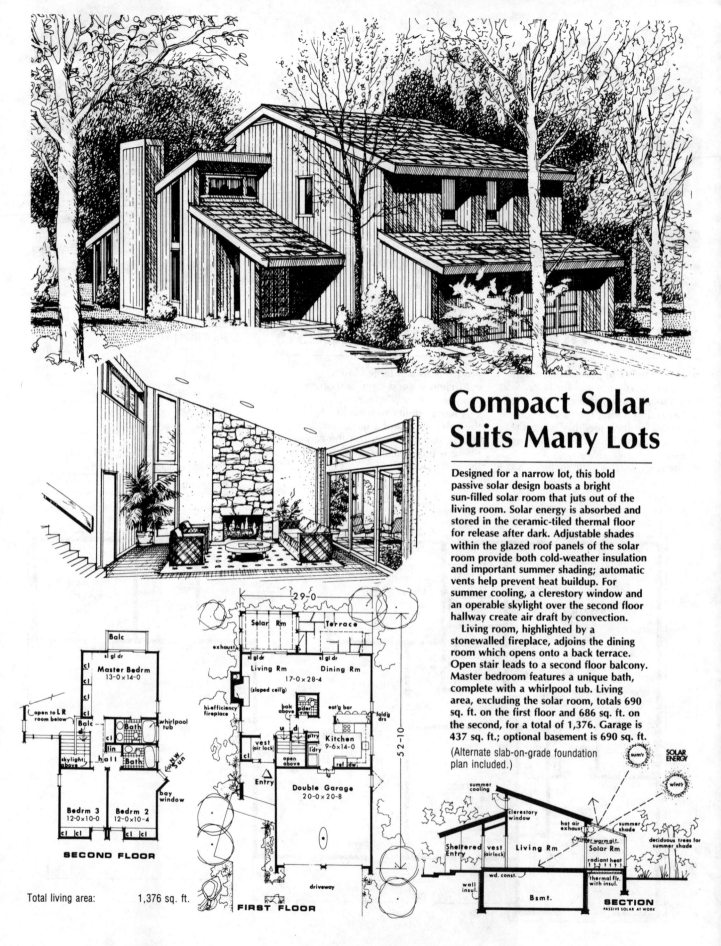

# Compact Solar Suits Many Lots

Designed for a narrow lot, this bold passive solar design boasts a bright sun-filled solar room that juts out of the living room. Solar energy is absorbed and stored in the ceramic-tiled thermal floor for release after dark. Adjustable shades within the glazed roof panels of the solar room provide both cold-weather insulation and important summer shading; automatic vents help prevent heat buildup. For summer cooling, a clerestory window and an operable skylight over the second floor hallway create air draft by convection.

Living room, highlighted by a stonewalled fireplace, adjoins the dining room which opens onto a back terrace. Open stair leads to a second floor balcony. Master bedroom features a unique bath, complete with a whirlpool tub. Living area, excluding the solar room, totals 690 sq. ft. on the first floor and 686 sq. ft. on the second, for a total of 1,376. Garage is 437 sq. ft.; optional basement is 690 sq. ft.

(Alternate slab-on-grade foundation plan included.)

**SOLAR ENERGY**

**SECTION**
PASSIVE SOLAR AT WORK

Total living area: 1,376 sq. ft.

**SECOND FLOOR**

Master Bedrm 13-0 x 14-0
Balc
whirlpool tub
open to LR room below
Bath
Bath
skylight above
hall
Balc
bay window
Bedrm 3 12-0 x 10-0
Bedrm 2 12-0 x 10-4

**FIRST FLOOR**

29-0
Solar Rm
Terrace
exhaust
Living Rm 17-0 x 28-4 (sloped ceil'g)
Dining Rm
hi-efficiency fireplace
Kitchen 9-6 x 14-0
eat'g bar
fold'g drs
vest (air lock)
open above
Entry
Double Garage 20-0 x 20-8
52-10
driveway

Blueprint Price Code A
## Plan K-521-C

**PRICES AND DETAILS**
**ON PAGES 12-15**

# Open Plan in Traditional Design

- This modest-sized design is popular for its simple yet stylish exterior, making it suitable for either country or urban settings.
- A covered front porch and gabled roof extension accent the facade while providing sheltered space for outdoor relaxing.
- Inside, the living room with a cathedral ceiling and fireplace is combined with an open dining area and kitchen with island to create one large gathering spot for family and guests.

- The master bedroom features a private bath, large closet and ample sleeping area.
- Two other bedrooms share a second full bath.
- A convenient utility area and walk-in pantry are found in the passageway to the carport; also note the large outdoor storage closet.

### Plan J-86155

| Bedrooms: 3 | Baths: 2 |
|---|---|

| Total living area: | 1,385 sq. ft. |
|---|---|
| Basement: | 1,385 sq. ft. |
| Carport: | 380 sq. ft. |

| Exterior Wall Framing: | 2x4 |
|---|---|

**Foundation options:**
Standard basement.
Crawlspace.
Slab.
(Foundation & framing conversion diagram available — see order form.)

| Blueprint Price Code: | A |
|---|---|

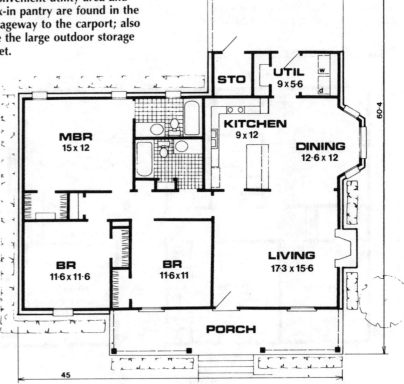

# Full-Width Veranda Welcomes Visitors

- A veranda invites you into this lovely traditionally styled ranch home.
- Inside, the entry allows a view through the dining room railing and straight back to the huge, central living room and backyard beyond.
- A massive stone fireplace, wood box and built-in bookshelves, plus exposed beams in the ceiling, highlight this main

living area.

- The formal dining room and kitchen combine for easy meal service, with a counter bar separating the two.
- The main hallway ends at the sleeping wing, which offers a large master bedroom and private bath, two extra bedrooms and a convenient, concealed washer/dryer.

| Plan E-1304 | |
|---|---|
| **Bedrooms:** 3 | **Baths:** 2 |
| **Space:** | |
| Main floor | 1,395 sq. ft. |
| **Total Living Area** | **1,395 sq. ft.** |
| Garage and Storage | 481 sq. ft. |
| **Exterior Wall Framing** | 2x4 |
| **Foundation options:** | |
| Crawlspace | |
| Slab | |
| (Foundation & framing conversion diagram available—see order form.) | |
| **Blueprint Price Code** | **A** |

73'-0"

37'-0"

MASTER B.R.
14'-0"x 13'-0"

KNEE SPACE

DRESS. ROOM

BATH

BATH

CLO.

SHVS

DRYER | WASH.

CLO.

LINEN

HALL

BED ROOM
12'-0"x 11'-0"

BED ROOM
12'-0"x 11'-0"

CLO.

CLO.

HEAT & A/C

ENTRY

CLO.

BEAM

LIVING
18'-0"x 17'-0"

POST W/ RAILING

BOOKS

STONE

WOOD BOX

STORAGE
7'-6"x 4'-0"

SHELVES

REF.

RANGE

DROPPED CEILING

DINING
12'-0"x 11'-0"

KITCHEN
12'-0"x 10'-0"

BAR

DW. | SINK

PATIO

DISAPPEARING STAIRS

W.H.

GARAGE
21'-0"x 21'-0"

PORCH
42'-0"x 7'-0"

Plan E-1304

**PRICES AND DETAILS ON PAGES 12-15**

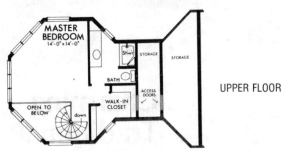

MASTER BEDROOM
14'-0" x 14'-0"

Shwr

STORAGE

STORAGE

BATH

UPPER FLOOR

OPEN TO BELOW

WALK-IN CLOSET

ACCESS DOORS

down

# Octagonal Vacation Retreat

- Octagonal shape offers a view on all sides.
- Living, dining, and meal preparation are combined in a single Great Room, interrupted only by a provocative spiral staircase.
- Winding staircase allows continuous observance of activities below.
- Extraordinary master suite is bordered by glass, a private bath, and dressing room.
- Attached garage has room for boat, camper, or extra automobile.

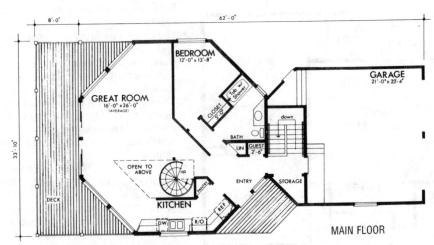

8'-0"    62'-0"

33'-10"

BEDROOM
12'-0" x 13'-8"

GARAGE
21'-0" x 23'-4"

GREAT ROOM
16'-0" x 26'-0"
(AVERAGE)

CLOSET 5'-0"

Tub w/ Shower

BATH

LIN

GUEST 2'-6"

down

OPEN TO ABOVE

up

DECK

ENTRY

STORAGE

KITCHEN

PANTRY

REF

DW

R/O

MAIN FLOOR

### Plans H-964-1A & -1B

| Bedrooms: 2-3 | Baths: 2-3 |
|---|---|

| Space: | |
|---|---|
| Upper floor: | 346 sq. ft. |
| Main floor: | 1,067 sq. ft. |

| Total living area: | 1,413 sq. ft. |
|---|---|
| Basement: | approx. 1,045 sq. ft. |
| Garage: | 512 sq. ft. |
| Storage (2nd floor) | 134 sq. ft. |

| Exterior Wall Framing: | 2x6 |
|---|---|

**Foundation options:**
Daylight basement (Plan H-964-1B).
Crawlspace (Plan H-964-1A).
Foundation & framing conversion diagram available — see order form.)

**Blueprint Price Code:**

| Without basement: | A |
|---|---|
| With basement: | C |

BEDROOM
22/0 x 10/0

CLOSET 4/0

CLOSET 4/0

RECREATION
16/0 x 21/6

BATH

up

LIN

W D LAUNDRY

CLOSET 7/6

STOR 3/6

STORAGE

WH

furnace

BASEMENT

0 1 2 3 4 5 6 7 8 9 10    15    20
SCALE

PATIO

PORCH
12' x 6'

DINING
12' x 12'

MASTER SUITE
16' x 12'

BAR

KITCHEN
12' x 10'
D W   SINK
REF
RANGE

BATH

CLO.

UTIL
9' x 6'
DRY   WASH
PANT
BRM
STOR

STORAGE
10' x 6'

CLO.

ENTRY

PORCH

LIVING
18' x 16'

WH

HEAT
& A/C

CLO.

BED RM.
14' x 12'

HALL

BATH

LIN

BED RM.
14' x 12'

CLO.

ATTIC
STAIRS

GARAGE
22' x 22'

50'

56'

**MAIN FLOOR**

# Charming Traditional

- The attractive facade of this traditional home greets visitors with warmth and charm.
- The entry area features a coat closet and a commanding view of the living room and a rear porch and patio, visible through French doors. A striking corner fireplace warms the living room.
- The bayed dining room boasts patio views and an eating bar. The U-shaped kitchen offers a nearby utility room, which includes a pantry and laundry facilities.
- The master suite has an angled window, a walk-in closet and a private bath with dual-sink vanity.
- Two additional bedrooms are secluded from the living areas with double doors. A full bath services this wing.

| Plan E-1428 | |
|---|---|
| **Bedrooms:** 3 | **Baths:** 2 |
| **Living Area:** | |
| Main floor | 1,415 sq. ft. |
| **Total Living Area:** | **1,415 sq. ft.** |
| Garage | 484 sq. ft. |
| Storage | 60 sq. ft. |
| **Exterior Wall Framing:** | 2x6 |
| **Foundation Options:** | |
| Crawlspace | |
| Slab | |
| (Typical foundation & framing conversion diagram available—see order form.) | |
| **BLUEPRINT PRICE CODE:** | A |

Plan E-1428

# Dramatic Skewed Prow

- This cleverly modified A-frame combines a dramatic exterior with an exciting interior that offers commanding views through its many windows.
- The central foyer opens to a spacious living room and dining room combination with a soaring cathedral ceiling and a massive stone fireplace.
- Directly ahead is the kitchen with sliding glass doors that open to the wraparound deck.
- Two bedrooms are located at the rear near the full bath and the laundry room.
- A third bedroom and a loft area that could sleep overnight guests are found on the upper level.

**Plan HFL-1160-CW**

| Bedrooms: 3 | Baths: 2 |
|---|---|
| **Space:** | |
| Upper floor | 400 sq. ft. |
| Main floor | 1,016 sq. ft. |
| **Total Living Area** | **1,416 sq. ft.** |
| **Exterior Wall Framing** | 2x4 |
| **Foundation options:** | |

Crawlspace
(Foundation & framing conversion diagram available—see order form.)

| **Blueprint Price Code** | **A** |
|---|---|

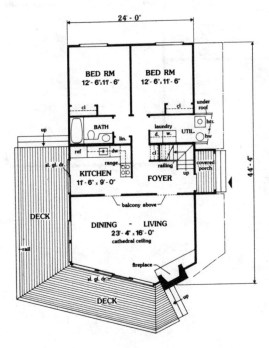

MAIN FLOOR

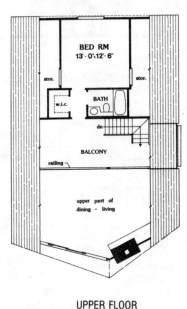

UPPER FLOOR

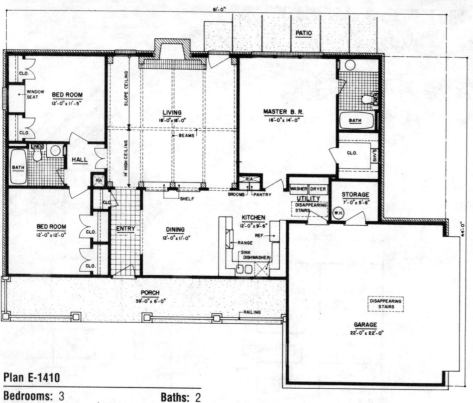

# Vaulted Ceiling in Living Room

- This home packs a lot of grace and space into 1,418 square feet.
- Note the large living room with its beamed, vaulted ceiling and massive fireplace.
- The formal dining room lies off the foyer, and adjoins the efficient kitchen, which also includes a pantry and utility area.
- The master suite features a large walk-in closet and roomy master bath.
- At the other end of the home, two secondary bedrooms with abundant closet space share another full bath.
- The house-spanning porch invites guests to come in for a relaxing visit.

**Plan E-1410**

| Bedrooms: 3 | Baths: 2 |
|---|---|

**Space:**

| | |
|---|---|
| **Total living area:** | 1,418 sq. ft. |
| Garage: | 484 sq. ft. |
| Storage: | 38 sq. ft. |
| Porch: | 238 sq. ft. |

| **Exterior Wall Framing:** | 2x4 |
|---|---|

**Foundation options:**
Crawlspace.
Slab.
(Foundation & framing conversion diagram available — see order form.)

| **Blueprint Price Code:** | A |
|---|---|

*TO ORDER THIS BLUEPRINT, CALL TOLL-FREE 1-800-547-5570*

## Plan E-1410

**PRICES AND DETAILS ON PAGES 12-15**

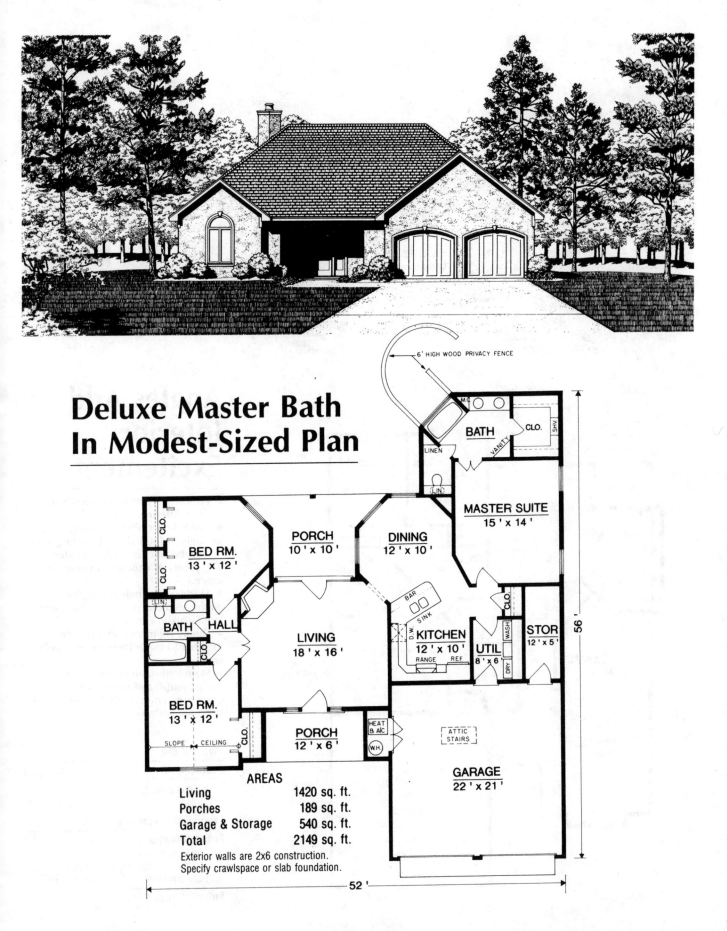

# Deluxe Master Bath In Modest-Sized Plan

6' HIGH WOOD PRIVACY FENCE

BATH

CLO.

SHV.

LINEN

VANITY

LIN.

MASTER SUITE
15' x 14'

CLO.

BED RM.
13' x 12'

CLO.

PORCH
10' x 10'

DINING
12' x 10'

BAR

LIN.

SINK

D.W.

KITCHEN
12' x 10'

CLO.

WASH

STOR
12' x 5'

LIVING
18' x 16'

RANGE

REF.

UTIL
8' x 6'

DRY

BATH

HALL

CLO.

BED RM.
13' x 12'

SLOPE    CEILING

CLO.

PORCH
12' x 6'

HEAT
& A/C

WH.

ATTIC
STAIRS

GARAGE
22' x 21'

56'

52'

## AREAS

| | |
|---|---|
| Living | 1420 sq. ft. |
| Porches | 189 sq. ft. |
| Garage & Storage | 540 sq. ft. |
| Total | 2149 sq. ft. |

Exterior walls are 2x6 construction.
Specify crawlspace or slab foundation.

Blueprint Price Code A

## Plan E-1426

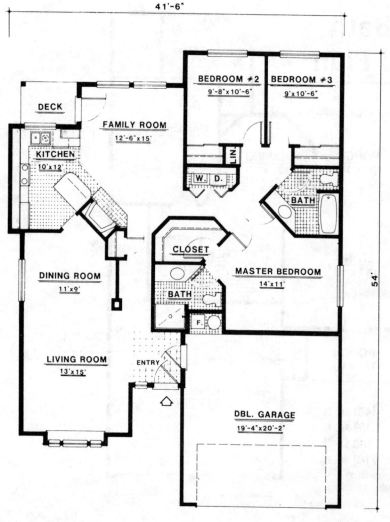

41'-6"

DECK

FAMILY ROOM
12'-6" x 15'

BEDROOM #2
9'-8" x 10'-6"

BEDROOM #3
9' x 10'-6"

KITCHEN
10' x 12'

W. D.

LIN.

BATH

DINING ROOM
11' x 9'

CLOSET

MASTER BEDROOM
14' x 11'

BATH

F.

54'

LIVING ROOM
13' x 15'

ENTRY

DBL. GARAGE
19'-4" x 20'-2"

# Angles Add Interior Excitement

- Eye-catching exterior leads into exciting interior.
- You'll find cathedral ceilings throughout the living and dining area.
- Angular kitchen includes eating bar, plenty of cabinet and counter space.
- Master suite includes angled double-door entry, private bath and large walk-in closet.
- Family room and kitchen join together to make large casual family area.
- Main bathroom continues the angled motif, and the washer and dryer are conveniently located in the bedroom hallway.

## Plan NW-864

| Bedrooms: 3 | Baths: 2 |
|---|---|
| **Total living area:** | 1,449 sq. ft. |
| Garage: | 390 sq. ft. |
| **Exterior Wall Framing:** | 2x6 |

**Foundation options:**
  Crawlspace only.
(Foundation & framing conversion diagram available — see order form.)

**Blueprint Price Code:** A

Plan NW-864

**PRICES AND DETAILS
ON PAGES 12-15**

# Cathedral Ceiling Featured

The open floor plan of this modified A-Frame design virtually eliminates wasted hall space. The centrally located Great Room features a 15'4" cathedral ceiling with exposed wood beams and large areas of fixed glass on both front and rear. Living and dining areas are visually separated by a massive stone fireplace.

The isolated master suite features a walk-in closet and sliding glass doors opening onto the front deck.

A walk-thru utility room provides easy access from the carport and outside storage area to the compact kitchen. On the opposite side of the Great Room are two additional bedrooms and a second full

bath. All this takes up only 1,454 square feet of heated living area. A full length deck and vertical wood siding with stone accents on the corners provide a rustic yet contemporary exterior.

Total living area: 1,454 sq. ft.
(Not counting basement or garage)

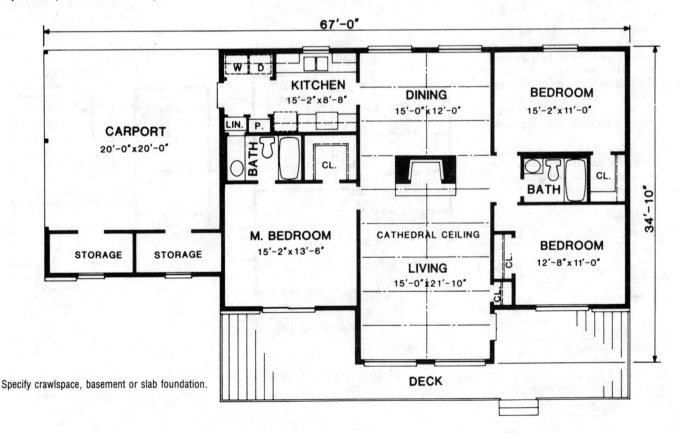

Specify crawlspace, basement or slab foundation.

# Private Decks Abound

- With two bedrooms opening to their own private deck, and another deck extending the full length of the living room, the scenic views can be fully enjoyed, both inside and out.
- The sunken living room features a fireplace, a dramatic 19-foot ceiling with skylights, and three sliding glass doors opening to the deck.
- The efficient kitchen overlooks the front yard and the rear view over the breakfast bar and dining room with opening to the living room.

**Plan CAR-81007**

| Bedrooms: 3 | Baths: 1½ |
|---|---|

**Space:**

| | |
|---|---|
| Upper floor: | 560 sq. ft. |
| Main floor: | 911 sq. ft. |

| | |
|---|---|
| Total living area: | 1,471 sq. ft. |
| Basement: | 911 sq. ft. |

| | |
|---|---|
| Exterior Wall Framing: | 2x6 |

**Foundation options:**
Standard basement.
(Foundation & framing conversion diagram available — see order form.)

| Blueprint Price Code: | A |
|---|---|

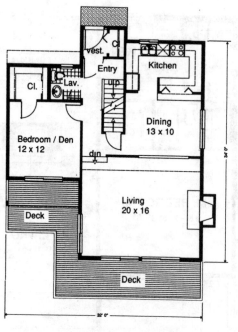

MAIN FLOOR

UPPER FLOOR

## Plan CAR-81007

**PRICES AND DETAILS ON PAGES 12-15**

# Eye-Catching Prow-Shaped Chalet

- Steep pitched roof lines and wide cornices give this chalet a distinct alpine appearance.
- Prowed shape, large windows, and 10' deck provide view and enhancement of indoor/outdoor living.
- Functional division of living and sleeping areas by hallway and first floor full bath.

- Laundry facilities conveniently located near bedroom wing.
- U-shaped kitchen and spacious dining/living areas make the main floor perfect for entertaining.

**UPPER FLOOR**

### Plans H-886-3 & -3A

| Bedrooms: 3 | Baths: 2 |
|---|---|

| Space: | |
|---|---|
| Upper floor: | 486 sq. ft. |
| Main floor: | 994 sq. ft. |

| Total without basement: | 1,480 sq. ft. |
|---|---|
| Basement: | approx. 715 sq. ft. |
| Garage: | 279 sq. ft. |

| Exterior Wall Framing: | 2x6 |
|---|---|

**Foundation options:**
Daylight basement (Plan H-886-3).
Crawlspace (Plan H-886-3A).
(Foundation & framing conversion diagram available — see order form.)

| Blueprint Price Code: | A |
|---|---|

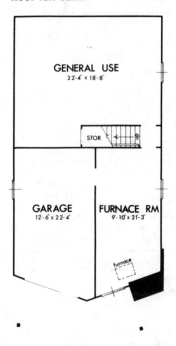

**BASEMENT**

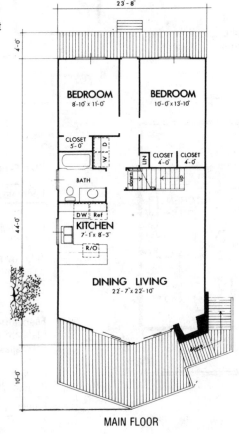

**MAIN FLOOR**

# Compact, Cozy, Inviting

- Liberal-sized living room is centrally located and features corner fireplace and sloped ceilings.
- Separate two-car garage is included with plan.
- Two-bedroom loft overlooks living room and entryway below.
- Full-width porches, both front and rear, invite guests and family alike for leisure time rest and relaxation.

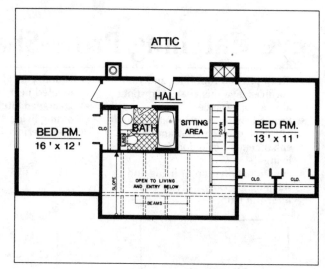

UPPER FLOOR

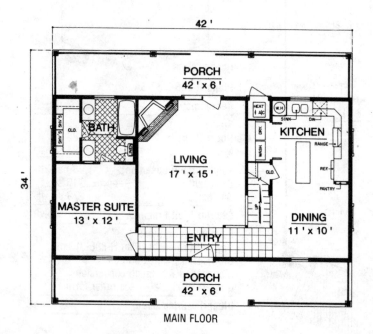

MAIN FLOOR

**Plan E-1421**

| Bedrooms: 3 | Baths: 2 |
|---|---|
| **Space:** | |
| Upper floor: | 561 sq. ft. |
| Main floor: | 924 sq. ft. |
| **Total living area:** | 1,485 sq. ft. |
| Basement: | approx. 924 sq. ft. |
| Porches: | 504 sq. ft. |
| **Exterior Wall Framing:** | 2x6 |

**Foundation options:**
Standard basement.
Crawlspace.
Slab.
(Foundation & framing conversion diagram available — see order form.)

**Blueprint Price Code:** A

Plan E-1421

**PRICES AND DETAILS ON PAGES 12-15**

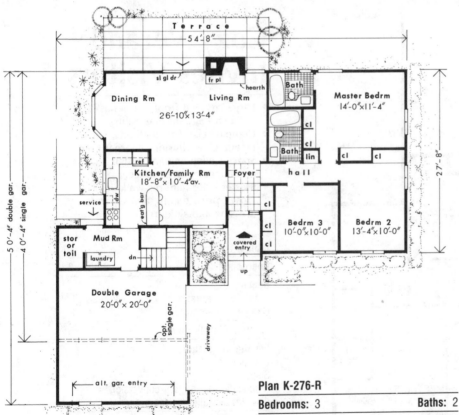

# Compact, Economical to Build

- This economically-structured L-shaped ranch puts a great many desirable features into a mere 1,193 sq. ft. of living space. A wood-burning fireplace highlights the living area. Sliding glass doors open to the backyard terrace.
- The kitchen/family room features an eating bar.
- Covered entry welcomes you to the central foyer for easy channeling to any part of the house.
- Located in a wing of their own are three bedrooms and two baths.
- For a narrow lot, the garage door could face the front.

**Plan K-276-R**

| Bedrooms: 3 | Baths: 2 |
|---|---|

| Space: | |
|---|---|
| Total living area: | 1,193 sq. ft. |
| Basement: | 1,193 sq. ft. |
| Garage, mud room, etc.: | 551 sq. ft. |

| Exterior Wall Framing: | 2x4 or 2x6 |
|---|---|

**Foundation options:**
Standard basement.
Crawlspace.
Slab.
(Foundation & framing conversion diagram available — see order form)

**Blueprint Price Code:** A

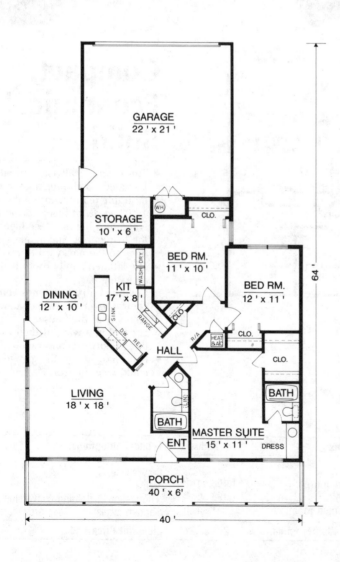

GARAGE
22' x 21'

STORAGE
10' x 6'

BED RM.
11' x 10'

BED RM.
12' x 11'

DINING
12' x 10'

KIT
17' x 8'

HALL

LIVING
18' x 18'

BATH

BATH

MASTER SUITE
15' x 11'

ENT

DRESS

PORCH
40' x 6'

64'

40'

# Cozy Veranda Invites Visitors

- Large covered front porch has detailed columns and railings.
- Compact size fits small lots, yet facade gives illusion of larger home.
- Space-saving angular design minimizes hallway space.
- Master suite features walk-in closet, private bath, and separate dressing and sink area.

**Plan E-1217**

| | |
|---|---|
| **Bedrooms:** 3 | **Baths:** 2 |

**Space:**
| | |
|---|---|
| **Total living area:** | 1,266 sq. ft. |
| Garage and storage: | 550 sq. ft. |

| **Exterior Wall Framing:** | 2x6 |
|---|---|

**Foundation options:**
Crawlspace.
Slab.
(Foundation & framing conversion diagram available — see order form.)

| **Blueprint Price Code:** | A |
|---|---|

*TO ORDER THIS BLUEPRINT,*
*CALL TOLL-FREE 1-800-547-5570*

Plan E-1217

*PRICES AND DETAILS*
*ON PAGES 12-15*

# L-Shaped Country-Style Home

- The classic L-shape and covered front porch with decorative railings and columns make this home reminiscent of the early 20th century farmhouse.
- The dormer windows give the home the look of a two-story, even though it is designed for convenient single-level living.
- The huge living room features ceilings that slope up to 13 feet. The beamed area of the ceiling is 8 feet high and creates a cozy atmosphere. A corner fireplace radiates warmth to both the living room and the dining room.
- The dining room overlooks the backyard patio and is open to the kitchen. Just off the kitchen is a large utility room.
- The master bedroom has a private bath. The two smaller bedrooms at the other end of the home share a full bath.

**Plan E-1412**

| | |
|---|---|
| **Bedrooms:** 3 | **Baths:** 2 |

**Space:**

| | |
|---|---|
| Main floor | **1,484 sq. ft.** |
| **Total Living Area** | **1,484 sq. ft.** |
| **Exterior Wall Framing** | **2x6** |

**Foundation options:**

Crawlspace

Slab

(Foundation & framing conversion diagram available—see order form.)

| **Blueprint Price Code** | **A** |
|---|---|

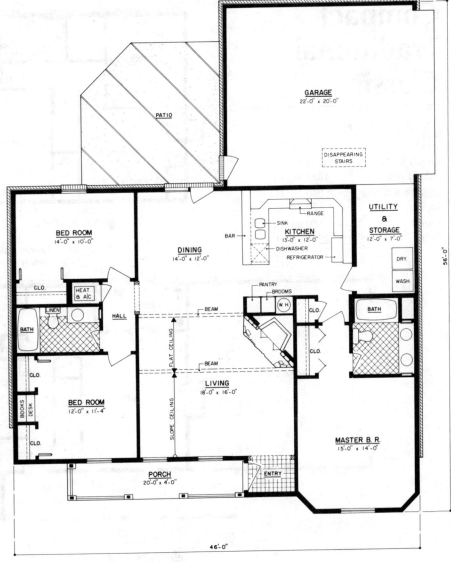

# Compact Traditional Classic

## AREAS

| | |
|---|---|
| Living-Lower | 767 sq. ft. |
| Living-Upper | 720 sq. ft. |
| Total Living | 1487 sq. ft. |
| Garage & Storage | 565 sq. ft. |
| Atrium | 72 sq. ft. |
| Porch | 180 sq. ft. |
| Total | 2304 sq. ft. |

**UPPER LEVEL**

Exterior walls are 2x6 construction.
Specify crawlspace or slab foundation.

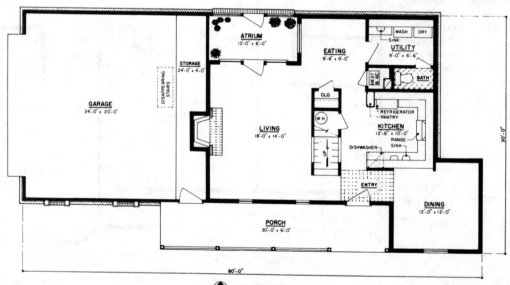

**LOWER LEVEL**

**TO ORDER THIS BLUEPRINT,
CALL TOLL-FREE 1-800-547-5570**

Blueprint Price Code A

# Plan E-1409

**PRICES AND DETAILS
ON PAGES 12-15**

# Unique, Dramatic Floor Plan

- An expansive and impressive Great Room, warmed by a wood stove, features an island kitchen that's completely open in design.
- A passive solar sun room is designed to collect and store heat from the sun, while also providing a good view of the surroundings.
- Upstairs, you'll see a glamorous master suite with a private bath and a huge walk-in closet.
- The daylight basement adds a sunny sitting room, a third bedroom and a large recreation room.

**UPPER FLOOR**

| Plans P-536-2A & -2D | |
|---|---|
| **Bedrooms:** 2-3 | **Baths:** 2-3 |

| **Space:** | |
|---|---|
| Upper floor: | 642 sq. ft. |
| Main floor: | 863 sq. ft. |

| **Total living area:** | 1,505 sq. ft. |
|---|---|
| Basement: | 863 sq. ft. |
| Garage: | 445 sq. ft. |

| **Exterior Wall Framing:** | 2x4 |
|---|---|

| **Foundation options:** | Plan # |
|---|---|
| Daylight basement | P-536-2D |
| Crawlspace | P-536-2A |

(Foundation & framing conversion diagram available — see order form.)

| **Blueprint Price Code:** | |
|---|---|
| Plan P-536-2A | B |
| Plan P-536-2D | C |

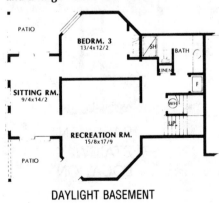

**DAYLIGHT BASEMENT**

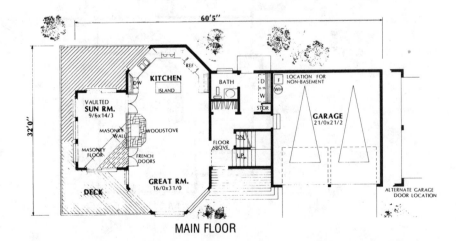

**MAIN FLOOR**

Photo by Mark Englund/HomeStyles

# Sunny and Sensational

- All of the living spaces in this spectacular home revolve around a sensational kitchen with an adjoining bay-windowed nook.
- The vaulted entry is strategically positioned to allow easy access to the bedroom wing, the kitchen and the vaulted living room. The latter offers a fireplace framed by picture windows. The open dining room is outlined by a dropped ceiling and has a pocket door closing it off from the family room.

- The spacious family room is further enlarged by a cathedral ceiling, a large picture window and sliders leading to a deck or patio.
- The sunny kitchen and nook are joined by a large island with a cooktop and a serving counter. In addition to its appealing bay windows, the nook offers a practical desk that is handy to the entry and the kitchen.
- The utility room is convenient to the bedrooms, plus provides an easy passageway between the garage and the kitchen.
- The master bedroom has a private bath, while the two remaining bedrooms share a full bath.

**Plans P-7758-2A & -2D**

| Bedrooms: 3 | Baths: 2 |
|---|---|
| **Living Area:** | |
| Main floor (crawlspace version) | 1,535 sq. ft. |
| Main floor (basement version) | 1,595 sq. ft. |
| **Total Living Area:** | **1,535/1,595 sq. ft.** |
| Daylight basement | 1,580 sq. ft. |
| Garage | 579 sq. ft. |
| **Exterior Wall Framing:** | 2x4 |
| **Foundation Options:** | **Plan #** |
| Daylight basement | P-7758-2D |
| Crawlspace | P-7758-2A |

(Typical foundation & framing conversion diagram available—see order form.)

**BLUEPRINT PRICE CODE:** **B**

**NOTE:**
The above photographed home may have been modified by the homeowner. Please refer to floor plan and/or drawn elevation shown for actual blueprint details.

60'0"

52'0"

SHWR

DRESSING

**BEDRM. 2**
10/0x10/0

**BEDRM. 3**
10/0x10/0

**GARAGE**
26/6x21/10

**BATH**

WH

LIN

TUB

F

**MASTER**
13/9x11/6

UTILITY

D W

**VAULTED LIVING**
15/6x17/0

**VAULTED ENTRY**

DESK

**KITCHEN**
10/0x11/0

**NOOK**
8/6x11/0

DW

REF

CEILING LINE

**DINING**
10/0x9/0

**VAULTED FAMILY**
17/4x12/0

**PATIO**

**MAIN FLOOR**

BATH

TUB

GARAGE

UTILITY

D W

**BASEMENT STAIRWAY LOCATION**

**TO ORDER THIS BLUEPRINT,**
**CALL TOLL-FREE 1-800-547-5570**
Plans P-7758-2A & -2D
**PRICES AND DETAILS**
**ON PAGES 12-15**

# Rustic Comfort

- While rustic in exterior appearance, this home is completely modern inside and loaded with the amenities preferred by today's builders.
- A large living room is made to seem immense by use of 16' ceilings, and an impressive fireplace and hearth dominate one end of the room.
- A formal dining room adds to the spaciousness, since it is separated from the living room only by a divider and a 6" step.
- The large U-shaped kitchen is adjoined by a convenient sewing and utility area, which in turn leads to the garage. A storage area is included in the garage, along with a built-in workbench.

- The sumptuous master suite features a sitting area, enormous walk-in closet and deluxe private bath.
- The two secondary bedrooms share another full bath and are zoned for privacy.

| Plan E-1607 | |
|---|---|
| Bedrooms: 3 | Baths: 2 |

| Space: | |
|---|---|
| **Total living area:** | 1,600 sq. ft. |
| Basement: | approx. 1,600 sq. ft. |
| Garage: | 484 sq. ft. |
| Storage: | 132 sq. ft. |
| Porch: | 295 sq. ft. |

| Exterior Wall Framing: | 2x6 |
|---|---|

**Foundation options:**
Standard basement.
Crawlspace.
Slab.
(Foundation & framing conversion diagram available — see order form)

| Blueprint Price Code: | B |
|---|---|

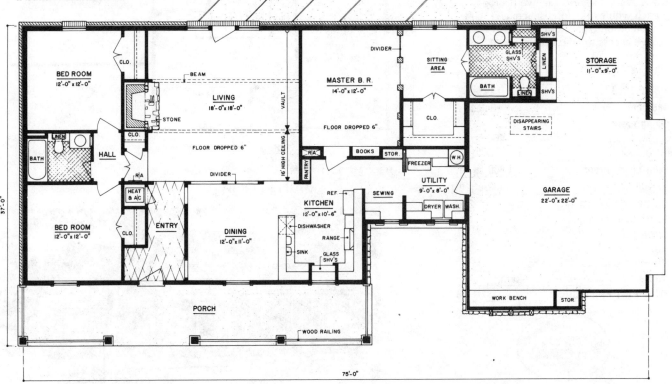

UPPER FLOOR

# Cost-Saving Style

- This country-style home has a classic exterior look and an open, space-saving floor plan.
- The U-shaped kitchen flows nicely into the dining room, where an angled hall stretches to the screened-in porch and the living room.
- The deluxe master bedroom is large for a home this size, and includes a separate sink and vanity area that adjoins the main bath.
- A good-sized utility room is convenient to the garage, which features a large storage area.
- The second floor offers two bedrooms, each with extra closet space, and another full bath. Both bedrooms also have access to attic storage space.

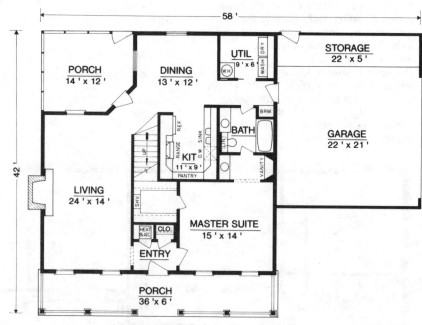

MAIN FLOOR

### Plan E-1626

| Bedrooms: 3 | Baths: 2 |
|---|---|
| **Living Area:** | |
| Upper floor | 464 sq. ft. |
| Main floor | 1,136 sq. ft. |
| **Total Living Area:** | **1,600 sq. ft.** |
| Garage | 462 sq. ft. |
| **Exterior Wall Framing:** | 2x6 |

**Foundation Options:**
Crawlspace
Slab
(Typical foundation & framing conversion diagram available—see order form.)

**BLUEPRINT PRICE CODE:** B

**\*\*NOTE:**
The above photographed home may have been modified by the homeowner. Please refer to floor plan and/or drawn elevation shown for actual blueprint details.

Plan E-1626

# Compact Three-Bedroom Home

- A stylish blend of traditional and contemporary architecture emanates from this compact, three-bedroom home.
- Two bedrooms and an adjoining bath occupy one corner of the main level, segregated from the living areas by a central hallway.
- Large living and dining area has sloped ceilings, wood stove, and access to side deck.
- Master suite occupies entire 516 sq. ft. second floor, features sloped ceilings, and overlooks the living room below.

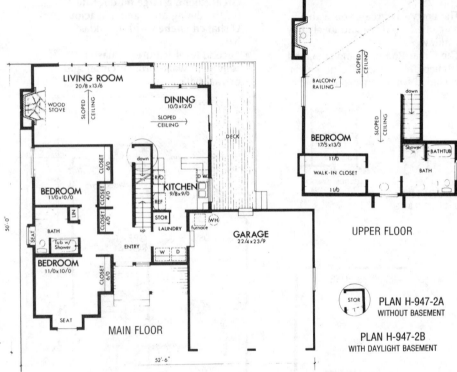

**MAIN FLOOR**

**UPPER FLOOR**

PLAN H-947-2A
WITHOUT BASEMENT

PLAN H-947-2B
WITH DAYLIGHT BASEMENT

### Plans H-947-2A & -2B

| Bedrooms: 3 | Baths: 2 |
|---|---|

**Space:**

| | |
|---|---|
| Upper floor: | 516 sq. ft. |
| Main floor: | 1,162 sq. ft. |
| **Total living area:** | **1,678 sq. ft.** |
| Basement: | approx. 1,162 sq. ft. |
| Garage: | 530 sq. ft. |

**Exterior Wall Framing:** 2x6

**Foundation options:**
Daylight basement (Plan H-947-2B).
Crawlspace (Plan H-947-2A).
(Foundation & framing conversion diagram available — see order form.)

**Blueprint Price Code:** B

# Ideal Home for a Narrow Lot

- This design features a room arrangement that is wide-open, yet confined to an economical width of only 28'.
- The entryway greets you with a balconied staircase and lovely bay window.
- The Great Room, dining area, and kitchen are arranged so no one is excluded from conversation or on-going activities.
- Other highlights include a woodstove/stone hearth in the Great Room, a large outdoor deck off the dining area, and a spacious U-shaped kitchen with breakfast bar.
- Second level features a master suite with walk-through closet and private bath.

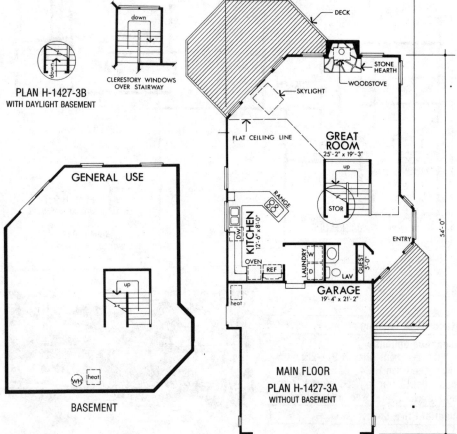

PLAN H-1427-3B
WITH DAYLIGHT BASEMENT

CLERESTORY WINDOWS
OVER STAIRWAY

GENERAL USE

BASEMENT

DECK

FLAT CEILING LINE

SKYLIGHT

STONE HEARTH

WOODSTOVE

GREAT ROOM
25'-2" x 19'-3"

28'-0"

54'-0"

STOR

KITCHEN
12'-6" x 8'-0"

RANGE

DW

OVEN

REF

LAUNDRY

W D

LAV

GUEST 5'-0"

ENTRY

heat

GARAGE
19'-4" x 21'-2"

MAIN FLOOR
PLAN H-1427-3A
WITHOUT BASEMENT

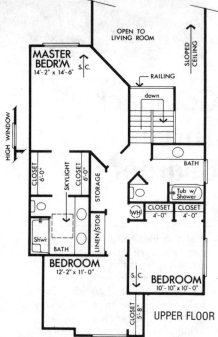

OPEN TO
LIVING ROOM

SLOPED CEILING

MASTER BEDR'M
14'-2" x 14'-6"

S.C.

RAILING

down

HIGH WINDOW

CLOSET 6'-0"

SKYLIGHT

CLOSET 6'-0"

STORAGE

LINEN/STOR

BATH

BATH

Tub w/ Shower

WH

CLOSET 4'-0"

CLOSET 4'-0"

Shw'r

BEDROOM
12'-2" x 11'-0"

S.C.

CLOSET 5'-8"

BEDROOM
10'-10" x 10'-0"

UPPER FLOOR

### Plans H-1427-3A & -3B

| Bedrooms: 3 | Baths: 2½ |
|---|---|
| **Space:** | |
| Upper floor: | 880 sq. ft. |
| Main floor: | 810 sq. ft. |
| **Total without basement:** | 1,690 sq. ft. |
| Basement: | 810 sq. ft. |
| **Total with basement:** | 2,500 sq. ft. |
| Garage: | 443 sq. ft. |

| **Exterior Wall Framing:** | 2x4 |
|---|---|

**Foundation options:**
Daylight basement.
Crawlspace.
Foundation & framing conversion diagram available — see order form.)

**Blueprint Price Code:**

| Without basement: | B |
|---|---|
| With basement: | D |

Photo by Mark Englund/HomeStyles

# Exciting Interior Angles

- A relatively modest-looking exterior encloses an exciting interior design that's loaded with surprises.
- The Y-shaped entry directs traffic to the more formal living/dining area or to the family room or bedroom wing.
- The family room features an unusual shape, a vaulted ceiling and a fireplace.
- The living room is brightened by a bay window, and also includes a fireplace.
- The dining area, the sun room, the family room and the outdoor patios are grouped around the large kitchen.
- The roomy master suite includes a deluxe bath and a large closet.
- The daylight-basement version adds 1,275 square feet of space.

### Plans P-7661-3A & -3D

| | |
|---|---|
| **Bedrooms: 2-3** | **Baths: 2** |
| **Space:** | |
| Main floor | 1,693 sq. ft. |
| **Total Living Area** | **1,693 sq. ft.** |
| Basement | 1,275 sq. ft. |
| Garage | 462 sq. ft. |
| **Exterior Wall Framing** | 2x4 |
| **Foundation options:** | **Plan #** |
| Daylight Basement | P-7661-3D |
| Crawlspace | P-7661-3A |
| (Foundation & framing conversion diagram available—see order form.) | |
| **Blueprint Price Code** | **B** |

**55'-0"**

**54'-0"**

PATIO

WALK IN WARDROBE

MASTER
13/0 x 15/6

VAULTED
FAMILY RM.
17/0 x 13/6

KITCHEN
13/0 x 10/0

LINEN

PATIO

WOODSTOVE

VAULTED
SUN RM.

PANTRY

ENTRY

DINING AREA

BEDRM. 2
10/0 x 10/0

DEN/
BEDRM. 3
10/0 x 11/6

W D

F WH

LIVING RM.
18/4 x 18/4

GARAGE
21/4 x 21/8

MAIN FLOOR
PLAN P-7661-3A
WITH CRAWLSPACE

**NOTE:**
The above photographed home may have been modified by the homeowner. Please refer to floor plan and/or drawn elevation shown for actual blueprint details.

BAR

MASTER

DN

PLAN P-7661-3D
WITH DAYLIGHT BASEMENT

# Fresh New Interior with an Old Favorite Exterior

This Louisiana-style raised cottage features a separate master suite with a connecting showplace bathroom fit for the most demanding taste.

Pairs of French doors in each of the front rooms invite family members and visitors to enjoy the cool and relaxing front porch. The tin roof adds to the comfort and nostalgic appeal of this Creole classic. An unusual, angled eating bar overlooks the cozy covered terrance via a bay window morning room.

The secondary bedroom wing has two full-size bedrooms, maximum closets, and a full-size bath.

This full-feature energy-efficient design is drawn on a raised crawlspace foundation. An alternate concrete slab foundation is available.

### PLAN E-1823
WITHOUT BASEMENT

Areas:

| | |
|---|---|
| Heated: | 1,800 sq. ft. |
| Unheated: | 1,100 sq. ft. |
| Total area: | 2,900 sq. ft. |

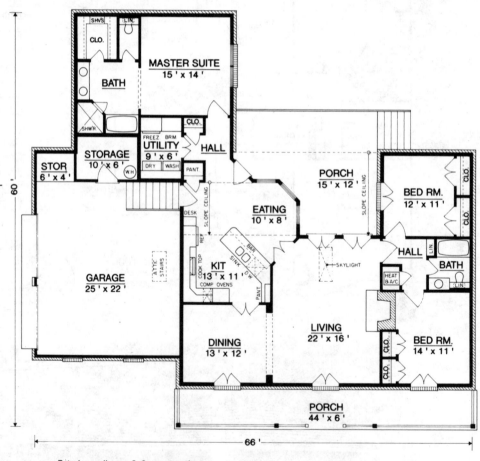

Exterior walls are 2x6 construction.
Specify crawlspace or slab foundation.

**TO ORDER THIS BLUEPRINT, CALL TOLL-FREE 1-800-547-5570**

Blueprint Price Code B
## Plan E-1823

**PRICES AND DETAILS ON PAGES 12-15**

# Raised Cottage Design Offers Large Covered Porches

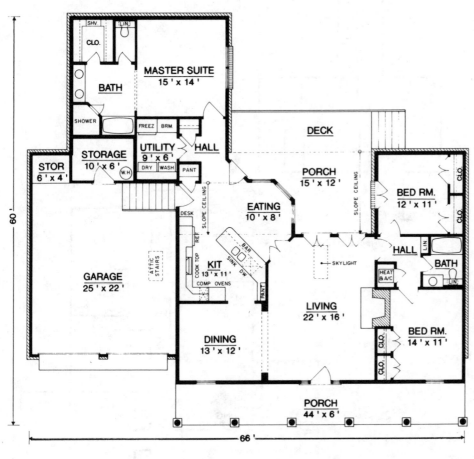

- Twin dormers and covered porch add drama to this raised one-story.
- Large centered living room features 12' ceilings and built-in skylights.
- Kitchen has unusual but functional angular design, sloped ceilings, bar, and eating area that overlooks the adjoining deck.
- Elegant master suite is conveniently located near kitchen.

**Plan E-1826**

| Bedrooms: 3 | Baths: 2 |
|---|---|

| Space: | |
|---|---|
| **Total living area:** | 1,800 sq. ft. |
| Garage: | 550 sq. ft. |
| Storage: | 84 sq. ft. |
| Porches: | 466 sq. ft. |

| **Exterior Wall Framing:** | 2x6 |
|---|---|

**Foundation options:**
Crawlspace.
Slab.
(Foundation & framing conversion diagram available — see order form.)

| **Blueprint Price Code:** | B |
|---|---|

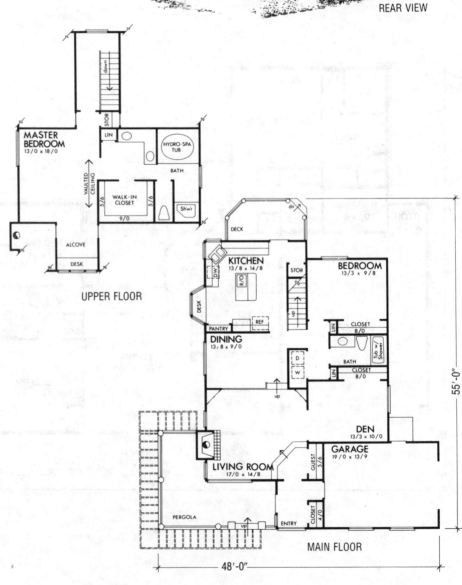

REAR VIEW

# Bungalow Style for Today

- Many of the features of the once-popular bungalow are preserved and improved upon in this plan.
- A special touch is the pergola — the wooden trelliswork attached to the porch roof and supported by tapered columns.
- The spacious foyer has doors opening from both the porch and the opposing garage.
- The sunken living room is separated from the dining room by a custom-designed handrail.
- French doors close off the den or third bedroom from the living room.
- The expansive kitchen features an island work center, a pantry, a bay window with built-in desk, and access to the rear deck.
- The master suite has numerous frills.

## Plans H-1459-1 & -1A

| Bedrooms: 2 | Baths: 2 |
|---|---|
| **Space:** | |
| Upper floor | 658 sq. ft. |
| Main floor | 1,201 sq. ft. |
| **Total Living Area** | **1,859 sq. ft.** |
| Basement | 630 sq. ft. |
| Garage | 280 sq. ft. |
| **Exterior Wall Framing** | 2x6 |

**Foundation options:**

Partial Basement
Crawlspace
(Foundation & framing conversion diagram available—see order form.)

| **Blueprint Price Code** | **B** |
|---|---|

## Plans H-1459-1 & -1A

**PRICES AND DETAILS**
**ON PAGES 12-15**

# Attainable Luxury

- This traditional ranch home offers a large, central living room with a volume ceiling, a corner fireplace and an adjoining patio.
- The U-shaped kitchen easily services both the formal dining room and the bayed eating area.
- The luxurious master suite features a large bath with separate vanities and dressing areas.
- A covered carport boasts a decorative brick wall, attic space above and two additional storage areas.

**Plan E-1812**

| Bedrooms: 3 | Baths: 2 |
|---|---|
| **Living Area:** | |
| Main floor | 1,860 sq. ft. |
| **Total Living Area:** | **1,860 sq. ft.** |
| Carport | 484 sq. ft. |
| **Exterior Wall Framing:** | 2x6 |

**Foundation Options:**
Crawlspace
Slab
(Typical foundation & framing conversion diagram available—see order form.)

**BLUEPRINT PRICE CODE:**      **B**

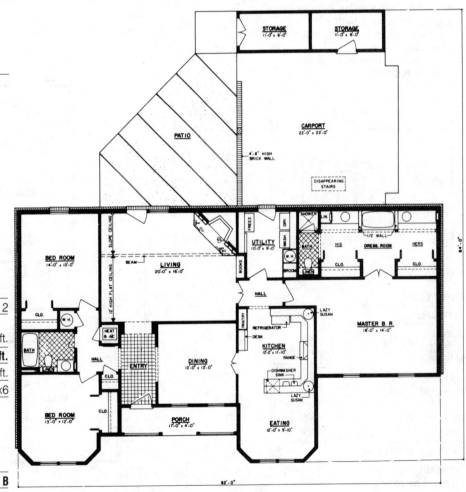

MAIN FLOOR

# Cost-Efficient Cottage with Luxury Features

- This country cottage is easy to build, economical and attractive.
- The basic rectangular shape simplifies construction, and the steeply pitched roof accommodates upstairs bedrooms in space that would often otherwise be simply attic overhead.
- A huge living room with fireplace dominates the main floor.
- The dining room, kitchen, utility area and half bath make an efficient and livable area for casual family life.
- The main-floor master suite includes a spacious private bath with separate tub and shower, and a large closet.
- Upstairs, two bedrooms share another full bath.

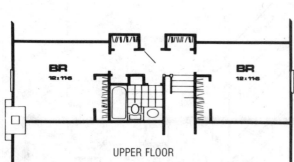

UPPER FLOOR

**Plan J-86131**

| Bedrooms: 3 | Baths: 2½ |
|---|---|
| **Space:** | |
| Upper floor: | 500 sq. ft. |
| Main floor: | 1,369 sq. ft. |
| **Total living area:** | **1,869 sq. ft.** |
| Basement: | 1,369 sq. ft. |
| Carport: | 416 sq. ft. |
| Storage: | 124 sq. ft. |
| Porch: | 258 sq. ft. |
| **Exterior Wall Framing:** | 2x4 |

**Foundation options:**
Standard basement.
Crawlspace.
Slab.
(Foundation & framing conversion diagram available — see order form.)

| **Blueprint Price Code:** | B |
|---|---|

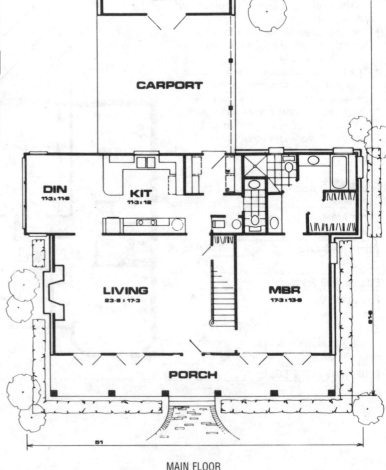

MAIN FLOOR

Plan J-86131

**PRICES AND DETAILS ON PAGES 12-15**

# Passive Solar with Many Orientation Options

This angled passive solar design is planned to suit almost any plot and many orientation alternatives. Exterior siding of vertical natural wood and a high front chimney give the house an interesting appearance.

Inside, the central focus is the light-filled south-facing sun garden that greets occupants and visitors as they enter the reception hall. The large combination living room and dining room are highlighted by a dramatic sloped ceiling and a high-efficiency wood-burning fireplace. Glass around and above the fireplace contributes more light and provides a panoramic view of the rear landscaping. Sharing a second fireplace is the informal area that includes the family room and U-shaped kitchen.

Three bedrooms are located in the left wing of the house. The large master suite has a cheerful sitting area which borders on the sun garden. Living area, excluding the sun garden, is 1,574 sq. ft.; optional basement is 1,522 sq. ft.; garage is 400 sq. ft.

Total living area:                 1,574 sq. ft.
(Not counting basement or garage)

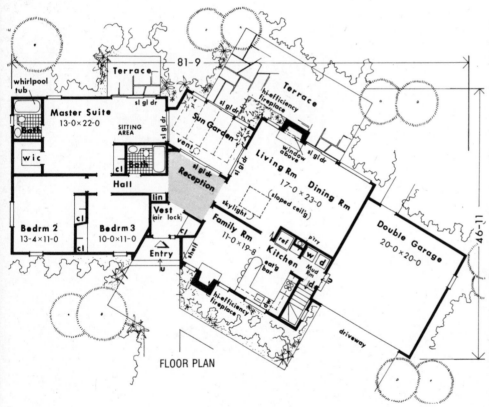

**FLOOR PLAN**

Master Suite 13-0×22-0
whirlpool tub
Terrace — 81-9
SITTING AREA
w i c
Bath
Hall
Bedrm 2 13-4×11-0
Bedrm 3 10-0×11-0
Vest (air lock)
Entry
Sun Garden
Reception
Family Rm 11-0×19-8
Kitchen
hi-efficiency fireplace
skylight
Living Rm   Dining Rm 17-0×23-0 (sloped ceil'g)
Terrace
hi-efficiency fireplace
Double Garage 20-0×20-0
driveway
46-11

SOLAR ENERGY
sum'r
win't'r
summer vent
summer shade to reflect sun
deciduous trees for summer shade
winter warm air
Terrace   Sun Garden   Recep   Vest air lock
Sheltered Entry
thermal flr. with insul. to store energy
wd. const.
Bsmt.
wall insulation

**SECTION**
**PASSIVE SOLAR AT WORK**

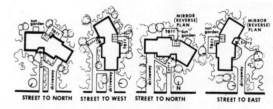

STREET TO NORTH   STREET TO WEST   STREET TO NORTH   STREET TO EAST
MIRROR (REVERSE) PLAN

**IMAGINE THE ORIENTATION POSSIBILITIES**

Blueprint Price Code B

# Plan K-526-C

# Angled Solar Design

- This passive solar design with a six-sided core is angled to capture as much sunlight as possible.
- Finished in natural vertical cedar planks and stone veneer, this contemporary three-bedroom requires minimum maintenance.
- Double doors at the entry open into the spacious living and dining areas.
- The formal area features a domed ceiling with skylights, a free-standing fireplace and three sets of sliding glass doors. The central sliders lead to a glass-enclosed sun room.
- The bright U-shaped kitchen is an extension of the den; sliding glass doors lead to one of two large backyard terraces.
- The master bedroom, in a quiet sleeping wing, boasts ample closets, a private terrace and a luxurious bath, complete with a whirlpool tub.

**VIEW OF LIVING ROOM LOOKING INTO DINING ROOM**

### Plan K-534-L

| Bedrooms: 3 | Baths: 2 |
|---|---|

| **Living Area:** | |
|---|---|
| Main floor | 1,647 sq. ft. |

| **Total Living Area:** | **1,647 sq. ft.** |
|---|---|
| Standard basement | 1,505 sq. ft. |
| Garage | 400 sq. ft. |

| **Exterior Wall Framing:** | 2x4 or 2x6 |
|---|---|

**Foundation Options:**
Standard basement
Slab
(Typical foundation & framing conversion diagram available—see order form.)

| **BLUEPRINT PRICE CODE:** | **B** |
|---|---|

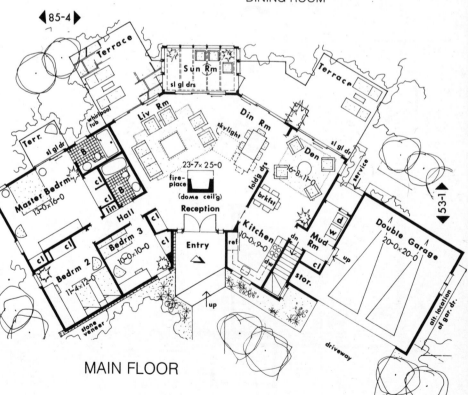

**MAIN FLOOR**

# Private Courtyard Protects Entry

| AREAS | |
|---|---|
| Living | 1497 sq. ft. |
| Porch | 24 sq. ft. |
| Garage & Storage | 528 sq. ft. |
| Total | 2049 sq. ft. |

Exterior walls are 2x6 construction.
Specify crawlspace or slab foundation.

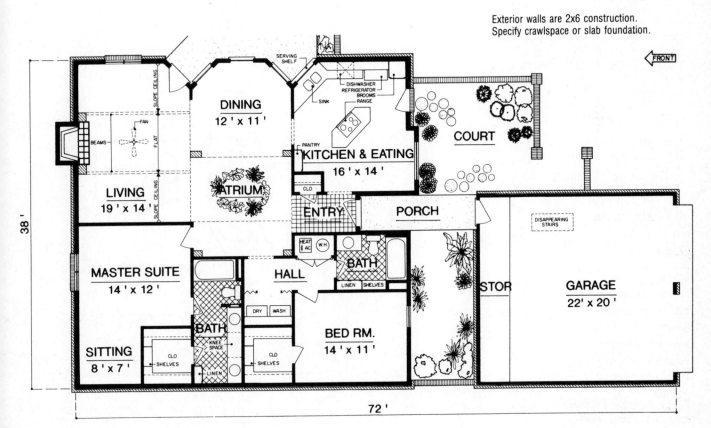

Blueprint Price Code A

Plan E-1418

**TO ORDER THIS BLUEPRINT,**
**CALL TOLL-FREE 1-800-547-5570**

**PRICES AND DETAILS**
**ON PAGES 12-15**

**67**

REAR VIEW

# For Vacation or Year-Round Casual Living

- More than 500 square feet of deck area across the rear sets the theme of casual outdoor living for this compact plan.
- The living/dining/kitchen combination is included in one huge, 15' x 39' Great Room, which is several steps down from the entry level for an even more dramatic effect.
- Two large downstairs bedrooms share a bath. Upstairs, a hideaway bedroom includes a private bath, a walk-in closet and a romantic private deck.
- A utility room is conveniently placed in the garage entry area.
- The optional basement features a large recreation room with a fireplace and sliders to a patio underneath the rear deck.
- A fourth bedroom and a third bath in the basement would be ideal for guests.
- At the front of the basement is a large area that could be used for a hobby room or a children's play area.

**Plans H-877-1 & -1A**

| Bedrooms: 3-4 | Baths: 2-3 |
|---|---|
| **Living Area:** | |
| Upper floor | 320 sq. ft. |
| Main floor | 1,200 sq. ft. |
| Daylight basement | 1,200 sq. ft. |
| **Total Living Area:** | **1,520/2,720 sq. ft.** |
| Garage | 155 sq. ft. |
| **Exterior Wall Framing:** | 2x6 |

**Foundation Options:**
Daylight basement
Crawlspace
(Typical foundation & framing conversion diagram available—see order form.)

| **BLUEPRINT PRICE CODE:** | B/D |
|---|---|

UPPER FLOOR

BASEMENT STAIRWAY LOCATION

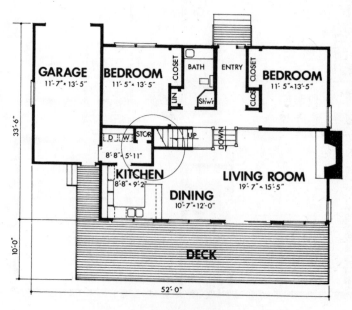

MAIN FLOOR

**TO ORDER THIS BLUEPRINT, CALL TOLL-FREE 1-800-547-5570**

Plan H-877-1 & -1A

**PRICES AND DETAILS ON PAGES 12-15**

Photo by James Erickson

# Rustic Styling, Comfortable Interior

- Front-to-back split level with large decks lends itself to steep sloping site, particularly in a scenic area.
- Compact, space-efficient design makes for economical construction.
- Great Room design concept utilizes the entire 36' width of home for the kitchen/dining/living area.
- Two bedrooms and a bath are up three steps, on the entry level.
- Upper level bedroom includes a compact bath and a private deck.

**\*\*NOTE:**
The above photographed home may have been modified by the homeowner. Please refer to floor plan and/or drawn elevation shown for actual blueprint details.

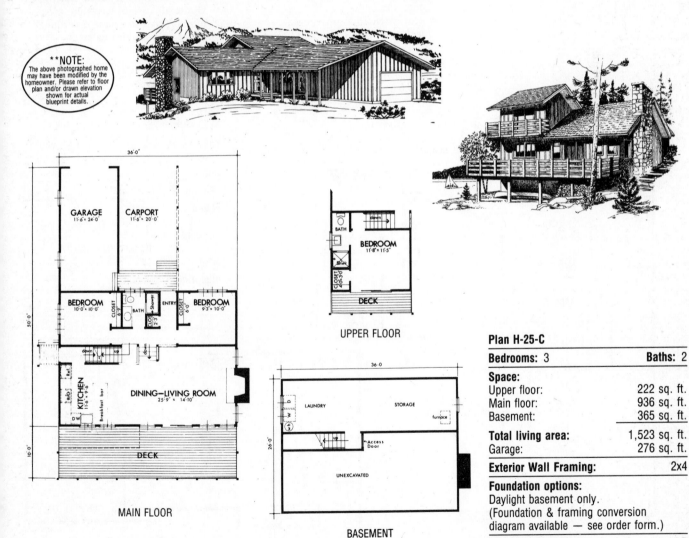

GARAGE 11'-6" x 24'-0"   CARPORT 11'-6" x 20'-0"

BEDROOM 10'-0" x 10'-0"   CLOSET   BATH   Shower   ENTRY   CLOSET   BEDROOM 9'-3" x 10'-0"

down   up   down

KITCHEN 11'-6" x 9'-6"   Breakfast bar   DINING—LIVING ROOM 25'-9" x 14'-10"

DW   Ref.

DECK

36'-0"

50'-0"

10'-0"

**MAIN FLOOR**

BATH   down

BEDROOM 11'-8" x 11'-5"

CLOSET 4'0"-3'0"   Shwr.

DECK

**UPPER FLOOR**

36'-0"

W   D

LAUNDRY   STORAGE   furnace

up   Access Door

UNEXCAVATED

26'-0"

**BASEMENT**

### Plan H-25-C

| Bedrooms: 3 | Baths: 2 |
|---|---|

| Space: | |
|---|---|
| Upper floor: | 222 sq. ft. |
| Main floor: | 936 sq. ft. |
| Basement: | 365 sq. ft. |

| Total living area: | 1,523 sq. ft. |
|---|---|
| Garage: | 276 sq. ft. |

| Exterior Wall Framing: | 2x4 |
|---|---|

**Foundation options:**
Daylight basement only.
(Foundation & framing conversion diagram available — see order form.)

| Blueprint Price Code: | B |
|---|---|

**FRONT VIEW**

# Economical Design

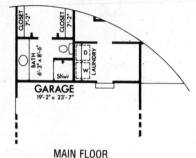

**MAIN FLOOR**
**PLAN H-868-1A**
WITHOUT BASEMENT

CLOSET 7'-2"   CLOSET 7'-2"
BATH 6'-3" x 8'-6"
D W LAUNDRY
Shwr
**GARAGE** 19'-2" x 23'-7"

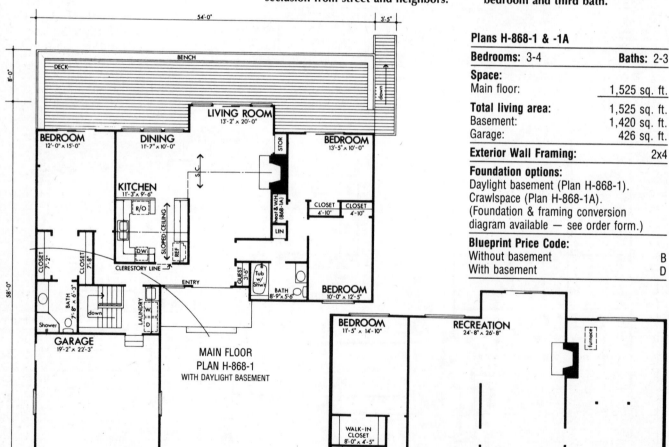

**REAR VIEW**

- Uninterrupted glass and a full, rear deck afford a sweeping view of the outdoors.
- Rear orientation provides a seclusion from street and neighbors.

- Open, flexible family living areas allow for efficient traffic flow.
- Optional daylight basement plan offers recreation room, additional bedroom and third bath.

### Plans H-868-1 & -1A

| Bedrooms: 3-4 | Baths: 2-3 |
|---|---|
| **Space:** | |
| Main floor: | 1,525 sq. ft. |
| **Total living area:** | 1,525 sq. ft. |
| Basement: | 1,420 sq. ft. |
| Garage: | 426 sq. ft. |
| **Exterior Wall Framing:** | 2x4 |

**Foundation options:**
Daylight basement (Plan H-868-1).
Crawlspace (Plan H-868-1A).
(Foundation & framing conversion diagram available — see order form.)

**Blueprint Price Code:**
| Without basement | B |
|---|---|
| With basement | D |

**MAIN FLOOR**
**PLAN H-868-1**
WITH DAYLIGHT BASEMENT

54'-0"   3'-5"
8'-0"
BENCH
DECK   down
LIVING ROOM 13'-2" x 20'-0"
BEDROOM 12'-0" x 15'-0"   DINING 11'-7" x 10'-0"   STOR   BEDROOM 13'-5" x 10'-0"
KITCHEN 11'-3" x 9'-6"
R/O
S.C.
SLOPED CEILING
DW   REF   Heat & W.H. (868-1A)
CLERESTORY LINE   LIN
58'-0"
CLOSET 7'-2"   CLOSET 7'-8"   ENTRY   CLOSET 4'-10"   CLOSET 4'-10"
BATH 7'-8" x 6'-3"   GUEST 3'-6"   Tub w/Shwr   BEDROOM 10'-0" x 12'-5"
Shower   down   LAUNDRY W D   BATH 8'-9" x 5'-6"
**GARAGE** 19'-2" x 22'-3"

CLERESTORY WINDOW OVER KITCHEN

**DAYLIGHT BASEMENT**

BEDROOM 11'-5" x 14'-10"   RECREATION 24'-8" x 26'-8"   furnace
WALK-IN CLOSET 8'-0" x 4'-5"
BATH
up
Shower   WH   STOR   WH   GENERAL USE 15'-3" x 24'-6"

# Open, Energy-Saving Design

- **Wrapped with heavy insulation beneath elegant horizontal siding, this handsome three-bedroom ranch helps generate and conserve natural energy.**

- **An expansive sun roof and sliding glass doors enlighten the informal family room adjoining a lavish U-shaped kitchen with bar and connecting eating area.**

- **A cathedral ceiling, wood-burning fireplace, sliding glass doors and two tall windows grace the formal living room.**

- **The isolated master bedroom boasts a private terrace and luxury bath; the secondary bedrooms share a second full bath.**

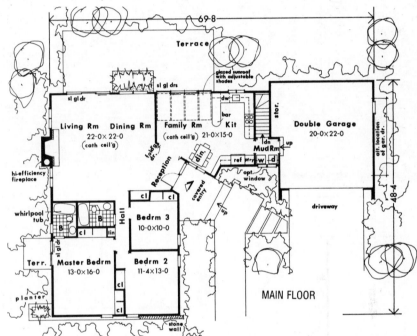

Terrace

69-8

Living Rm 22-0×22-0 (cath ceil'g)

Dining Rm

Family Rm (cath ceil'g) 21-0×15-0

Kit

Double Garage 20-0×22-0

glazed sunroof with adjustable shades

sl gl dr

sl gl drs

dw

bar

stor.

Mud Rm

alt. location of gar. dr.

hi-efficiency fireplace

Reception

ref

w

d

opt. window

whirlpool tub

B

B

cl

lin

Hall

cl

cl

Bedrm 3 10-0×10-0

covered entry

up

up

driveway

Terr.

Master Bedrm 13-0×16-0

sl gl drs

Bedrm 2 11-4×13-0

cl

cl

planter

cl

stone wall

**MAIN FLOOR**

48-4

| Plan K-538-L | |
|---|---|
| **Bedrooms:** 3 | **Baths:** 2 |
| **Space:** | |
| **Total living area:** | 1,532 sq. ft. |
| Optional basement: | 1,570 sq. ft. |
| Garage, mudroom: | 550 sq. ft. |
| **Exterior Wall Framing:** | 2x4 or 2x6 |
| **Foundation options:** Standard basement. Slab. (Foundation & framing conversion diagram available — see order form.) | |
| **Blueprint Price Code:** | B |

FRONT VIEW

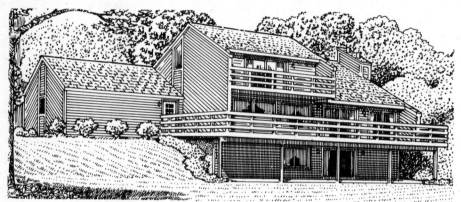

REAR VIEW

# Hillside Design Fits Contours

- The daylight-basement version of this popular plan is perfect for a scenic, sloping lot.
- A large, wraparound deck embraces the rear-oriented living areas, accessed through sliding glass doors.
- The spectacular living room boasts a corner fireplace, a sloped ceiling and outdoor views to the side and rear.
- The secluded master suite upstairs offers a walk-in closet, a private bath and sliders to a sun deck.
- The daylight basement (not shown) includes a fourth bedroom with private bath and walk-in closet, as well as a recreation room with fireplace and sliders to a rear patio.
- The standard basement (not shown) includes a recreation room with fireplace and a room for hobbies or child's play.
- Both basements also have a large unfinished area below the main-floor bedrooms.

UPPER FLOOR

| Plans H-877-4, -4A & -4B | |
|---|---|
| **Bedrooms:** 3-4 | **Baths:** 2-3 |
| **Living Area:** | |
| Upper floor | 333 sq. ft. |
| Main floor | 1,200 sq. ft. |
| Basement (finished portion) | 591 sq. ft. |
| **Total Living Area:** | **1,533/2,124 sq. ft.** |
| Basement (unfinished portion) | 493 sq. ft. |
| Garage | 480 sq. ft. |
| **Exterior Wall Framing:** | 2x6 |
| **Foundation Options:** | **Plan #** |
| Daylight basement | H-877-4B |
| Standard basement | H-877-4 |
| Crawlspace | H-877-4A |
| (Typical foundation & framing conversion diagram available—see order form.) | |
| **BLUEPRINT PRICE CODE:** | **B/C** |

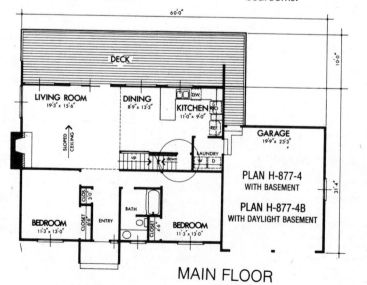

PLAN H-877-4
WITH BASEMENT

PLAN H-877-4B
WITH DAYLIGHT BASEMENT

PLAN H-877-4A
WITHOUT BASEMENT

MAIN FLOOR

**TO ORDER THIS BLUEPRINT, CALL TOLL-FREE 1-800-547-5570**

# Plans H-877-4, -4A & -4B

**PRICES AND DETAILS ON PAGES 12-15**

UPPER FLOOR

# Chalet for All Seasons

- Rustic exterior makes this design suitable for a lakefront, beach, or wooded setting.
- Patterned railing and wood deck edge the front and side main level, while a smaller deck assumes a balcony role.
- Designed for relaxed, leisure living, the main level features a large L-shaped Great Room warmed by a central free-standing fireplace.
- Upper level offers a second bath and added sleeping accommodations.

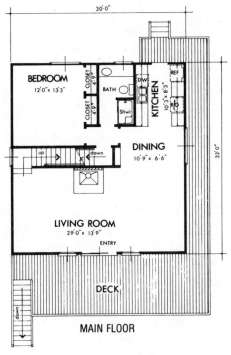

MAIN FLOOR

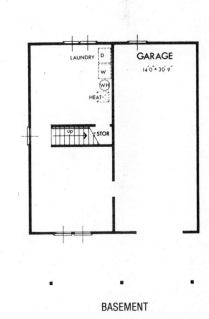

BASEMENT

## Plan H-858-2

| Bedrooms: 3 | Baths: 2 |
|---|---|

| Space: | |
|---|---|
| Upper floor: | 576 sq. ft. |
| Main floor: | 960 sq. ft. |

| Total living area: | 1,536 sq. ft. |
|---|---|
| Basement: | 530 sq. ft. |
| Garage: | 430 sq. ft. |

| Exterior Wall Framing: | 2x6 |
|---|---|

**Foundation options:**
Daylight basement.
(Foundation & framing conversion diagram available — see order form.)

| Blueprint Price Code: | B |
|---|---|

# Solarium Adds Extra Touch of Luxury

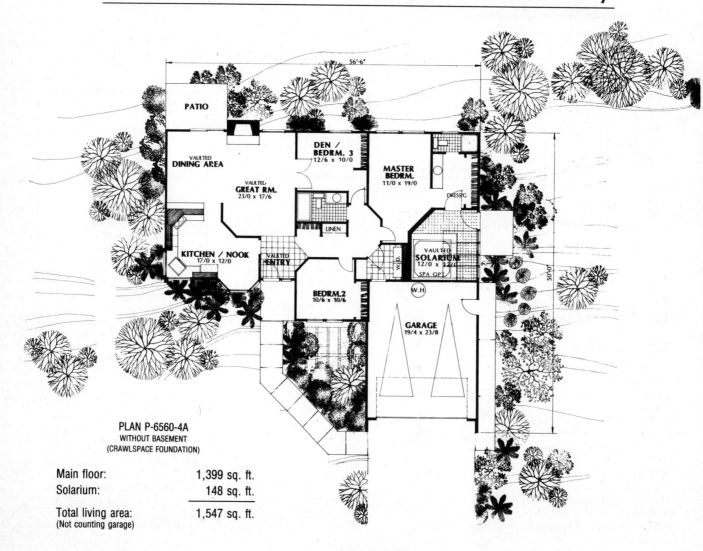

**PLAN P-6560-4A**
WITHOUT BASEMENT
(CRAWLSPACE FOUNDATION)

Main floor:                    1,399 sq. ft.
Solarium:                        148 sq. ft.

Total living area:           1,547 sq. ft.
(Not counting garage)

Blueprint Price Code B
## Plan P-6560-4A

**TO ORDER THIS BLUEPRINT,**
**CALL TOLL-FREE 1-800-547-5570**

*PRICES AND DETAILS*
*ON PAGES 12-15*

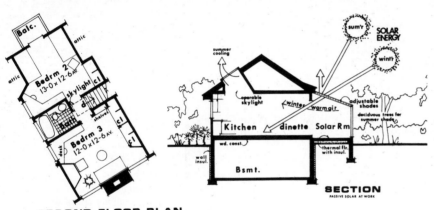

**SECOND FLOOR PLAN**

**SECTION**
PASSIVE SOLAR AT WORK

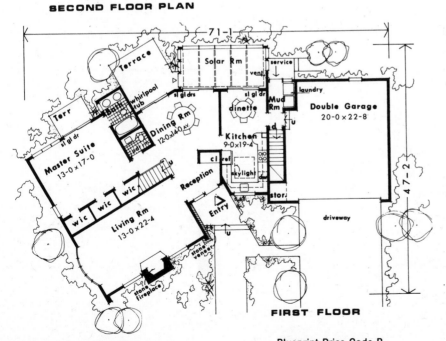

**FIRST FLOOR**

# Passive Solar Home Meets Modern Demands

The exterior of this two-story plan is thoroughly contemporary. The layout is angled to give it added distinction in any neighborhood. Optional orientations in relation to the street allow this plan to adapt to a variety of plot shapes. Inside, the reception hall immediately presents a pleasing view of the rear terrace and solar room. To the left is the living room, which is graced by a stone fireplace.

In winter months, light and solar heat enter through the glass and heat is stored in the ceramic tiled floor of the solar room; after the sun sets, this warmth is released to the house. In summer months, the sun rises higher and its rays are blocked by adjustable shades built into glazed ceiling panels; automatic vent guards against heat buildup.

Generously sized, the master bedroom features extensive glass to the south side, a personal bath and sliding glass doors that lead out to a private terrace.

Total living area, excluding the solar room, is 1,132 sq. ft. on the first floor and 416 sq. ft. on the second. Optional basement is 1,176 sq. ft.; garage, mud room, etc., come to 560 sq. ft. (Alternate slab-on-grade foundation plan is included.)

Total living area: 1,548 sq. ft.

# Open Kitchen/Family Room Combination

- This compact plan is designed to provide maximum casual living space for a small but busy family.
- A large family room/kitchen combination opens onto a large deck.
- The great room features an impressive corner fireplace and a vaulted ceiling and adjoins the dining room to create a liberal space for entertaining.
- Upstairs, the master suite includes a private bath and large closet.
- Bedroom 2 boasts a large gable window, two closets and easy access to a second upstairs bath.
- The loft area is available for study, play, an exercise area or third bedroom.

| Plan B-88006 | |
|---|---|
| **Bedrooms: 2-3** | **Baths: 2½** |
| **Space:** | |
| Upper floor: | 732 sq. ft. |
| Main floor: | 818 sq. ft. |
| **Total living area:** | 1,550 sq. ft. |
| Basement: | 818 sq. ft. |
| Garage: | 374 sq. ft. |
| **Exterior Wall Framing:** | 2x4 |

**Foundation options:**
Standard basement only.
(Foundation & framing conversion diagram available — see order form.)

| **Blueprint Price Code:** | B |
|---|---|

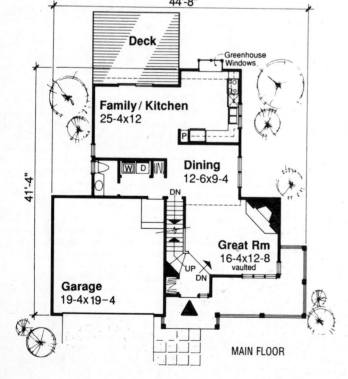

MAIN FLOOR

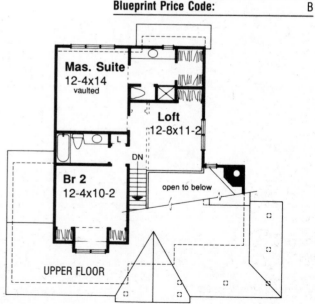

UPPER FLOOR

*TO ORDER THIS BLUEPRINT, CALL TOLL-FREE 1-800-547-5570*

Plan B-88006

*PRICES AND DETAILS ON PAGES 12-15*

# Cozy, Rustic Comfort

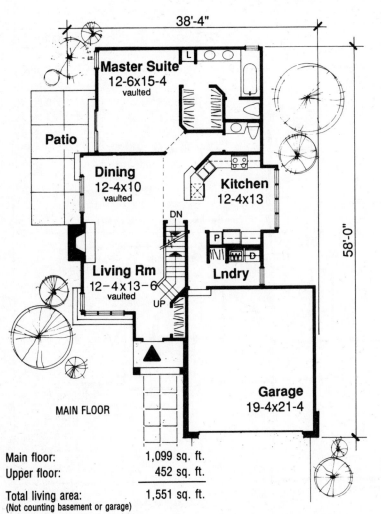

**38'-4"**

**Master Suite**
12-6x15-4
*vaulted*

L

**Patio**

**Dining**
12-4x10
*vaulted*

**Kitchen**
12-4x13

DN

**Living Rm**
12-4x13-6
*vaulted*

P

**Lndry**

W D

UP

▲

**58'-0"**

**Garage**
19-4x21-4

**MAIN FLOOR**

Main floor: 1,099 sq. ft.
Upper floor: 452 sq. ft.

Total living area: 1,551 sq. ft.
(Not counting basement or garage)

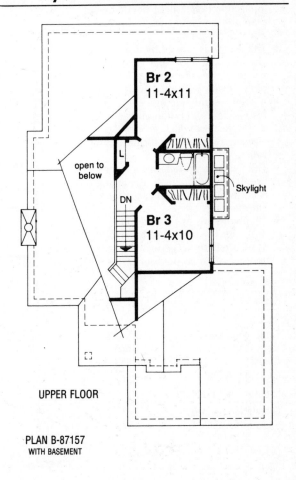

**Br 2**
11-4x11

open to
below

L

DN

Skylight

**Br 3**
11-4x10

**UPPER FLOOR**

**PLAN B-87157**
WITH BASEMENT

# Open Plan Includes Circular Dining Room

- Innovative architectural features and a functional, light-filled floor plan are the hallmarks of this attractive design.
- The facade is graced by a stone chimney and a circular glass bay which houses the spectacular dining room with its domed ceiling.
- A bright, sunny kitchen is set up for efficient operation and adjoins a dinette area which echoes the circular shape of the formal dining room.
- The living room features a stone fireplace, and opens to the dining room to make a great space for entertaining.
- The bedrooms are zoned to the left, with the master suite including a private bath, large walk-in closet and access to an outdoor terrace.

**Plan K-663-N**

| Bedrooms: 3 | Baths: 2 |
|---|---|

| Space: | |
|---|---|
| **Total living area:** | **1,560 sq. ft.** |
| Basement: | 1,645 sq. ft. |
| Garage: | 453 sq. ft. |
| Mudroom & stairs: | 122 sq. ft. |

| **Exterior Wall Framing:** | 2x4/2x6 |
|---|---|

**Foundation options:**
Standard basement.
Slab.
(Foundation & framing conversion diagram available — see order form.)

| **Blueprint Price Code:** | B |
|---|---|

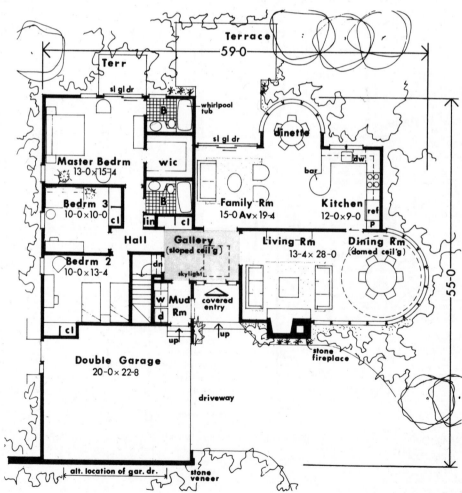

*TO ORDER THIS BLUEPRINT,*
*CALL TOLL-FREE 1-800-547-5570*

Plan K-663-N

*PRICES AND DETAILS*
*ON PAGES 12-15*

**DINING**
11'-0" x 12'-0"

**KITCHEN**

**LIVING ROOM**
19'-8" x 15'-4"

SLOPED CEILING

DECK

up
down
down

STOR

**LAUNDRY**
W D

GUEST

**BATH**
10'-3" x 8'-9"

LINEN

CLOSET
8'-4"

**BEDROOM**
11'-6" x 13'-7"

**BEDROOM**
11'-6" x 13'-7"

ENTRY

STORAGE

CLOSET
6'-6"

**GARAGE**
12'-10" x 23'-8"

**MAIN FLOOR**
1217 SQUARE FEET

**PLAN H-925-2**
WITH DAYLIGHT BASEMENT

DECK

WALK-IN CLOSET
7'-5" x 5'-0"

SLOPED C. CEILING

Shwr

**BATH**
9'-0" x 5'-0"

**BEDROOM**
14'-0" x 14'-0"

down

**SECOND FLOOR**
360 SQUARE FEET

STOR
w/ heat

**PLAN H-925-2A**
WITHOUT BASEMENT
(CRAWLSPACE FOUNDATION)

| | |
|---|---:|
| First floor: | 1,217 sq. ft. |
| Second floor: | 360 sq. ft. |
| **Total living area:** | 1,577 sq. ft. |
| (Not counting basement or garage) | |

# Economical and Convenient

In an effort to merge the financial possibilities and the space requirements of the greatest number of families, the designers of this home restricted themselves to just over 1,200 sq. ft. of ground cover (exclusive of garage), and still managed to develop a superior three-bedroom design.

From a covered walkway, one approaches a centralized entry hall which effectively distributes traffic throughout the home without causing interruptions. Two main floor bedrooms and bath as well as the stairway to the second floor master suite are immediately accessible to the entry. Directly forward and four steps down finds one in the main living area, consisting of a large living room with vaulted ceiling and a dining-kitchen combination with conventional ceiling height. All these rooms have direct access to an outdoor living deck of over 400 sq. ft. Thus, though modest and unassuming from the street side, this home evolves into eye-popping expansion and luxury toward the rear.

To ease homemaking chores, whether this is to be a permanent or vacation home, the working equipment, including laundry space, is all on the main floor. Yet the homemaker remains part of the family scene because there is only a breakfast counter separating the work space from the living area.

Tucked away upstairs, in complete privacy, one finds a master bedroom suite equipped with separate bath, walk-in wardrobe and a romantic private deck.

The plan is available with or without a basement and is best suited to a lot that slopes gently down from the road.

**TO ORDER THIS BLUEPRINT,**
**CALL TOLL-FREE 1-800-547-5570**

Blueprint Price Code B
## Plans H-925-2 & -2A

*PRICES AND DETAILS*
*ON PAGES 12-15*

**79**

# Low-Cost Comfort

- Designed for the energy-conscious, this passive solar home provides year-round comfort at much lower fuel costs.
- The open, airy interior is a delight. In winter, sunshine penetrates deeply into the living spaces. In summer, wide overhangs shade the interior.
- The family room/breakfast/kitchen combination is roomy and bright for family activities.
- The living/dining areas flow together for more bright, open space.
- The master suite includes a private bath and walk-in closet. Two other bedrooms share another full bath.

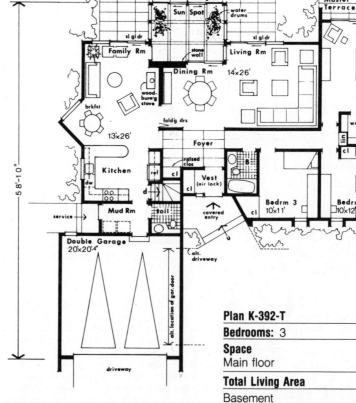

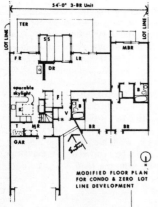

MODIFIED FLOOR PLAN FOR CONDO & ZERO LOT LINE DEVELOPMENT

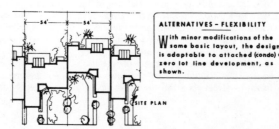

SITE PLAN

**ALTERNATIVES – FLEXIBILITY**

With minor modifications of the same basic layout, the design is adaptable to attached (condo) or zero lot line development, as shown.

| Plan K-392-T | |
|---|---|
| **Bedrooms: 3** | **Baths:** 2½ |
| **Space** | |
| Main floor | 1,592 sq. ft. |
| **Total Living Area** | **1,592 sq. ft.** |
| Basement | 634 sq. ft. |
| Garage | 407 sq. ft. |
| **Exterior Wall Framing** | 2x4/2x6 |

**Foundation options:**
Partial Basement
Slab
(Foundation & framing conversion diagram available—see order form.)

| **Blueprint Price Code** | B |
|---|---|

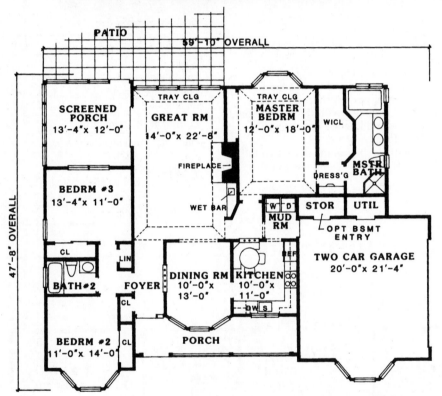

# Single-Story with Sparkle

- A lovely front porch with decorative posts, a cameo front door, bay windows and dormers give this country-style home extra sparkle.
- The Great Room is at the center of the floor plan, where it merges with the dining room, kitchen and screened porch. The Great Room features a tray ceiling, a wall of windows facing the patio, a fireplace and a built-in wet bar.
- The eat-in kitchen has a half-wall that keeps it open to the Great Room and hallway. The dining room has a half-wall facing the foyer and a bay window overlooking the front porch.
- The delectable master suite is isolated from the other bedrooms and includes a charming bay window, a tray ceiling and a luxurious private bath.
- The two smaller bedrooms are off the main foyer and separated by a full bath.
- A mud room with washer and dryer is accessible from the two-car garage, disguised with another bay window.

| Plan AX-91312 | |
|---|---|
| Bedrooms: 3 | Baths: 2 |
| Space: | |
| Main floor | 1,595 sq. ft. |
| **Total Living Area** | **1,595 sq. ft.** |
| Screened Porch | 178 sq. ft. |
| Basement | 1,595 sq. ft. |
| Garage, Storage and Utility | 508 sq. ft. |
| **Exterior Wall Framing** | 2x4 |
| **Foundation options:** | |
| Standard Basement | |
| Slab | |
| (Foundation & framing conversion diagram available—see order form.) | |
| **Blueprint Price Code** | B |

**View into Great Room from dining room**

# Tradition Updated

- Traditional lines, materials, and even a front porch create a nostalgic exterior appeal.
- The interior breaks the traditional mold, however. You won't find the small, boxy, low ceilinged rooms of older homes here. Rather, all of the living areas blow open with dramatic cathedral ceilings with skylights.

- The formal living/dining spaces flow together oriented to the front. The family room shares a three-sided fireplace with the living room.
- The island kitchen opens to a spacious breakfast room.
- The three bedrooms share two full baths in the sleeping wing of the plan.

**Plan AX-90303-A**

| Bedrooms: 3 | Baths: 2 |
|---|---|
| **Space:** | |
| **Total living area:** | 1,615 sq. ft. |
| Optional basement: | 1,615 sq. ft. |
| Garage: | 412 sq. ft. |
| **Exterior Wall Framing:** | 2x4 |

**Foundation options:**
Standard basement.
Crawlspace.
(Foundation & framing conversion diagram available — see order form.)

| **Blueprint Price Code:** | B |
|---|---|

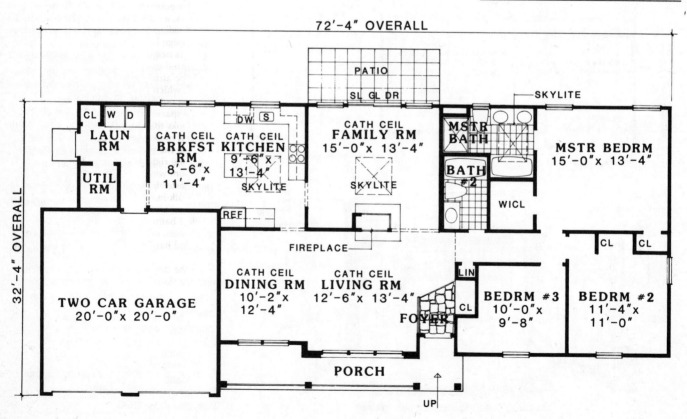

# A Home for Sun Lovers

This open plan home, brightened by a landscaped atrium, also has a vaulted, glass-ceiling solarium with an optional spa, offering a sunny garden room for sitting or soaking — a bonus in a three-bedroom home of only 1,621 sq. ft.

Intersecting hip roofs with corner notches, a clerestory dormer, vertical board siding and a covered front walkway add design interest and set the house apart from its neighbors. Inside the vaulted, skylighted entry, the hallway angles left past the atrium into the vaulted great room, which has a fireplace and a door leading out to a wood deck or patio.

The spacious L-shaped kitchen also overlooks the atrium and has an adjacent vaulted nook with solarium window and a door to the garage.

To the right of the entry hall is the bedroom wing. Double doors open into the master bedroom, with a private bath and walk-in closet. Doors lead to the solarium and the front courtyard. A second bathroom serves the other two bedrooms, one of which can double as a den and has doors opening into the great room.

In the daylight basement version of the plan, a stairway replaces the atrium.

| | |
|---|---|
| Main floor: | 1,497 sq. ft. |
| Solarium: | 124 sq. ft. |
| Total living area: (Not counting basement or garage) | 1,621 sq. ft. |
| Basement: | 1,514 sq. ft. |

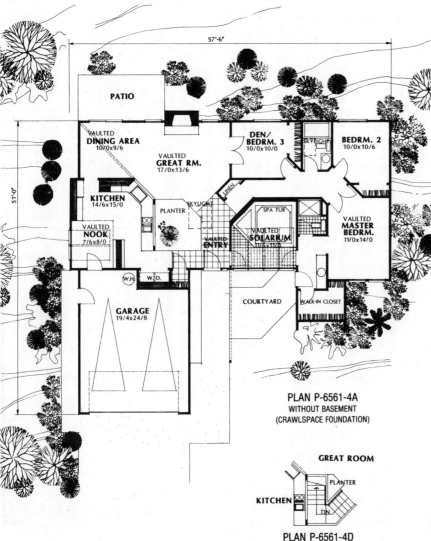

**PLAN P-6561-4A**
WITHOUT BASEMENT
(CRAWLSPACE FOUNDATION)

**PLAN P-6561-4D**
WITH DAYLIGHT BASEMENT

Blueprint Price Code B

**Plans P-6561-4A & -4D**

*TO ORDER THIS BLUEPRINT,*
*CALL TOLL-FREE 1-800-547-5570*

*PRICES AND DETAILS*
*ON PAGES 12-15*

**83**

# Covered Wraparound Deck Featured

- A covered deck spans this home from the main entrance to the kitchen door.
- An over-sized fireplace is the focal point of the living room, which merges into an expandable dining area.
- The kitchen is tucked into one corner, but open counter space allows visual contact with living areas beyond.
- Two good-sized main-floor bedrooms are furnished with sufficient closet space.
- The basement level adds a third bedroom in an additional 673 sq. ft. of living space.

| Plan H-806-2 | |
| --- | --- |
| **Bedrooms:** 3 | **Baths:** 1 |
| **Living Area:** | |
| Main floor | 952 sq. ft. |
| Daylight basement | 673 sq. ft. |
| **Total Living Area:** | **1,625 sq. ft.** |
| Garage | 279 sq. ft. |
| **Exterior Wall Framing:** | 2x6 |
| **Foundation Options:** | |
| Daylight basement | |
| (Typical foundation & framing conversion diagram available—see order form.) | |
| **BLUEPRINT PRICE CODE:** | **B** |

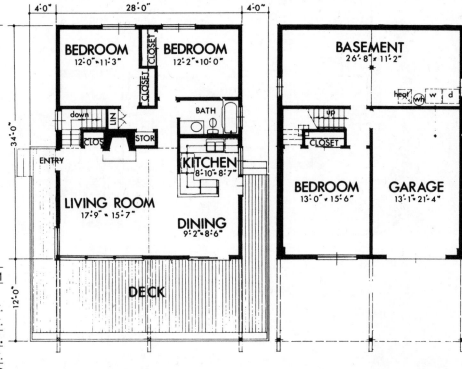

MAIN FLOOR          DAYLIGHT BASEMENT

*TO ORDER THIS BLUEPRINT, CALL TOLL-FREE 1-800-547-5570*

Plan H-806-2

*PRICES AND DETAILS ON PAGES 12-15*

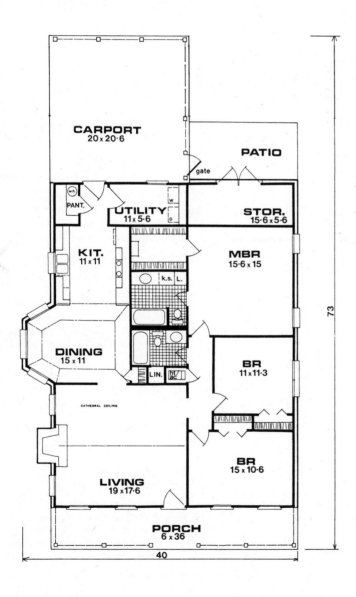

**CARPORT**
20 x 20·6

**PATIO**

gate

w.h.
**PANT.**

**UTILITY**
11 x 5·6

W
D

**STOR.**
15·6 x 5·6

**KIT.**
11 x 11

**MBR**
15·6 x 15

k.s. L.

**DINING**
15 x 11

LIN.
h.l.
a.c.

**BR**
11 x 11·3

CATHEDRAL CEILING

**LIVING**
19 x 17·6

**BR**
15 x 10·6

**PORCH**
6 x 36

40

73

# Traditional Design Fits Narrow Lot

- This compact, cozy and dignified plan makes great use of a small lot, while also offering an exciting interior design.
- Note the bay-windowed dining area, which joins the living room to provide a large space for entertaining.
- The living room features a warm fireplace and a cathedral ceiling.
- The master suite includes a deluxe private bath and large walk-in closet.
- Two secondary bedrooms share another bath in the hallway.
- Also note the pantry and utility space adjoining the kitchen, and the storage area off the rear patio.

**Plan J-86161**

| Bedrooms: 3 | Baths: 2 |
|---|---|
| **Space:** | |
| Main floor | 1,626 sq. ft. |
| **Total Living Area** | **1,626 sq. ft.** |
| Basement | 1,626 sq. ft. |
| Carport | 410 sq. ft. |
| Storage | 104 sq. ft. |
| Porch | 216 sq. ft. |
| **Exterior Wall Framing** | 2x4 |

**Foundation options:**
Standard Basement
Crawlspace
Slab
(Foundation & framing conversion diagram available—see order form.)

**Blueprint Price Code**      **B**

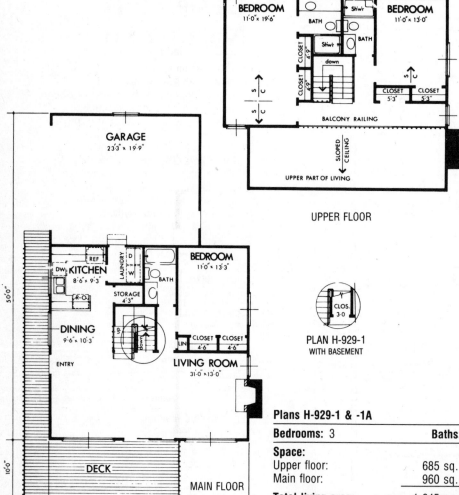

**GARAGE**
23'3" x 19'9"

**KITCHEN**
8'6" x 9'3"

REF

DW

LAUNDRY

D
W

BATH

STORAGE
4'3"

R-O

**BEDROOM**
11'0" x 13'3"

**DINING**
9'6" x 10'3"

ENTRY

Down

**LIVING ROOM**
31'0" x 13'0"

CLOSET
4'6"

CLOSET
4'6"

LIN

**DECK**

**MAIN FLOOR**

50'0"

10'0"

4'0"

32'0"

**UPPER FLOOR**

**BEDROOM**
11'0" x 19'6"

Sh'w'r

**BATH**

**BEDROOM**
11'0" x 13'0"

Sh'w'r

**BATH**

CLOSET
4'9"

CLOSET
4'9"

down

CLOSET
5'3"

CLOSET
5'3"

S C

S C

S C

S C

**BALCONY RAILING**

SLOPED CEILING

**UPPER PART OF LIVING**

CLOS.
3-0

**PLAN H-929-1**
WITH BASEMENT

# Contemporary Retreat

- Main floor plan revolves around an open, centrally located stairway.
- Spaciousness prevails throughout entire home with open kitchen and combination dining/living room.
- Living room features a great-sized fireplace and access to two-sided deck.
- Separate baths accommodate each bedroom.
- Upstairs hallway reveals an open balcony railing to oversee activities below.

### Plans H-929-1 & -1A

| Bedrooms: 3 | | Baths: 3 |
|---|---|---|

**Space:**

| | |
|---|---|
| Upper floor: | 685 sq. ft. |
| Main floor: | 960 sq. ft. |

| | |
|---|---|
| **Total living area:** | 1,645 sq. ft. |
| Basement: | approx. 960 sq. ft. |
| Garage: | 459 sq. ft. |

| **Exterior Wall Framing:** | 2x6 |
|---|---|

**Foundation options:**
Daylight basement (Plan H-929-1).
Crawlspace (Plan H-929-1A).
(Foundation & framing conversion diagram available — see order form.)

| **Blueprint Price Code:** | B |
|---|---|

# Comfortable, Open Plan

- A central Great Room features a cathedral ceiling and is visually separated from the dining area by a huge fireplace.
- A wing on the left includes two secondary bedrooms which share a bath.
- In the right wing, you'll find a spacious master bedroom with private bath and walk-in closet.
- The kitchen is roomy and well-planned,

with a utility room in the garage entry area.
- A house-spanning front deck adds an extra welcoming touch to the plan.

| Plan C-8160 | | |
| --- | --- | --- |
| **Bedrooms:** 3 | | **Baths:** 2 |
| **Space:** | | |
| Main floor | | 1,669 sq. ft. |
| **Total Living Area** | | **1,669 sq. ft.** |
| Basement | (approx.) | 1,660 sq. ft. |
| Carport | | 413 sq. ft. |
| Storage | (approx.) | 85 sq. ft. |
| **Exterior Wall Framing** | | 2x4 |
| **Foundation options:** | | |
| Standard Basement | | |
| Crawlspace | | |
| Slab | | |
| (Foundation & framing conversion diagram available—see order form.) | | |
| **Blueprint Price Code** | | **B** |

# Great Room Featured

- In this rustic design, the centrally located Great Room features a cathedral ceiling with exposed wood beams. Living and dining areas are separated by a massive fireplace.
- The isolated master suite features a walk-in closet and compartmentalized bath.
- The galley type kitchen is between the breakfast room and formal dining area. A large utility room and storage room complete the garage area.
- On the opposite side of the Great Room are two additional bedrooms and a second full bath.

**Plan C-8460**

| | |
|---|---|
| **Bedrooms:** 3 | **Baths:** 2 |

**Space:**

| | |
|---|---|
| **Total living area:** | 1,670 sq. ft. |
| Basement: | approx. 1,600 sq. ft. |
| Garage: | 427 sq. ft. |
| Storage: | 63 sq. ft. |

**Exterior Wall Framing:** 2x4

**Foundation options:**
Standard basement.
Crawlspace.
Slab.
(Foundation & framing conversion diagram available — see order form)

**Blueprint Price Code:** B

# Covered Porch Offers Three Entries

- Showy window treatments, columns and covered front and rear porches give this Southern-style home a welcoming exterior. Entry is possible through three separate front entrances.
- 12' ceilings in the living room, the dining area and the kitchen add volume to the economical 1,600+ square feet of living space.
- A corner fireplace and a rear view to the back porch are found in the living room. A counter bar separates the kitchen from the formal dining area and from the informal eating area on the opposite side.
- The private master suite offers a cathedral ceiling, a walk-in closet and a large luxury bath. Two additional bedrooms are located at the opposite end of the home and share a second bath.

**Plan E-1602**

| Bedrooms: 3 | Baths: 2 |
|---|---|
| **Space:** | |
| Main floor | 1,672 sq. ft. |
| **Total Living Area** | **1,672 sq. ft.** |
| Basement | 1,672 sq. ft. |
| Garage | 484 sq. ft. |
| **Exterior Wall Framing** | 2x6 |

**Foundation options:**

Standard Basement
Crawlspace
Slab
(Foundation & framing conversion diagram available—see order form.)

| **Blueprint Price Code** | B |
|---|---|

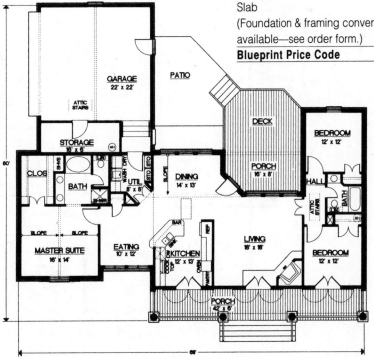

# Design Reflects Finesse

This especially handsome yet simple ranch house attracts admiration with its exterior facade of stone, shingles, and natural tone (unpainted) wood, all used with finesse. The house layout is practical, but with many imaginative touches. There are two entries to the house, one through the mud room, the other a formal, covered front entranceway.

To the left of the welcoming gallery is the dining room-living room area, with elegant cathedral ceiling. The living room has an optional entrance to the family room, covered by folding doors. The dinette, with a curved wall of stock-size windows overlooking the terrace, also has a screen or partition shielding it from the family room. The family room offers a sliding glass exit to the terrace and a built-in fireplace.

To the right of the gallery lie the three bedrooms. The master suite contains a walk-in closet and a surprise: a skylight above the dressing alcove. The master bedroom has its own bath while the other two bedrooms share a bath. There is plenty of closet and storage space throughout. The basic house is 1,672 sq. ft.; optional basement is 1,672 sq. ft.; garage, etc., is 546 sq. ft.

| | |
|---|---|
| Living area: | 1,672 sq. ft. |
| Basement (opt.) | 1,672 sq. ft. |
| Garage, mud room, etc.: | 546 sq. ft. |

(Alternate slab-on-grade foundation plan included.)

**79'-4"**

**Terrace**

dinette
10'-0"x8'-8"av.

d  w  cl

Mud Rm

sl gl dr

fireplace

Family Rm
13'-4"x18'-0"

vanity

dress'g

skylite above

Bath

Master Suite
13'-4"x16'-2"

wic

service

dn

Kitchen
10'-0"x12'-0"

opt. open'g w/fold'g drs

Bath

cl

lin

Double Garage
20'-0"x20'-4"

hall

ref

Gallery

cl

stor

Dining Rm
10'-4"x13'-0"

Living Rm
12'-0"x18'-0"

Bedrm 3
10'-0"x13'-0"

cl

cl

cl

Bedrm 2
11'-0"x13'-4"

cathedral ceil'g

covered entry

up

**37'-0"**

driveway

Blueprint Price Code B
## Plan K-162-J

**PRICES AND DETAILS ON PAGES 12-15**

FRONT VIEW

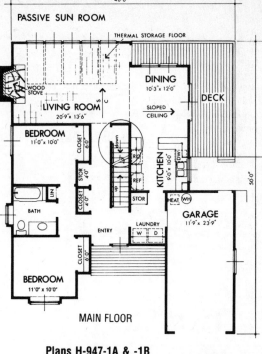

PASSIVE SUN ROOM

40'-0"

THERMAL STORAGE FLOOR

DINING
10'-3" x 12'-0"

DECK

WOOD STOVE

LIVING ROOM
20'-9" x 13'-6"

SLOPED CEILING

BEDROOM
11'-0" x 10'-0"

CLOSET

STOR

CLOSET

down

KITCHEN
9'-0" x 10'-0"

50'-0"

BATH

LIN

up

REF

STOR

HEAT WH

GARAGE
11'-9" x 23'-9"

ENTRY

LAUNDRY
W D

CLOSET

BEDROOM
11'-0" x 10'-0"

MAIN FLOOR

# Sunny Family Living

- Pleasant-looking and unassuming from the front, this plan breaks into striking, sun-catching angles at the rear.
- The living room sun roof gathers passive solar heat, which is stored in the tile floor and the two-story high masonry backdrop to the wood stove.
- A 516-square-foot master suite with private bath and balcony makes up the second floor.
- The main floor offers two more bedrooms and a full bath.

PASSIVE SUN ROOM BELOW

SLOPED CEILING

BALCONY RAILING

BEDROOM
17'-3" x 13'-3"

down

Shwr

BATH

WALK-IN CLOSET
10'-9" x 6'-6"

UPPER FLOOR

STOR

WITHOUT BASEMENT
(CRAWLSPACE FOUNDATION)

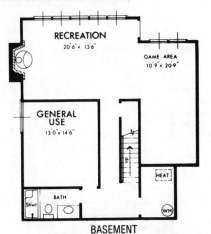

RECREATION
20'-6" x 13'-6"

GAME AREA
10'-9" x 20'-9"

GENERAL USE
13'-0" x 14'-6"

up

HEAT

Shwr

BATH

WH

BASEMENT

## Plans H-947-1A & -1B

| Bedrooms: 3 | Baths: 2-3 |
|---|---|

| Space: | |
|---|---|
| Upper floor: | 516 sq. ft. |
| Main floor: | 1,162 sq. ft. |

| Total without basement: | 1,678 sq. ft. |
|---|---|
| Daylight basement: | 966 sq. ft. |

| Total with basement: | 2,644 sq. ft. |
|---|---|
| Garage: | 279 sq. ft. |

| Exterior Wall Framing: | 2x6 |
|---|---|

**Foundation options:**
Daylight basement (H-947-1B).
Crawlspace (H-947-1A).
(Foundation & framing conversion diagram available — see order form.)

**Blueprint Price Code:**
Without basement:         B
With basement:             D

REAR VIEW

# Two-Story with Victorian Touch

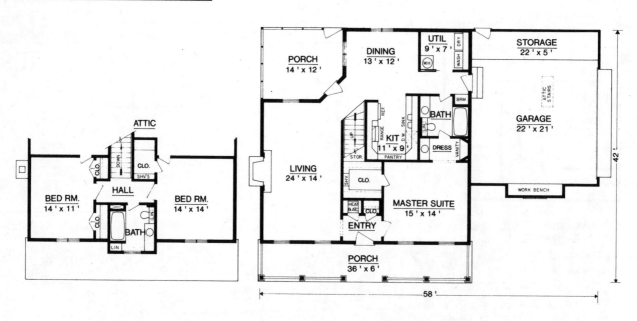

UPPER FLOOR

MAIN FLOOR

| | |
|---|---|
| Living area: | 1,686 sq. ft. |
| Porches: | 393 sq. ft. |
| Garage & storage: | 592 sq. ft. |
| Total area: | 2,671 sq. ft. |

Specify crawlspace or slab foundation.

Blueprint Price Code B
## Plan E-1631

*PRICES AND DETAILS*
*ON PAGES 12-15*

# Rustic Home With Porches Means Relaxation

A spacious screened porch serves as a great place to eat out during warm summer days and nights, while the front porch is ideal for relaxed rocking or a swing. The Great Room to the left of the entry has a fireplace and connects to the dining area and country kitchen. The large master bedroom features a private bath and ample closets.

For entertaining large groups, the combined dining area, living room and screened porch provide lots of space. Also note the large kitchen/utility and pantry area.

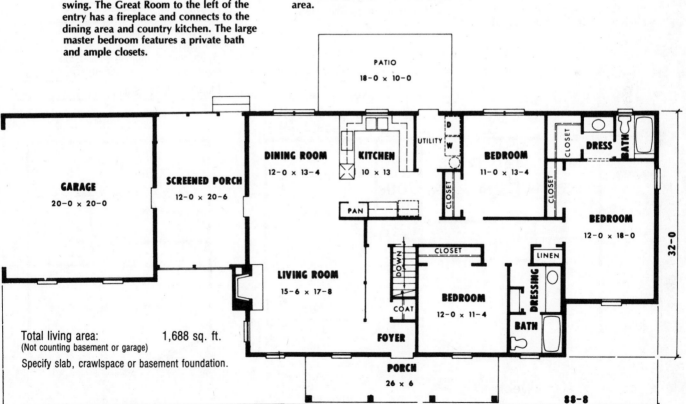

PATIO
18-0 x 10-0

GARAGE
20-0 x 20-0

SCREENED PORCH
12-0 x 20-6

DINING ROOM
12-0 x 13-4

KITCHEN
10 x 13

UTILITY

D W

CLOSET

BEDROOM
11-0 x 13-4

CLOSET

DRESS

BATH

CLOSET

BEDROOM
12-0 x 18-0

32-0

PAN

LIVING ROOM
15-6 x 17-8

DOWN

CLOSET

LINEN

DRESSING

COAT

BEDROOM
12-0 x 11-4

BATH

FOYER

Total living area: 1,688 sq. ft.
(Not counting basement or garage)

Specify slab, crawlspace or basement foundation.

PORCH
26 x 6

88-8

# Panoramic Prow View

- A glass-filled prow gable design is almost as spectacular as the panoramic view from inside. The two-story window-wall floods the living room with light and views.
- The open-feeling corner kitchen has the right angle to enjoy the dining room and the family room, including views of the front and rear decks.
- Two main level bedrooms share a full bath.
- The entire upper floor is a private master bedroom suite with large bath, dressing area and balcony opening to the two-story glass wall, a real "good morning" view.

| Plan NW-196 | |
|---|---|
| **Bedrooms:** 3 | **Baths:** 2 |

| Space: | |
|---|---|
| Upper floor | 394 sq. ft. |
| Main floor: | 1,317 sq. ft. |

| **Total living area:** | **1,711 sq. ft.** |
|---|---|

| **Exterior Wall Framing:** | 2x6 |
|---|---|

**Foundation options:**
Crawlspace.
(Foundation & framing conversion diagram available — see order form.)

| **Blueprint Price Code:** | B |
|---|---|

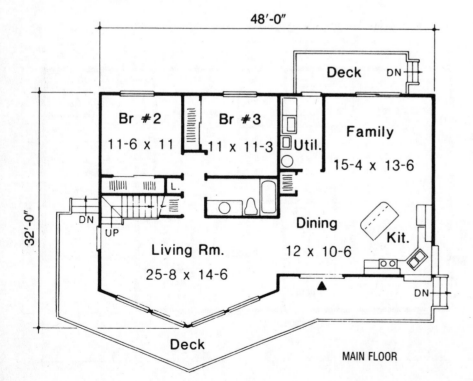

MAIN FLOOR

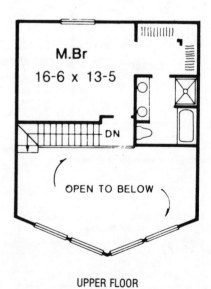

UPPER FLOOR

**TO ORDER THIS BLUEPRINT, CALL TOLL-FREE 1-800-547-5570**

Plan NW-196

**PRICES AND DETAILS ON PAGES 12-15**

# Panoramic View Embraces Outdoors

- This geometric design takes full advantage of scenic sites.
- Living area faces a glass-filled wall and wrap-around deck.
- Open dining/living room arrangement is complemented by vaulted ceilings, an overhead balcony, and a 5-ft-wide fireplace.
- 12' deep main deck offers generous space for outdoor dining and entertaining.

**PLAN H-855-1A**
WITHOUT BASEMENT

SCALE

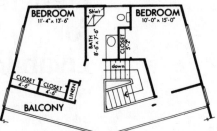

UPPER FLOOR

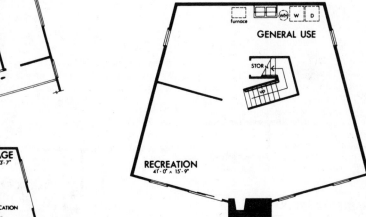

BASEMENT

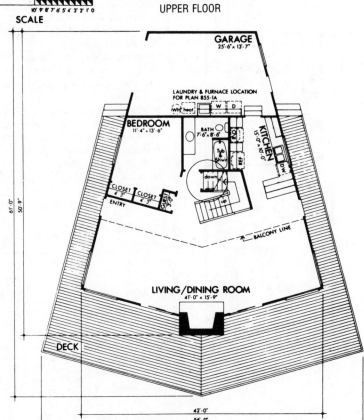

MAIN FLOOR

## Plans H-855-1 & -1A

| | |
|---|---|
| **Bedrooms:** 3 | **Baths:** 2 |

| **Space:** | |
|---|---|
| Upper floor: | 625 sq. ft. |
| Main floor: | 1,108 sq. ft. |
| **Total living area:** | 1,733 sq. ft. |
| Basement: | approx. 1,108 sq. ft. |
| Garage: | 346 sq. ft. |

| **Exterior Wall Framing:** | 2x6 |
|---|---|

**Foundation options:**
Daylight basement (Plan H-855-1).
Crawlspace (Plan H-855-1A).
(Foundation & framing conversion diagram available — see order form.)

**Blueprint Price Code:**

| | |
|---|---|
| Without basement | B |
| With basement | D |

# Designed for Livability

- As you enter this excitingly spacious traditional home you see through the extensive windows to the backyard.
- This four-bedroom home was designed for the livability of the maturing family with the separation of the master suite.
- The formal dining room expands spatially to the living room while being framed by the column and plant shelves.
- The bay that creates the morning room and the sitting area for the master suite also adds excitement to this plan, both inside and out.
- The master bath offers an exciting oval tub under glass and a separate shower, as well as a spacious walk-in closet and a dressing area.

**Plan DD-1696**

| Bedrooms: 4 | Baths: 2 |
|---|---|
| **Living Area:** | |
| Main floor | 1,748 sq. ft. |
| **Total Living Area:** | **1,748 sq. ft.** |
| Standard basement | 1,748 sq. ft. |
| Garage | 393 sq. ft. |
| **Exterior Wall Framing:** | 2x4 |

**Foundation Options:**
Standard basement
Crawlspace
Slab
(Typical foundation & framing conversion diagram available—see order form.)

**BLUEPRINT PRICE CODE:** B

## Floor Plan

PATIO

54'10"

SITTING

MORNING
9⁸ x 9⁴

MASTER BEDROOM
14⁴ x 18⁰

KITCHEN
9⁴ x 14⁰

LIVING
15⁰ x 19⁸

BEDROOM 3
12⁴ x 11⁰

BATH 2

M BATH

UTIL

50'5"

DINING
11⁴ x 11⁴

BEDROOM 4
10⁰ x 10⁴

GARAGE
19⁸ x 20⁰

BEDROOM 2
12⁴ x 10⁴

MAIN FLOOR

**TO ORDER THIS BLUEPRINT,
CALL TOLL-FREE 1-800-547-5570**

**PRICES AND DETAILS
ON PAGES 12-15**

Plan DD-1696

# Efficient Dining-Kitchen-Nook Combination

- Here's a four-bedroom design that is beautiful in its simplicity and ease of construction.
- All on one floor, it offers ample space for both family life and entertaining.
- A huge living room soars aloft with vaulted, beamed ceilings and features a massive fireplace to give a Great Room feel to the area.
- The roomy, efficient kitchen is flanked by a sunny informal eating

area protruding into the back yard and a front-facing formal dining room that is right off the elegant foyer.
- A deluxe master suite includes a dressing room, large closet and private bath.
- The three secondary bedrooms are larger than average and also offer ample closet space.
- Convenient storage and utility areas are segmented off the two-car garage.

| Plan E-1702 | |
| --- | --- |
| **Bedrooms:** 4 | **Baths:** 2 |
| **Space:** | |
| **Total living area:** | 1,751 sq. ft. |
| Porch: | 64 sq. ft. |
| Garage: | 484 sq. ft. |
| Storage: | 105 sq. ft. |
| **Exterior Wall Framing:** | 2x4 |

**Foundation options:**
Crawlspace.
Slab.
(Foundation & framing conversion diagram available — see order form)

| **Blueprint Price Code:** | B |
| --- | --- |

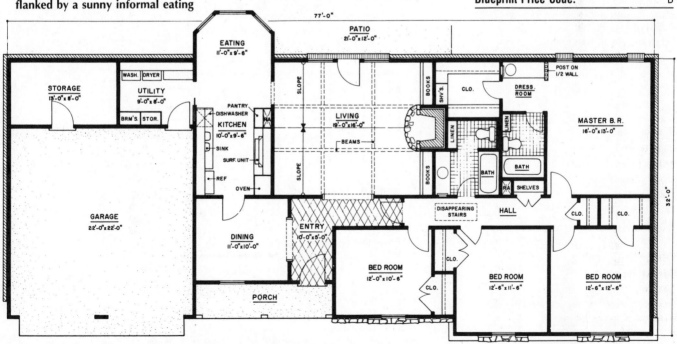

# Rustic Home Offers Comfort, Economy

- Rustic and compact, this home offers economy of construction and good looks.
- The homey front porch, multi-paned windows, shutters and horizontal siding combine to create a rustic exterior.
- An L-shaped kitchen is open to the dining room and also to the living room to create a Great Room feel to the floor plan.
- The living room includes a raised-hearth fireplace.
- The main-floor master suite features a large walk-in closet and a double vanity in the master bath.
- An open two-story-high foyer leads to the second floor, which includes two bedrooms with walk-in closets and a full bath with two linen closets.

| Plan C-8339 | |
|---|---|
| **Bedrooms:** 3 | **Baths:** 2 |
| **Space:** | |
| Upper floor | 660 sq. ft. |
| Main floor | 1,100 sq. ft. |
| **Total Living Area** | **1,760 sq. ft.** |
| Basement | approx. 1,100 sq. ft. |
| Garage | Included in basement |
| **Exterior Wall Framing** | 2x4 |
| **Foundation options:** | |
| Daylight Basement (Foundation & framing conversion diagram available—see order form.) | |
| **Blueprint Price Code** | **B** |

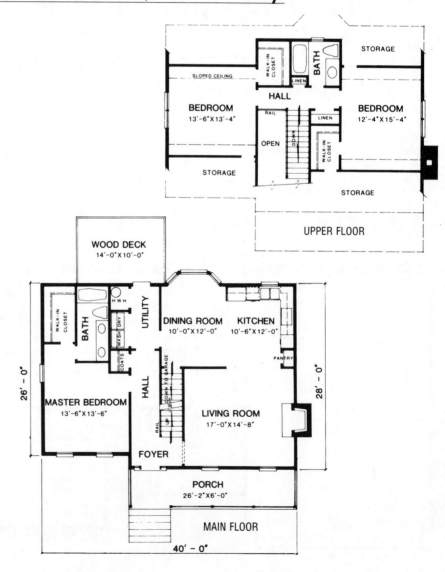

**TO ORDER THIS BLUEPRINT, CALL TOLL-FREE 1-800-547-5570**

Plan C-8339

**PRICES AND DETAILS ON PAGES 12-15**

# Rustic Home for Relaxed Living

A screened-in breezeway provides a cool place to dine out on warm summer days and nights, and the rustic front porch is ideal for relaxed rocking or a swing. A Great Room to the left of the entry has a fireplace and connects the dining area to the country kitchen.

The large master suite contains separate shower, garden tub, vanities and walk-in closets.

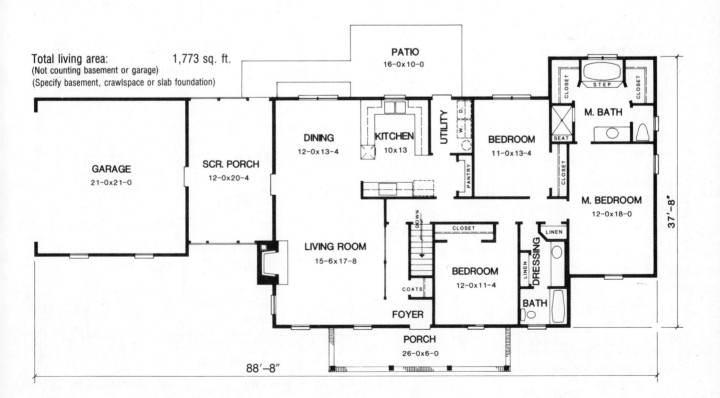

Total living area: 1,773 sq. ft.
(Not counting basement or garage)
(Specify basement, crawlspace or slab foundation)

PATIO
16-0x10-0

GARAGE
21-0x21-0

SCR. PORCH
12-0x20-4

DINING
12-0x13-4

KITCHEN
10x13

UTILITY

BEDROOM
11-0x13-4

M. BATH

STEP

CLOSET

CLOSET

SEAT

PANTRY

CLOSET

M. BEDROOM
12-0x18-0

LIVING ROOM
15-6x17-8

DOWN

CLOSET

LINEN

LINEN

DRESSING

BEDROOM
12-0x11-4

BATH

COATS

FOYER

PORCH
26-0x6-0

37'-8"

88'-8"

## Plan J-8895

| Bedrooms: 3 | Baths: 2½ |
|---|---|

**Space:**

| | |
|---|---|
| Upper floor: | 860 sq. ft. |
| Main floor: | 919 sq. ft. |

| | |
|---|---|
| **Total living area:** | **1,779 sq. ft.** |
| Basement: | 919 sq. ft. |
| Optional carport: | 462 sq. ft. |
| Porch: | 466 sq. ft. |

| **Exterior Wall Framing:** | 2x4 |
|---|---|

**Foundation options:**
Standard basement.
Crawlspace.
Slab.
(Foundation & framing conversion
diagram available — see order form.)

| **Blueprint Price Code:** | B |
|---|---|

# Expansive Porch Offers Warm Welcome

- This gracious design conjures up images of family and friends sipping iced tea on the veranda during warm summer evenings.
- Inside, a relatively compact floor plan still offers abundant space for family life and entertaining.
- The spacious living room includes a fireplace and built in cabinetry.

- The open kitchen/dining room design provides space for food preparation, eating and cleanup without the confined feeling found in many kitchens.
- The second floor consists of three good-sized bedrooms, two mirror-image baths and a hobby area.

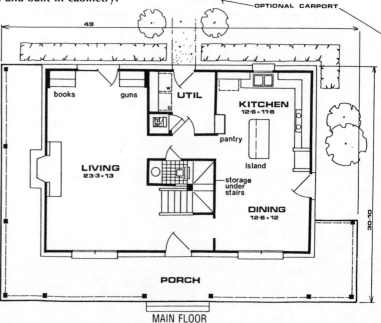

UPPER FLOOR

MAIN FLOOR

Plan J-8895

*PRICES AND DETAILS*
*ON PAGES 12-15*

# Classic Country-Style

- At the center of this rustic country home is an enormous living room with vaulted ceilings, a massive stone fireplace and entrance to a rear porch.
- The adjoining eating area and kitchen provide plenty of room for dining and meal preparation. A sloped ceiling with false beams, porch overlook, pantry, spice cabinet and counter bar are some

attractions found here.
- Formal dining and entertaining can take place in the dining room off the entry.
- For privacy, you'll find the secluded master suite rewarding; it offers a private bath with dressing area, walk-in closet and isolated toilet and tub.
- The two additional bedrooms also have abundant walk-in closet space.

| Plan E-1808 | |
|---|---|
| **Bedrooms:** 3 | **Baths:** 2 |
| **Space:** | |
| Main floor | 1,800 sq. ft. |
| **Total Living Area** | **1,800 sq. ft.** |
| Garage and storage | 605 sq. ft. |
| Porches | 354 sq. ft. |
| **Exterior Wall Framing** | 2x4 |
| **Foundation options:** | |
| Crawlspace | |
| Slab | |
| (Foundation & framing conversion diagram available—see order form.) | |
| **Blueprint Price Code** | **B** |

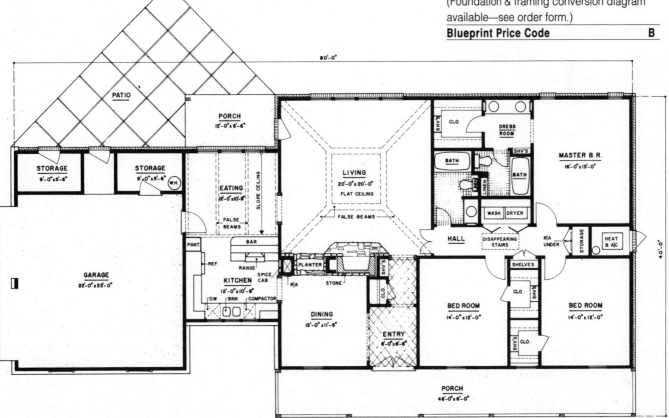

FRONT VIEW

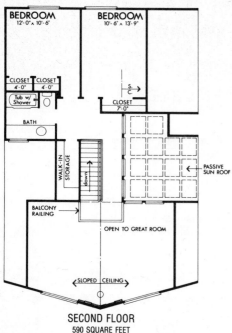

BEDROOM
12'-0" x 10'-6"

BEDROOM
10'-6" x 13'-9"

CLOSET
4'-0"

CLOSET
4'-0"

Tub w/
Shower

CLOSET
7'-0"

S.
C.

BATH

WALK-IN
STORAGE

down

PASSIVE
SUN ROOF

BALCONY
RAILING

OPEN TO GREAT ROOM

SLOPED CEILING

SECOND FLOOR
590 SQUARE FEET

| | |
|---|---|
| First floor: | 1,074 sq. ft. |
| Passive sun room: | 136 sq. ft. |
| Second floor: | 590 sq. ft. |
| Total living area: | 1,800 sq. ft. |
| (Not counting basement or garage) | |

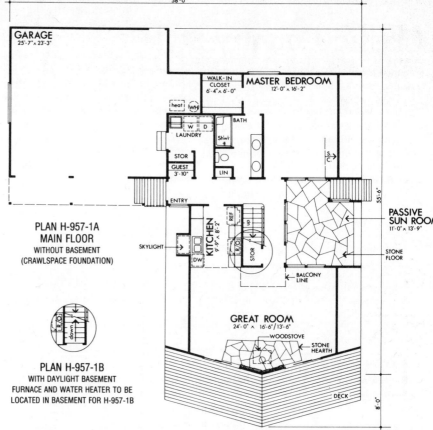

58'-0"

GARAGE
25'-7" x 23'-3"

WALK-IN
CLOSET
6'-4" x 6'-0"

MASTER BEDROOM
12'-0" x 16'-2"

heat    WH

BATH

W   D

Sh'wr

LAUNDRY

STOR

GUEST
3'-10"

LIN

S.
C.

ENTRY

55'-6"

PASSIVE
SUN ROOM
11'-0" x 13'-9"

STONE
FLOOR

SKYLIGHT

REF

UP

KITCHEN
9'-9" x 8'-2"

STOR

DW

BALCONY
LINE

PLAN H-957-1A
MAIN FLOOR
WITHOUT BASEMENT
(CRAWLSPACE FOUNDATION)

GREAT ROOM
24'-0" x 16'-6"/13'-6"

WOODSTOVE

STONE
HEARTH

down

DECK

8'-0"

PLAN H-957-1B
WITH DAYLIGHT BASEMENT
FURNACE AND WATER HEATER TO BE
LOCATED IN BASEMENT FOR H-957-1B

# A Truly Livable Retreat

For a number of years the A-Frame idea has enjoyed great acceptance and popularity, especially in recreational areas. Too often, however, hopeful expectations have led to disappointment because

economic necessity resulted in small and restricted buildings. Not so with this plan. Without ignoring the need for economy, the designers allowed themselves enough freedom to create a truly livable and practical home with a main floor of 1,210 sq. ft., exclusive of the garage area. The second floor has 590 sq. ft., and includes two bedrooms, a bath and ample storage space.

Take special note of the multi-use passive sun room. Its primary purpose is to collect, store and redistribute the sun's heat, not only saving a considerable

amount of money but contributing an important function of keeping out dampness and cold when the owners are elsewhere. Otherwise the room might serve as a delightful breakfast room, a lovely arboretum, an indoor exercise room or any of many other functions limited only by the occupants' ingenuity.

A truly livable retreat, whether for weekend relaxation or on a daily basis as a primary residence, this passive solar A-Frame is completely equipped for the requirements of today's active living.

Exterior walls are framed with 2x6 studs.

Blueprint Price Code B

Plans H-957-1A & -1B

TO ORDER THIS BLUEPRINT,
CALL TOLL-FREE 1-800-547-5570

PRICES AND DETAILS
ON PAGES 12-15

# Terrific Tri-Level

- A covered front porch with columns, interesting windows and a varied roofline give this tri-level home great curb appeal.
- A volume entry leads to a partially open stairway. The front parlor is a nostalgic return to the formal sitting room, with the informal living areas stationed to the rear of the home.
- The island kitchen includes a corner pantry and merges with the dining room. The sunny dining area offers a coffered ceiling and a bay window. The lower-level family room is warmed by a fireplace and has sliding glass doors opening to the patio.
- Upstairs, the roomy master suite features a large walk-in closet and a private bath with a double-sink vanity, a spa tub and a separate shower.
- Two more bedrooms share a hall bath. A handy laundry chute is nearby.

**Plan NW-450**

| Bedrooms: 3 | Baths: 2½ |
|---|---|
| **Living Area:** | |
| Upper floor | 830 sq. ft. |
| Main floor | 983 sq. ft. |
| **Total Living Area:** | **1,813 sq. ft.** |
| Garage | 448 sq. ft. |
| **Exterior Wall Framing:** | 2x6 |

**Foundation Options:**

Crawlspace
(Typical foundation & framing conversion diagram available—see order form.)

| **BLUEPRINT PRICE CODE:** | **B** |
|---|---|

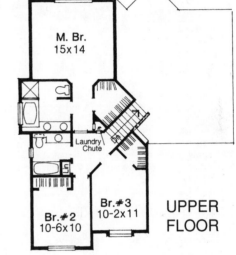

UPPER FLOOR

M. Br. 15x14

Laundry Chute

Br.#2 10-6x10

Br.#3 10-2x11

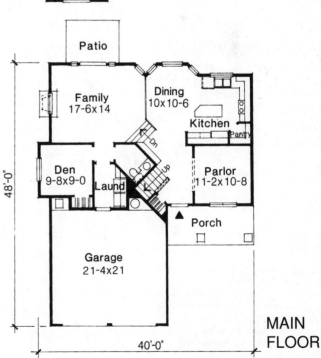

MAIN FLOOR

Patio

Family 17-6x14

Dining 10x10-6

Kitchen

Pantry

Den 9-8x9-0

Laund

Parlor 11-2x10-8

Porch

Garage 21-4x21

48'-0"

40'-0"

# Great Value

"Lots of house for the money" is what you get with this practical plan. It efficiently utilizes every inch of space to make it a real winner. Features include a formal living room, formal dining room, kitchen with a 4-person bar, family room, master suite with a large dressing area sporting a tub and shower, two additional bedrooms and a den that doubles as a fourth bedroom.

The traffic flow is very convenient, with the sleeping rooms at one end, the work and family areas at the other, and the formal entertaining area in the middle. With the addition of two 6' x 12' sunrooms on the south side, it will score high in solar efficiency also.

This truly is a spacious house for gracious living, captured in only 1,819 sq. ft. With the traditional northwest styling that is so attractive, this house will be a good value for years to come.

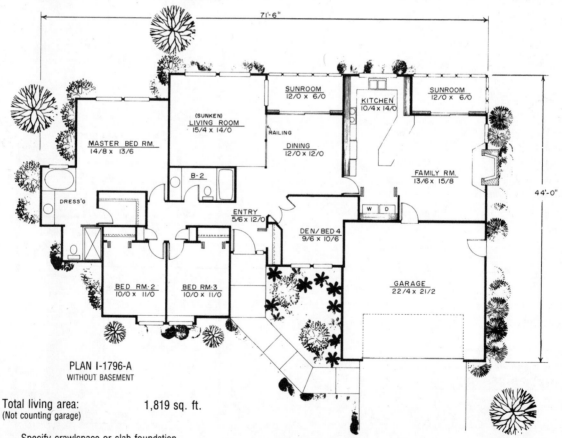

PLAN I-1796-A
WITHOUT BASEMENT

Total living area: 1,819 sq. ft.
(Not counting garage)

Specify crawlspace or slab foundation.

Blueprint Price Code B

## Plan I-1796-A

TO ORDER THIS BLUEPRINT,
CALL TOLL-FREE 1-800-547-5570

PRICES AND DETAILS
ON PAGES 12-15

# Unique Inside and Out

- This delightful design is striking from both inside and out.
- The huge "Grand Room" is flanked by two equally impressive master suites, both of which feature a vaulted ceiling, a sunny window seat, a walk-in closet and a private bath. Double doors in each of the suites open to a sun deck.
- The centrally located kitchen offers easy access from any part of the home, and a full bath, a laundry area and the entrance to the garage are nearby.
- Upstairs, two guest suites overlook the vaulted "Great Room" below.

### Plan EOF-13

| Bedrooms: 4 | Baths: 3 |
|---|---|

| **Living Area:** | |
|---|---|
| Upper floor | 443 sq. ft. |
| Main floor | 1,411 sq. ft. |

| **Total Living Area:** | **1,854 sq. ft.** |
|---|---|
| Garage | 264 sq. ft. |
| Storage | 50 sq. ft. |

| **Exterior Wall Framing:** | 2x6 |
|---|---|

**Foundation Options:**

Crawlspace

(Typical foundation & framing conversion diagram available—see order form.)

| **BLUEPRINT PRICE CODE:** | B |
|---|---|

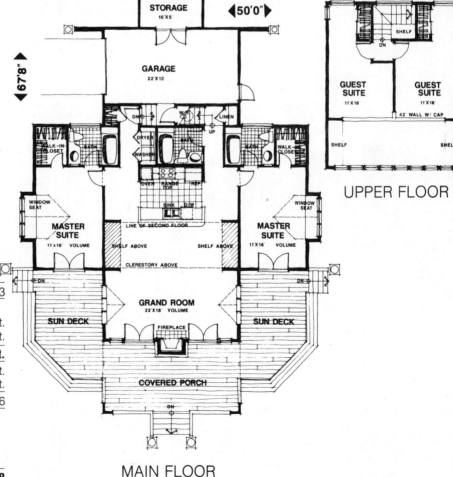

MAIN FLOOR

UPPER FLOOR

# Octagonal Dining Bay

- Classic traditional styling is recreated with a covered front porch and triple dormers with half-round windows.
- Once inside, the interior feels open, airy and bright.
- The living room with fireplace leads into the formal dining room with octagonal bay windows.
- The island kitchen overlooks the breakfast bay and family room with second fireplace and sliders to the rear deck.
- A skylit hallway connects the four upstairs bedrooms and two full baths.

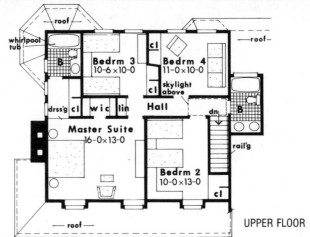

**Plan K-680-R**

| Bedrooms: 4 | Baths: 2½ |
|---|---|
| **Space:** | |
| Upper floor | 853 sq. ft. |
| Main floor | 1,015 sq. ft. |
| **Total Living Area** | **1,868 sq. ft.** |
| Basement | 1,015 sq. ft. |
| Garage & Mud Room | 504 sq. ft. |
| **Exterior Wall Framing** | 2x4 |

**Foundation options:**

Standard Basement

Slab

(Foundation & framing conversion diagram available—see order form.)

| **Blueprint Price Code** | **B** |
|---|---|

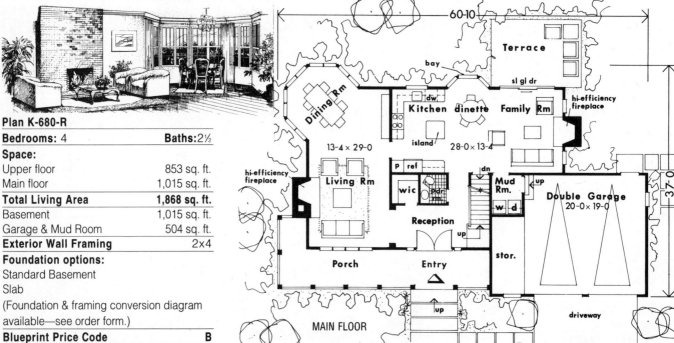

UPPER FLOOR

MAIN FLOOR

**TO ORDER THIS BLUEPRINT,**
**CALL TOLL-FREE 1-800-547-5570**

## Plan K-680-R

**PRICES AND DETAILS**
**ON PAGES 12-15**

# A Garden Home with a View

- This clever design proves that privacy doesn't have to be compromised even in high-density urban neighborhoods. From within, all views are oriented to the sideyard and to a lush entry courtyard.
- The exterior view is sheltered, but still offers a warm, welcoming look.
- The innovate interior design centers on a unique kitchen, which directs traffic away from the working areas while still serving the entire home.
- The large sunken family room features a vaulted ceiling and large fireplace.
- The master suite is highlighted by a sumptuous master bath, with separate shower and whirlpool tub, plus a large walk-in closet.
- The formal living room is designed and placed in such a way that it can become a third bedroom, den, office or study room, depending on family needs and lifestyles.

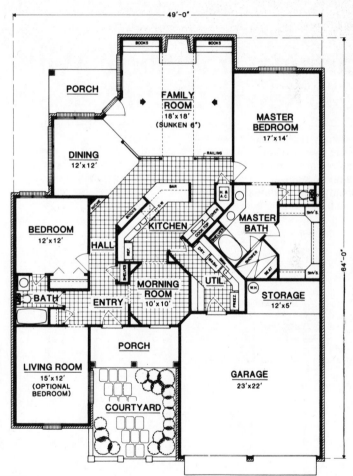

**Plan E-1824**

| Bedrooms: 2-3 | Baths: 2 |
| --- | --- |

**Space:**

| Total living area: | 1,891 sq. ft. |
| --- | --- |
| Garage: | 506 sq. ft. |
| Storage: | 60 sq. ft. |
| Porches: | 184 sq. ft. |

| Exterior Wall Framing: | 2x4 |
| --- | --- |

| Ceiling Heights: | 9' |
| --- | --- |

**Foundation options:**
Crawlspace.
Slab.
(Foundation & framing conversion diagram available — see order form.)

| Blueprint Price Code: | B |
| --- | --- |

# Charming Traditional With Great Room, Country Kitchen

- Huge family room features exposed beams in its high cathedral ceilings and a fireplace flanked by French doors and windows.
- A formal living room is partially divided by the dining area with a half-wall.
- Kitchen offers an abundance of work space, further expanded by an eating nook.
- Three large bedrooms complete the plan.

**Plan E-1815**

| Bedrooms: 3 | Baths: 2 |
|---|---|
| **Space:** | |
| Total living area: | 1,898 sq. ft. |
| Garage and porch: | 608 sq. ft. |
| **Exterior Wall Framing:** | 2x4 |

**Foundation options:**
Crawlspace.
Slab.
(Foundation & framing conversion diagram available — see order form.)

| **Blueprint Price Code:** | B |
|---|---|

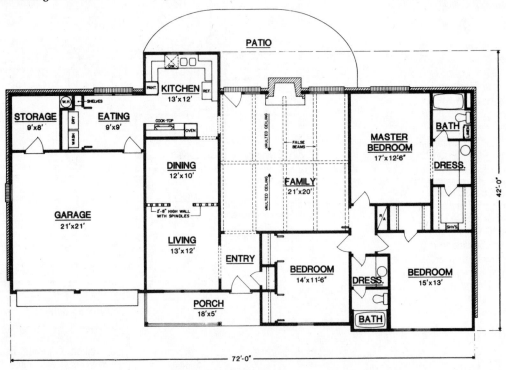

Plan E-1815

*PRICES AND DETAILS ON PAGES 12-15*

# Soaring Design
# Lifts the Human Spirit

- Suitable for level or sloping lots, this versatile design can be expanded or finished as time and budget allow.
- Surrounding deck accessible from all main living areas.
- Great living room enhanced by vaulted ceilings, second-floor balcony, skylights and dramatic window wall.
- Rear entrance has convenient access to full bath and laundry room.
- Two additional bedrooms on upper level share second bath and balcony room.

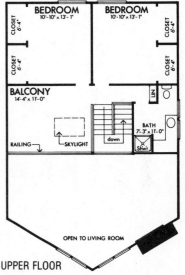

**UPPER FLOOR**

### Plans H-930-1 & -1A

| Bedrooms: 3 | Baths: 2 |
|---|---|

**Space:**

| | |
|---|---|
| Upper floor: | 710 sq. ft. |
| Main floor: | 1,210 sq. ft. |
| **Total living area:** | **1,920 sq. ft.** |
| Basement: | 605 sq. ft. |
| Garage/shop: | 605 sq. ft. |

| **Exterior Wall Framing:** | **2x6** |
|---|---|

**Foundation options:**
Daylight basement (Plan H-930-1).
Crawlspace (Plan H-930-1A).
(Foundation & framing conversion diagram available — see order form.)

**Blueprint Price Code:**

| Without basement: | B |
|---|---|
| With basement: | D |

**BASEMENT**
**PLAN H-930-1**
WITH BASEMENT

**PLAN H-930-1A**
WITHOUT BASEMENT
(CRAWLSPACE FOUNDATION)

**MAIN FLOOR**

*TO ORDER THIS BLUEPRINT,*
*CALL TOLL-FREE 1-800-547-5570*

Plans H-930-1 & -1A

*PRICES AND DETAILS*
*ON PAGES 12-15*

**109**

# Farmhouse for Today

- An inviting veranda and charming dormer windows lend traditional warmth to this attractive design.
- An up-to-date interior includes ample space for entertaining as well as for family life.
- An elegant foyer is flanked on one side by a formal, sunken living room and a sunken family room with fireplace on the other.
- A dining room joins the living room to increase the space available for parties.
- A roomy and efficient kitchen/nook/utility area combination with a half bath forms a spacious area for casual family life and domestic chores.
- Upstairs, a grand master suite includes a compartmentalized bath with separate tub and shower and a large closet.
- A second full bath serves the two secondary bedrooms.

### Plan U-87-203

| Bedrooms: 3 | Baths: 2½ |
|---|---|

**Space:**

| | |
|---|---|
| Upper floor: | 857 sq. ft. |
| Main floor: | 1,064 sq. ft. |

| **Total living area:** | **1,921 sq. ft.** |
|---|---|
| Basement: | 1,064 sq. ft. |
| Garage: | 552 sq. ft. |

| **Exterior Wall Framing:** | 2x4 & 2x6 |
|---|---|

**Foundation options:**
Standard basement.
Crawlspace.
Slab.
(Foundation & framing conversion diagram available — see order form.)

| **Blueprint Price Code:** | B |
|---|---|

DECK

SHLVS

TUB

DRESSING

TUB

BDRM. 2
12/2 x 11/6

MASTER
13/2 x 14/2

RAILING    DN

BDRM. 3
10/8 x 11/6

DESK

FOYER BELOW

UPPER FLOOR

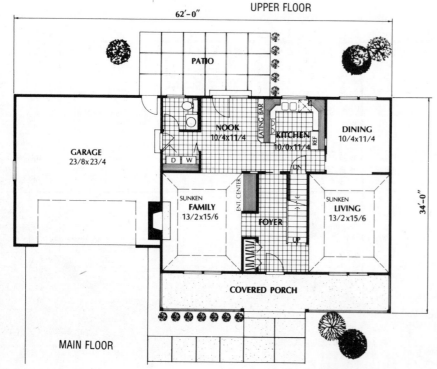

62'-0"

PATIO

34'-0"

GARAGE
23/8 x 23/4

NOOK
10/4 x 11/4

EATING BAR

KITCHEN
10/0 x 11/4

REF

DINING
10/4 x 11/4

D    W

ENT. CENTER

SUNKEN
FAMILY
13/2 x 15/6

UP

DN

FOYER

SUNKEN
LIVING
13/2 x 15/6

UP

COVERED PORCH

MAIN FLOOR

## Plan U-87-203

*PRICES AND DETAILS*
*ON PAGES 12-15*

# An Octagonal Home with a Lofty View

- There's no better way to avoid the ordinary than by building an octagonal home and escaping from square corners and rigid rooms.
- The roomy main floor offers plenty of space for full-time family living or for a comfortable second home retreat.
- The vaulted entry hall leads to the bedrooms on the right or down the hall to the Great Room.
- Warmed by a wood stove, the Great Room offers a panoramic view of the surrounding scenery.
- The center core of the main floor houses two baths, one of which contains a spa tub and is private to the master bedroom.
- This plan also includes a roomy kitchen and handy utility area.
- A large loft is planned as a recreation room, also with a wood stove.
- The daylight basement version adds another bedroom, bath, garage and large storage area.

## Plans P-532-3A & -3D

| Bedrooms: 3-4 | Baths: 2-3 |
|---|---|

**Space:**

| | |
|---|---|
| Upper floor: | 355 sq. ft. |
| Main floor: | 1,567 sq. ft. |

| | |
|---|---|
| **Total living area:** | 1,922 sq. ft. |
| Basement living area: | 430 sq. ft. |
| Garage (included in basement): | |
| | approx. 735 sq. ft. |
| Storage: | approx. 482 sq. ft. |

| Exterior Wall Framing: | 2x6 |
|---|---|

**Foundation options:**
Daylight basement (Plan P-532-3D).
Crawlspace (Plan P-532-3A).
(Foundation & framing conversion diagram available — see order form.)

**Blueprint Price Code:**

| | |
|---|---|
| Without basement: | B |
| With basement: | C |

FRONT VIEW

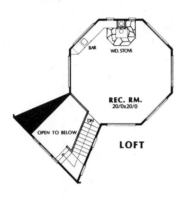

BAR / WD. STOVE / REC. RM. 20/0x20/0 / OPEN TO BELOW / DN

LOFT

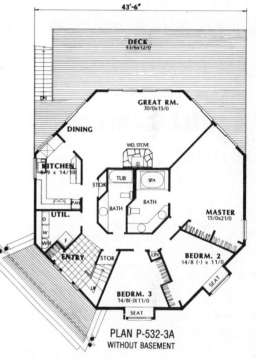

43'-6"

DECK 43/6x12/0

GREAT RM. 30/0x15/0

DINING

KITCHEN 8/9 x 14/10

WD. STOVE

STOR / TUB / SPA

BATH / BATH

UTIL.

MASTER 15/0x21/0

ENTRY / STOR / LIN

BEDRM. 2 14/8 (-) x 11/0

BEDRM. 3 14/8(-)X11/0

SEAT

PLAN P-532-3A
WITHOUT BASEMENT

BEDRM. 4 11/9x14/8

GARAGE 17/6x42/0

STORAGE

BATH

PLAN P-532-3D
WITH DAYLIGHT BASEMENT

REAR VIEW

# Imposing Form... Outstanding Floor Plan

- Stately and imposing, this one-story design boasts an attractive wood and brick exterior.
- The focal point is a grand, spacious family room with a beamed cathedral ceiling, slate-hearth fireplace and sliding glass doors to a rear terrace.
- The large living room features a sloped ceiling and high glass panels to the front.
- The luxurious master suite includes a sky-lit dressing room, private bath and large closet.
- The beautiful kitchen adjoins a sunny dinette area which protrudes onto the rear terrace.

### Plan K-278-M

| Bedrooms: 3 | Baths: 2½ |
|---|---|
| **Space:** | |
| Main floor | 1,926 sq. ft. |
| **Total Living Area** | **1,926 sq. ft.** |
| Basement | 1,778 sq. ft. |
| Garage | 463 sq. ft. |
| **Exterior Wall Framing** | 2x4/2x6 |

**Foundation options:**

Standard Basement

Slab

(Foundation & framing conversion diagram available—see order form.)

| **Blueprint Price Code** | **B** |
|---|---|

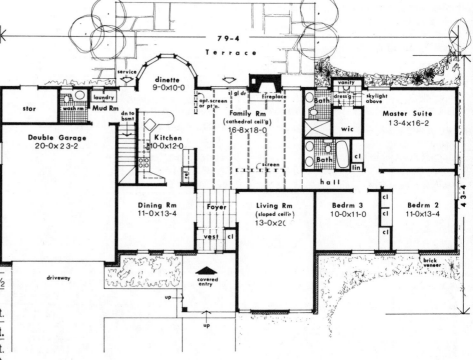

Plan K-278-M

*PRICES AND DETAILS ON PAGES 12-15*

# Decked Out for Fun

- Spacious deck surrounds this comfortable cabin/chalet.
- Sliding glass doors and windows blanket the living-dining area, indulged with raised hearth and a breathtaking view.
- Dining area and compact kitchen separated by breakfast bar.
- Master bedroom, laundry room and bath complete first floor; two additional bedrooms located on second floor.
- Upper level also features impressive balcony room with exposed beams.

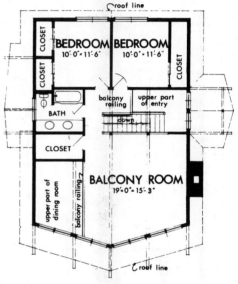

UPPER FLOOR

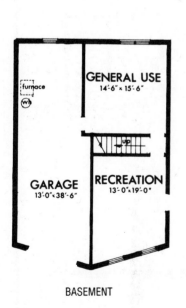

BASEMENT

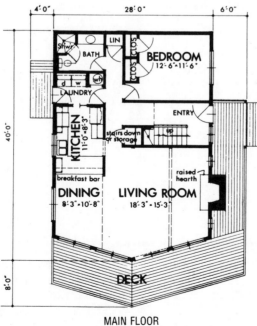

MAIN FLOOR

**Plans H-919-1 & -1A**

| Bedrooms: 3 | Baths: 2 |
|---|---|
| **Space:** | |
| Upper floor: | 869 sq. ft. |
| Main floor: | 1,064 sq. ft. |
| **Total living area:** | **1,933 sq. ft.** |
| Basement: | 475 sq. ft. |
| Garage: | 501 sq. ft. |
| **Exterior Wall Framing:** | 2x6 |

**Foundation options:**
Daylight basement (Plan H-919-1).
Crawlspace (Plan H-919-1A).
(Foundation & framing conversion diagram available — see order form.)

**Blueprint Price Code:**
| Without basement: | B |
| With basement: | C |

# Cozy L-Shaped Bungalow

This pleasing L-shaped design packs a smooth-flowing floor plan into 1,950 sq. ft. The master suite includes garden tub, shower, his and her vanities and separate walk-in closets. Two other bedrooms and a full bath complete the sleeping wing.

A large family room, foyer and separate living-dining room combine to form the center section. U-shaped kitchen, breakfast nook with bay window and separate utility complete the plan.

Total living area: 1,950 sq. ft.
(Not counting basement or garage)

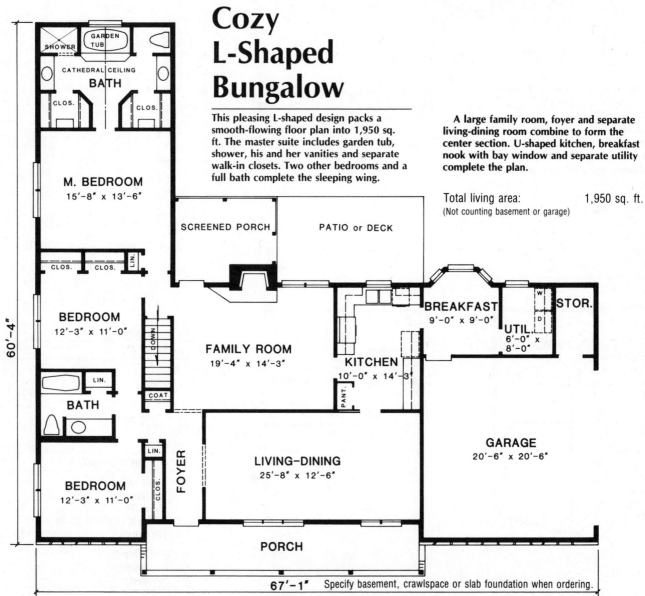

Specify basement, crawlspace or slab foundation when ordering.

Blueprint Price Code B

# Plan C-8620

# Excellent Family Design

- Long sloping rooflines and bold design features make this home attractive for any neighborhood.
- Inside, a vaulted entry takes visitors into an impressive vaulted Great Room with a wood stove and window-wall facing the house-spanning rear deck.
- Clerestory windows flanking the stove area and large windows front and rear flood the Great Room with natural light.
- The magnificent kitchen includes a stylish island and opens to the informal dining area which in turn flows into the Great Room.
- Two bedrooms on the main floor share a full bath, and bedroom #2 boasts easy access to the rear deck which spans the width of the house.
- The upstairs comprises an "adult retreat," with a roomy master suite, luxurious bath with double sinks, and a large walk-in closet.
- A daylight basement version adds another 1,410 sq. ft. of space for entertaining and recreation, plus a fourth bedroom and a large shop/storage area.

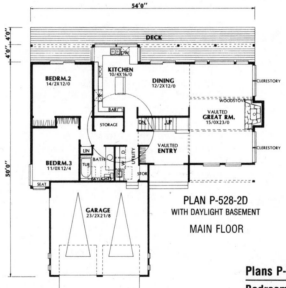

**PLAN P-528-2D**
WITH DAYLIGHT BASEMENT
**MAIN FLOOR**

**UPPER FLOOR**

**PLAN P-528-2A**
WITHOUT BASEMENT
(CRAWLSPACE FOUNDATION)

**BASEMENT**

### Plans P-528-2A & -2D

| Bedrooms: 3-4 | Baths: 2-3 |
|---|---|
| **Space:** | |
| Upper floor: | 498 sq. ft. |
| Main floor: | 1,456 sq. ft. |
| **Total living area:** | 1,954 sq. ft. |
| Basement: | 1,410 sq. ft. |
| Garage: | 502 sq. ft. |
| **Exterior Wall Framing:** | 2x6 |

**Foundation options:**
Daylight basement (Plan P-528-2D).
Crawlspace (Plan P-528-2A).
(Foundation & framing conversion diagram available — see order form.)

**Blueprint Price Code:**

| | |
|---|---|
| Without basement: | B |
| With basement: | E |

# Indoor/Outdoor Living on A Sloping Lot

- The wood siding, the front deck, and the multi-paned exterior of this Northwest contemporary will beckon you up to the entry stairs and inside.
- The two-story entry opens up to a vaulted living room with tall windows, exposed beam ceiling and adjoining dining area which accesses the hand-railed deck.
- An updated kitchen offers a walk-in

pantry, eating bar and breakfast nook with sliders to a rear deck.
- A fireplace and rear patio highlight the attached family room.
- A washer/dryer in the upper level bath is convenient to all three bedrooms, making laundry a breeze.

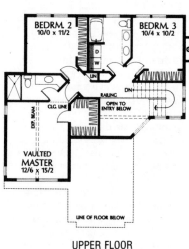

UPPER FLOOR

### Plan P-7737-4D

| Bedrooms: 3 | Baths: 2½ |
|---|---|
| **Space:** | |
| Upper floor: | 802 sq. ft. |
| Main floor: | 1,158 sq. ft. |
| **Total living area:** | 1,960 sq. ft. |
| Garage/basement: | 736 sq. ft. |
| **Exterior Wall Framing:** | 2x6 |

**Foundation options:**
Crawlspace.
(Foundation & framing conversion diagram available — see order form.)

| **Blueprint Price Code:** | B |
|---|---|

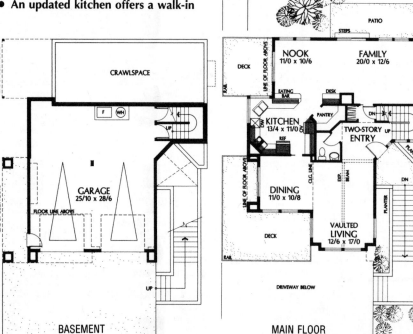

BASEMENT

MAIN FLOOR

## Plan P-7737-4D

# Passive Solar Design . . . from the Foundation Up

Designed to embrace the warming sun, this two-story passive solar house is constructed of standard lumber, and its dramatic exterior is finished in vertical wood siding and roof shingles. Focal point of the concept is a glass-enclosed, south-facing sun garden that is visible from the entrance gallery and is wrapped by the living, dining and family rooms. The open plan provides for a cheerful well-organized kitchen, situated to serve the dining room and family room. A library (or guest room) and bath are located off the entrance gallery.

Isolated on the second floor are three bedrooms and two baths with a balcony that overlooks the living and dining rooms. Solar energy is absorbed and stored in the masonry wall and dense floor for heating. The sun garden generates heat to the adjacent areas by opening the sliding doors. Direct heat gain is maintained through glazed walls that face south. For summer cooling, eave overhang keeps out unwanted sun. Operable vents in the clerestory draw air out of the house by convection to provide natural ventilation. Many other energy saving features are planned into the house to assure a high retention of heat, and a back-up heating system is provided for use as needed. Total living area, excluding the sun garden, is 1,214 sq. ft. on the first floor and 762 sq. ft. on the second; garage and mudroom, 536 sq. ft.; optional basement, 848 sq. ft.

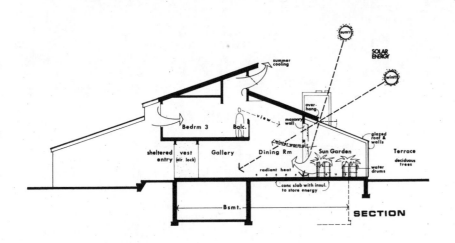

**SECTION**

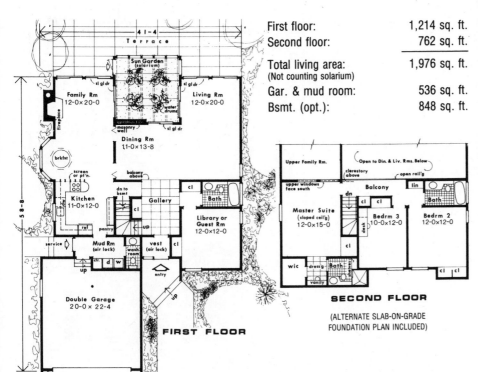

| First floor: | 1,214 sq. ft. |
| Second floor: | 762 sq. ft. |
| Total living area:<br>(Not counting solarium) | 1,976 sq. ft. |
| Gar. & mud room: | 536 sq. ft. |
| Bsmt. (opt.): | 848 sq. ft. |

**FIRST FLOOR**

**SECOND FLOOR**

(ALTERNATE SLAB-ON-GRADE FOUNDATION PLAN INCLUDED)

Blueprint Price Code B

## Plan K-279-T

PRICES AND DETAILS ON PAGES 12-15

FRONT VIEW

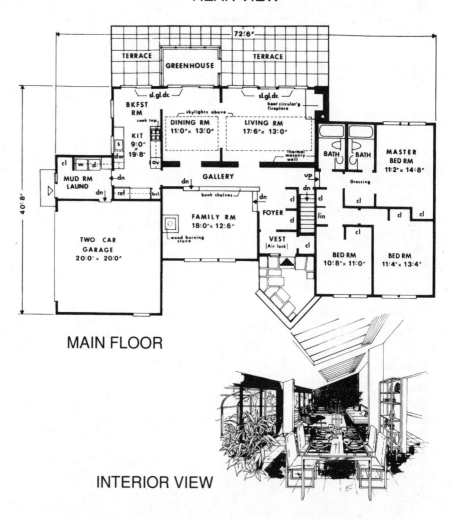

REAR VIEW

# Unique Solar Design

- This passive-solar design combines the use of heat-storing materials, a greenhouse and site orientation to capture the sun's energy.
- Large skylights and clerestory windows in the central formal living areas focus the sun's rays on a thick masonry wall that stores the heat. Heat can be further distributed by opening the sliding glass doors in the greenhouse.
- A recirculating fireplace in the living room and a wood-burning stove in the family room further supplement the energy savings. Cathedral ceilings grace the large formal area and the sunken family room.
- The walk-through kitchen adjoins a sunny breakfast room at the rear, which opens to an expansive terrace.
- Two steps up, the bedroom wing includes a large master suite with a private bath and two secondary bedrooms that share another bath.

## Plan HFL-1310-MA

| Bedrooms: 3 | Baths: 2 |
|---|---|
| **Living Area:** | |
| Main floor | 1,988 sq. ft. |
| **Total Living Area:** | **1,988 sq. ft.** |
| Partial basement | 756 sq. ft. |
| Garage | 400 sq. ft. |
| **Exterior Wall Framing:** | 2x4 |

**Foundation Options:**

Partial basement

Slab

(Typical foundation & framing conversion diagram available—see order form.)

| **BLUEPRINT PRICE CODE:** | B |
|---|---|

MAIN FLOOR

INTERIOR VIEW

Plan HFL-1310-MA

*PRICES AND DETAILS ON PAGES 12-15*

# Visual Surprises

- The exterior of this two-story, four-bedroom design is boldly accented with a dramatic roof cavity, while the inside features wall angles that enhance the efficiency of the floor plan and offer visual variety.
- The double-door entry opens into a bright reception area, leading to the sloped-ceilinged living room.
- The efficient kitchen conveniently serves the formal dining room and the cheerful breakfast dinette.
- Off the reception area is a powder room and a large laundry space which could be finished to serve as a hobby room.
- Four bedrooms are isolated on the second level; a connecting balcony is open to the living room below.
- The master suite is fully equipped; sliding glass doors yield access to the open wood deck that is literally carved into the roof.

## Plan K-540-L

| Bedrooms: 4 | Baths: 2½ |
|---|---|
| **Space:** | |
| Upper floor: | 884 sq. ft. |
| Main floor: | 1,106 sq. ft. |
| **Total living area:** | 1,990 sq. ft. |
| Basement: | 1,106 sq. ft. |
| Garage: | 400 sq. ft. |
| Storage, laundry: | 254 sq. ft. |

| Exterior Wall Framing: | 2x4/2x6 |
|---|---|

**Foundation options:**
Standard basement.
Slab.
(Foundation & framing conversion diagram available — see order form)

| **Blueprint Price Code:** | B |
|---|---|

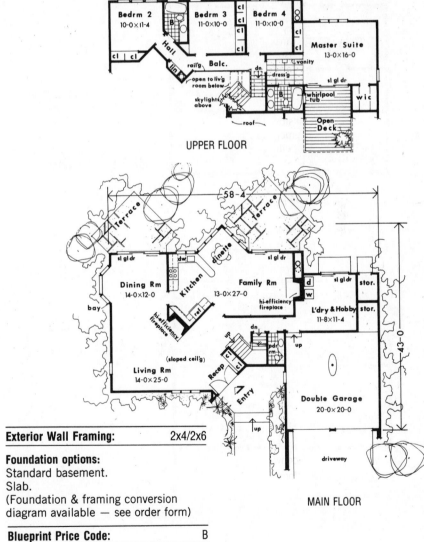

UPPER FLOOR

MAIN FLOOR

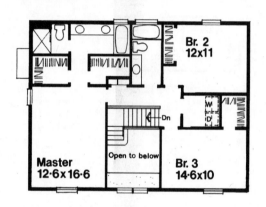

**Br. 2**
12x11

**Master**
12·6 x 16·6

**Br. 3**
14·6x10

W
D

Dn

Open to below

## UPPER FLOOR

# Relax on the Front Porch

- Summer evenings will be a breeze on the quaint front porch of this affordable two story home.
- A very efficient floor plan keeps hallways at a minimum and living spaces at a maximum.
- The front entry opens into a dramatic two story space with stairway, plant shelf and transom windows. To the left and right of the entry are the formal living and dining rooms.
- The informal family room with fireplace is only a half-wall away from the island kitchen and breakfast eating area.
- The upper floor feels spacious with the open stairwell. It houses three bedrooms, two full baths and a handy laundry room.

**Plan AGH-1997**

| | |
|---|---|
| **Bedrooms:** 3 | **Baths:** 2 ½ |
| **Space:** | |
| Upper floor | 933 sq. ft. |
| Main floor | 1,064 sq. ft. |
| **Total Living Area** | **1,997 sq. ft.** |
| Basement | 1,064 sq. ft. |
| Garage | 662 sq. ft. |
| **Exterior Wall Framing** | 2x4 |
| **Foundation options:** | |
| Standard Basement | |
| (Foundation & framing conversion diagram available—see order form.) | |
| **Blueprint Price Code** | B |

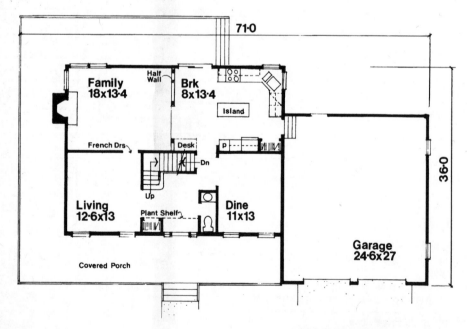

71·0

36·0

**Family**
18x13·4

Half Wall

**Brk**
8x13·4

Island

French Drs

Desk

P

Up

Dn

**Living**
12·6x13

Plant Shelf

**Dine**
11x13

**Garage**
24·6x27

Covered Porch

## MAIN FLOOR

# Plan AGH-1997

# Interior Angles Add Excitement

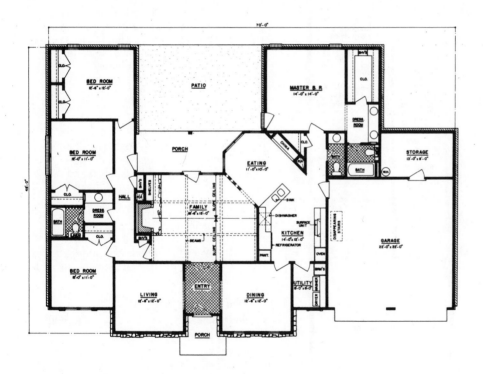

- Interior angles add a touch of excitement to this one-story home.
- A pleasantly charming exterior combines wood and stone to give the plan a solid, comfortable look for any neighborhood.
- Formal living and dining rooms flank the entry, which leads into a large family room complete with fireplace, vaulted and beamed ceiling and built-in bookshelves.
- The adjoining family-eating area with a built-in china cabinet angles off the spacious kitchen.
- Note the pantry and convenient utility area.
- The master bedroom suite is both large and private, and includes a dressing room, large walk-in closet and deluxe bath.
- The three secondary bedrooms are zoned for privacy, also, and share a second full bath.

**Plan E-1904**

| Bedrooms: 4 | Baths: 2 |
|---|---|

**Space:**

| Total living area: | 1,997 sq. ft. |
|---|---|
| Garage: | 484 sq. ft. |
| Storage: | 104 sq. ft. |
| Porches: | 157 sq. ft. |

| Exterior Wall Framing: | 2x4 |
|---|---|

**Foundation options:**
Crawlspace.
Slab.
(Foundation & framing conversion diagram available — see order form)

| Blueprint Price Code: | B |
|---|---|

# Great Room Overlooks Patio

- Handsome gables acented with keystones and arched transom windows highlight the exterior of this contemporary three-bedroom home.
- Inside, the well-integrated main living areas are geared for views to the covered patio, which is the perfect complement to a pool area.
- The home features 10-ft. ceilings throughout, with the exception of the vaulted ceilings in the dining room, Great Room, kitchen and nook.
- The open, airy plan is packed with extras, such as the concrete columns framing the dining room, the pass-through between the kitchen and the Great Room, and the optional fireplace in the living room.
- The master suite offers private access to the patio, a walk-in closet and a wonderful bath with a Roman tub.
- The two smaller bedrooms are separated by another full bath at the opposite end of the home.

| Plan HDS-99-170 | |
| --- | --- |
| **Bedrooms: 3** | **Baths: 2** |
| **Living Area:** | |
| Main floor | 2,005 sq. ft. |
| **Total Living Area:** | **2,005 sq. ft.** |
| Garage | 400 sq. ft. |
| **Exterior Wall Framing:** | 8" concrete block |
| **Foundation Options:** | |
| Slab | |

(Typical foundation & framing conversion diagram available—see order form.)

| **BLUEPRINT PRICE CODE:** | C |
| --- | --- |

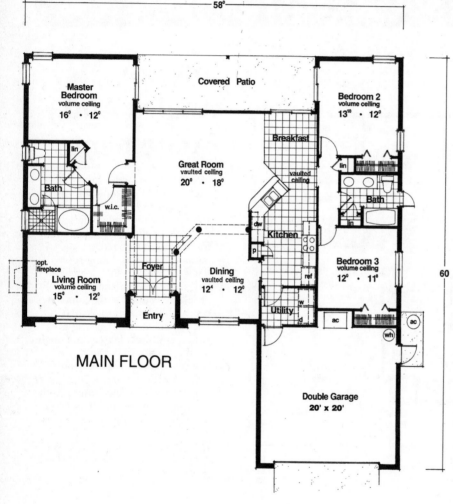

**MAIN FLOOR**

Plan HDS-99-170

PRICES AND DETAILS
ON PAGES 12-15

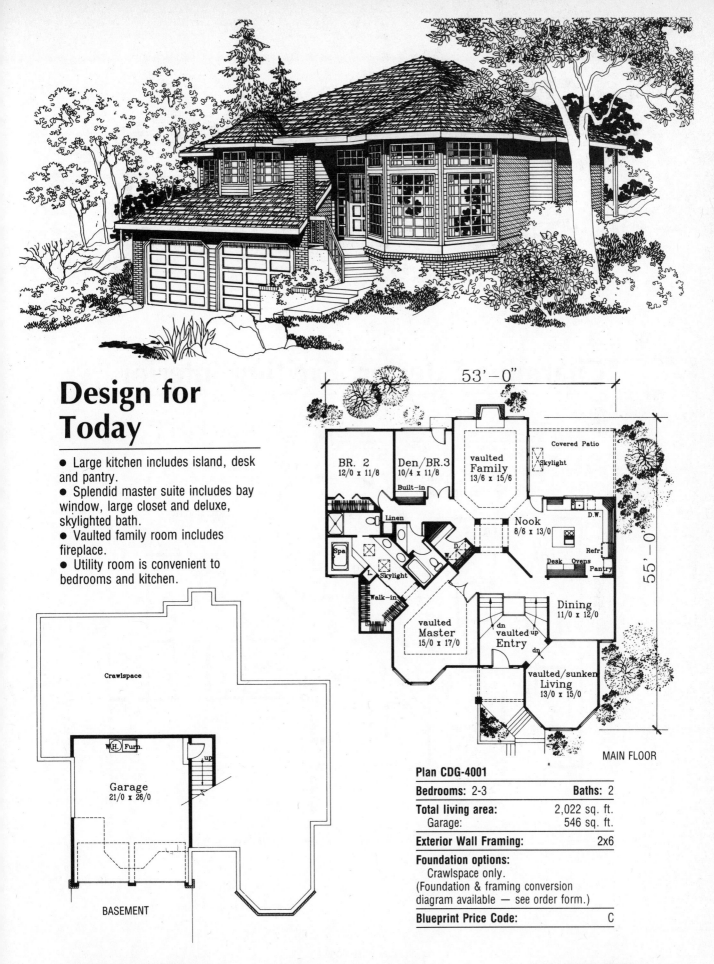

# Design for Today

- Large kitchen includes island, desk and pantry.
- Splendid master suite includes bay window, large closet and deluxe, skylighted bath.
- Vaulted family room includes fireplace.
- Utility room is convenient to bedrooms and kitchen.

**Crawlspace**

W.H. Furn.

up

**Garage**
21/0 x 26/0

**BASEMENT**

53'-0"

55'-0"

BR. 2
12/0 x 11/8

Den/BR.3
10/4 x 11/8

Built-in

vaulted
Family
13/6 x 15/6

Covered Patio

Skylight

Linen

D.W.

Nook
8/6 x 13/0

Spa

Refr.

Desk    Ovens

Pantry

Skylight

Walk-in

vaulted
Master
15/0 x 17/0

dn
vaulted
Entry
dn

up

Dining
11/0 x 12/0

vaulted/sunken
Living
13/0 x 15/0

MAIN FLOOR

**Plan CDG-4001**

| | |
|---|---|
| **Bedrooms:** 2-3 | **Baths:** 2 |

| **Total living area:** | 2,022 sq. ft. |
|---|---|
| Garage: | 546 sq. ft. |

| **Exterior Wall Framing:** | 2x6 |
|---|---|

**Foundation options:**
   Crawlspace only.
(Foundation & framing conversion
diagram available — see order form.)

| **Blueprint Price Code:** | C |
|---|---|

**TO ORDER THIS BLUEPRINT,**
**CALL TOLL-FREE 1-800-547-5570**

Plan CDG-4001

**PRICES AND DETAILS**
**ON PAGES 12-15**

123

# Charming Exterior, Exciting Interior

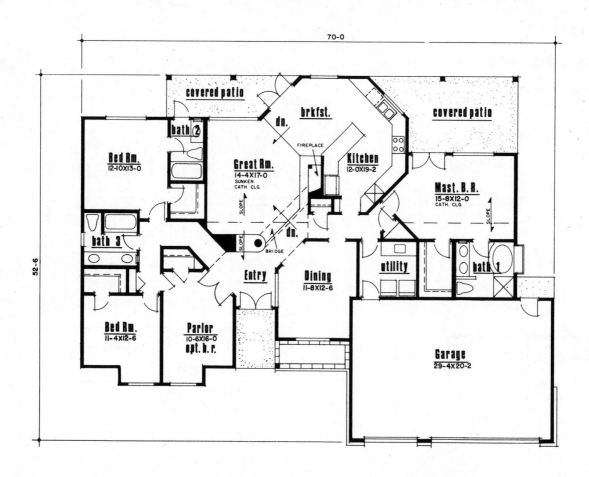

70-0

covered patio

bath 2

Bed Rm.
12-10X13-0

Great Rm.
14-4X17-0
SUNKEN
CATH. CLG.

brkfst.

dn.

FIREPLACE

Kitchen
12-0X19-2

covered patio

Mast. B.R.
15-8X12-0
CATH. CLG.

bath 3

SLOPE

SLOPE

dn.

BRIDGE

52-6

Entry

Dining
11-8X12-6

utility

bath 1

SLOPE

Bed Rm.
11-4X12-6

Parlor
10-6X16-0
opt. b.r.

Garage
29-4X20-2

Total living area:
(Not counting garage)

2,033 sq. ft.

Plan Q-2033-1A
WITHOUT BASEMENT
(SLAB-ON-GRADE FOUNDATION)

Blueprint Price Code C

## Plan Q-2033-1A

# A Glorious Blend of New and Old

This three-bedroom, two and one-half-bath home is a glorious blend of contemporary and traditional lines. Inside, its 2,035 sq. ft. are wisely distributed among amply proportioned, practically appointed rooms. A vaulted entry gives way to a second reception area bordering on a broad, vaulted living room nearly 20' long.

With its walls of windows overlooking the back yard, this grand room's centerpiece is a massive woodstove, whose central location contributes extra energy efficiency to the home — upstairs as well as down. The dining room offers quiet separation from the living room, while still enjoying the warmth from its woodstove. Its sliding door accesses a large wraparound covered patio to create a cool, shady refuge.

For sun-seeking, another wraparound patio at the front is fenced but uncovered, and elegantly accessed by double doors from a well-lighted, vaulted nook.

Placed conveniently between the two dining areas is a kitchen with all the trimmings: pantry, large sink window, and an expansive breakfast bar.

A stylish upstairs landing overlooks the living room on one side and the entry on the other, and leads to a master suite that rambles over fully half of the second floor.

Adjacent to the huge bedroom area is a spacious dressing area bordered by an abundance of closet space and a double-sink bath area. Unusual extras include walk-in wardrobe in the third bedroom and the long double-sink counter in the second upstairs bath.

Note also the exceptional abundance of closet space on both floors, and the separate utility room that also serves as a clean-up room connecting with the garage.

| | |
|---|---|
| Upper floor: | 1,085 sq. ft. |
| Main floor: | 950 sq. ft. |
| Total living area: | 2,035 sq. ft. |
| (Not counting basement or garage) | |

## Floor Plans

**MASTER SUITE** 17/8x15/8

OPEN TO LIVING BELOW

RAILING

DRESSING

RAILING

SHWR

BATH

OPEN TO ENTRY BELOW

DN

LIN

BATH

TUB

LIN

BEDRM. 3 10/6x12/8

BEDRM. 2 10/6x13/2

**UPPER FLOOR**

**PLAN P-6597-2A**
WITHOUT BASEMENT
(CRAWLSPACE FOUNDATION)

**PLAN P-6597-2D**
(WITH DAYLIGHT BASEMENT)

UP
DN

40'0"

PATIO

BUILDING LINE ABOVE

VAULTED LIVING RM. 19/4x17/4

CEILING LINE

DINING 12/0x10/0

WOODSTOVE

OPEN

UP

KITCHEN 12/5x12/0

OV

REF

DW

PANTRY

BAR

VAULTED ENTRY

BATH

D

W

UTILITY

WH

F

VAULTED NOOK 10/0x11/0

GARAGE 21/4x28/0

PATIO

54'0"

**MAIN FLOOR**

# Country Kitchen and Great Room

- Highlights of this home's pleasant exterior include a cozy front porch, two dormers, stylish shutters and multi-paned windows. The side-loading garage keeps the front of the home beautiful and uncluttered.
- The interior features a central Great Room with fireplace and an eat-in country kitchen with island counter and bay windows.
- A view to the wood deck is possible from the Great Room and the adjoining dining room.
- The main-floor master suite boasts a walk-in closet and private access to a compartmentalized bath with oversized linen closet.
- Upstairs, two bedrooms with window seats share a full bath. A large storage area is found above the garage.

### Plan C-8040

| Bedrooms: 3 | Baths: 2 |
|---|---|
| **Living Area:** | |
| Upper floor: | 718 sq. ft. |
| Main floor | 1,318 sq. ft. |
| **Total Living Area:** | **2,036 sq. ft.** |
| Standard basement | 1,221 sq. ft. |
| Garage | 436 sq. ft. |
| **Exterior Wall Framing:** | 2x4 |

**Foundation Options:**

Standard basement
Crawlspace
Slab
(Typical foundation & framing conversion diagram available—see order form.)

| **BLUEPRINT PRICE CODE:** | C |
|---|---|

UPPER FLOOR

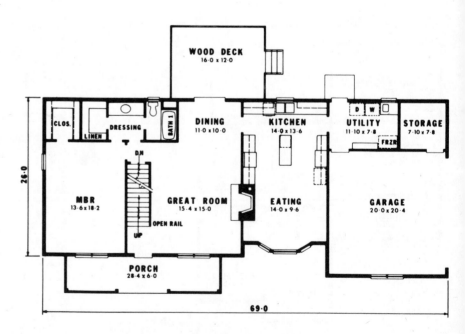

MAIN FLOOR

*TO ORDER THIS BLUEPRINT, CALL TOLL-FREE 1-800-547-5570*

Plan C-8040

*PRICES AND DETAILS ON PAGES 12-15*

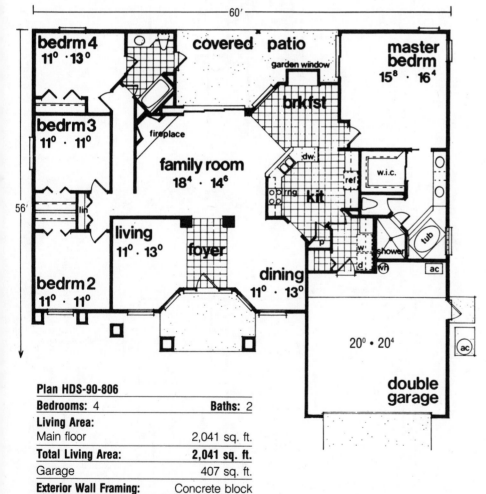

bedrm 4
11⁰ · 13⁰

covered patio

garden window

master bedrm
15⁸ · 16⁴

bedrm 3
11⁰ · 11⁰

brkfst

fireplace

family room
18⁴ · 14⁶

dw

w.i.c.

ref

rng

kit

lin

living
11⁰ · 13⁰

foyer

tub

shower

bedrm 2
11⁰ · 11⁰

dining
11⁰ · 13⁰

ac

20⁰ · 20⁴

ac

double garage

60'

56'

**Plan HDS-90-806**

| | |
|---|---|
| **Bedrooms:** 4 | **Baths:** 2 |

**Living Area:**

| | |
|---|---|
| Main floor | 2,041 sq. ft. |
| **Total Living Area:** | **2,041 sq. ft.** |
| Garage | 407 sq. ft. |
| **Exterior Wall Framing:** | Concrete block |

**Foundation Options:**

Slab

(Typical foundation & framing conversion diagram available—see order form.)

**BLUEPRINT PRICE CODE:** C

# Elaborate Entryway

- An important-looking covered entry greets guests with heavy, banded support columns, sunburst transom windows and dual sidelights flanking the front door.
- Once inside, the formal living and dining rooms open up to the left and right of the foyer, while straight ahead, through columns, lies the family room.
- The family room features a vaulted ceiling, fireplace and sliders to the rear covered patio.
- The kitchen overlooks the family room and breakfast eating area which has a garden window focal point.
- The master suite is well-separated on the opposite side of the plan from the three secondary bedrooms. It features sliding-door patio access, a large walk-in closet and private bath with corner platform tub and separate shower.

*TO ORDER THIS BLUEPRINT,*
*CALL TOLL-FREE 1-800-547-5570*

Plan HDS-90-806

*PRICES AND DETAILS*
*ON PAGES 12-15*

127

# Geometric Gem

- This striking contemporary flaunts a unique exterior of vertical siding, shed roofs and glass. With the tuck-under garage, the home would be ideal for a sloping lot. Without the garage, it may be built on a level lot.
- A semi-circular silo houses the stairway to the private master suite on the upper floor, which features a skylighted bath and a private balcony.
- The skylighted foyer opens to a huge Great Room, also with skylights. A cathedral ceiling, a large fireplace and lots of glass are other highlights. Sliders at the rear access the expansive backyard deck.
- The centrally located kitchen is open to the Great Room and includes a functional snack counter, a work desk, a pantry and its own deck access.
- A full bath, a discreet laundry closet and three bedrooms are located in the sleeping wing.

## Plan AX-98489

| Bedrooms: 4 | Baths: 2 |
|---|---|
| **Living Area:** | |
| Upper floor | 485 sq. ft. |
| Main floor | 1,560 sq. ft. |
| **Total Living Area:** | **2,045 sq. ft.** |
| Standard basement | 1,218 sq. ft. |
| Tuck-under garage | 342 sq. ft. |
| **Exterior Wall Framing:** | 2x4 |

**Foundation Options:**

Standard basement

(Typical foundation & framing conversion diagram available—see order form.)

| **BLUEPRINT PRICE CODE:** | C |
|---|---|

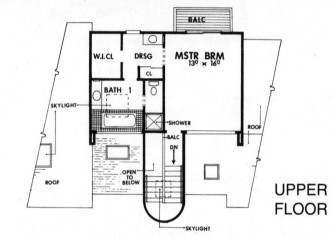

UPPER FLOOR

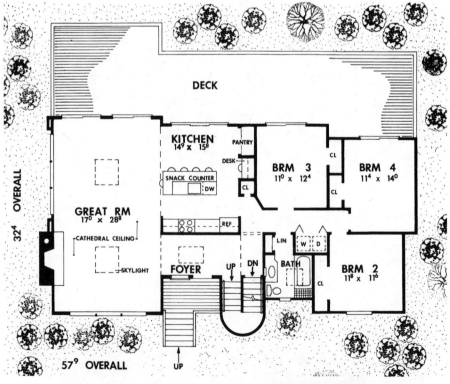

MAIN FLOOR

*TO ORDER THIS BLUEPRINT, CALL TOLL-FREE 1-800-547-5570*

Plan AX-98489

*PRICES AND DETAILS ON PAGES 12-15*

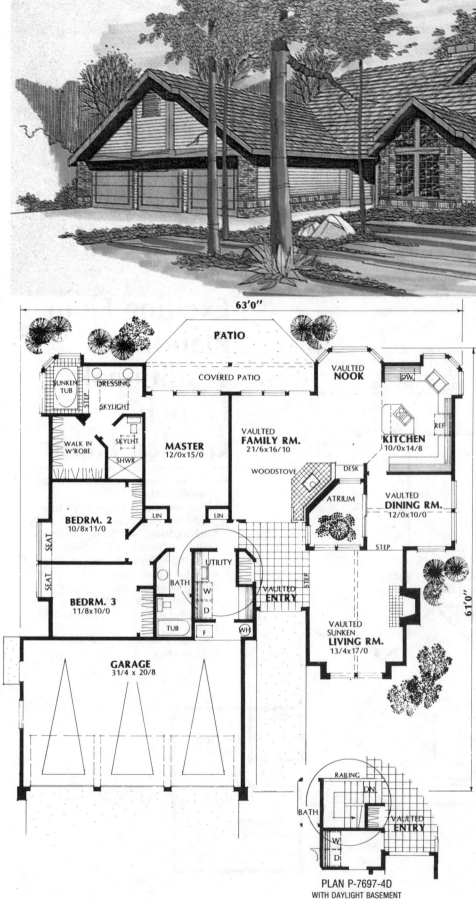

**63'0"**

PATIO

COVERED PATIO

VAULTED NOOK

SUNKEN TUB

DRESSING

SKYLIGHT

WALK IN W'ROBE

SKYLHT

SHWR

MASTER
12/0x15/0

VAULTED
FAMILY RM.
21/6x16/10

KITCHEN
10/0x14/8

DW.

REF

WOODSTOVE

DESK

ATRIUM

VAULTED
DINING RM.
12/0x10/0

LIN

LIN

BEDRM. 2
10/8x11/0

SEAT

SEAT

UTILITY

W D

BATH

VAULTED
ENTRY

STEP

STEP

BEDRM. 3
11/8x10/0

TUB

F

WH

VAULTED
SUNKEN
LIVING RM.
13/4x17/0

61'0"

GARAGE
31/4 x 20/8

RAILING

DN

BATH

VAULTED
ENTRY

W D

PLAN P-7697-4D
WITH DAYLIGHT BASEMENT

# Soaring Spaces under Vaulted Ceilings

- A dignified exterior and a gracious, spacious interior combine to make this an outstanding plan for today's families.
- The living, dining, family rooms and breakfast nook all feature soaring vaulted ceilings.
- An interior atrium provides an extra touch of elegance, with its sunny space for growing plants and sunbathing.
- The master suite is first class all the way, with a spacious sleeping area, opulent bath, large skylight and enormous walk-in closet.
- A gorgeous kitchen includes a large work/cooktop island, corner sink with large corner windows and plenty of counter space.

**Plans P-7697-4A & -4D**

| Bedrooms: 3 | Baths: 2 |
|---|---|

| Space: | |
|---|---|
| Main floor (crawlspace version): | 2,003 sq. ft. |
| Main floor (basement version): | 2,030 sq. ft. |
| Basement: | 2,015 sq. ft. |
| Garage: | 647 sq. ft. |

| **Exterior Wall Framing:** | 2x4 |
|---|---|

**Foundation options:**
Daylight basement (Plan P-7697-4D).
Crawlspace (Plan P-7697-4A).
(Foundation & framing conversion diagram available — see order form.)

| **Blueprint Price Code:** | C |
|---|---|

Photo by Mark Englund/HomeStyles

**Plan E-2004**

| | |
|---|---|
| **Bedrooms:** 3 | **Baths:** 2 |

**Space:**

| | |
|---|---|
| **Total living area:** | 2,023 sq. ft. |
| Garage: | 484 sq. ft. |
| Storage & Porches: | 423 sq. ft. |

| **Exterior Wall Framing:** | 2x6 |

**Foundation options:**
Crawlspace.
Slab.
(Foundation & framing conversion diagram available — see order form.)

| **Blueprint Price Code:** | C |

# Exciting Floor Plan In Traditional French Garden Home

- Creative, angular design permits an open floor plan.
- Living and dining rooms open to a huge covered porch.
- Kitchen, living and dining rooms feature impressive 12′ ceilings accented by extensive use of glass.
- Informal eating nook faces a delightful courtyard.
- Luxurious master bath offers a whirlpool tub, shower, and walk-in closet.
- Secondary bedrooms also offer walk-in closets.

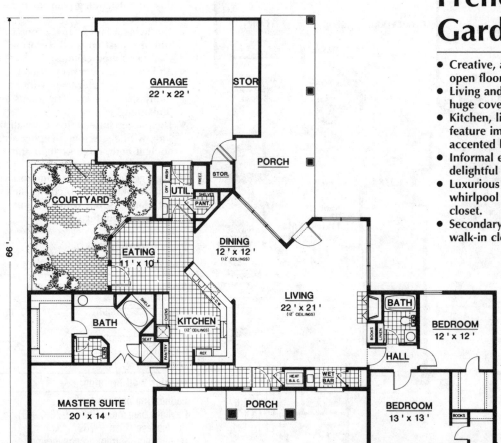

**\*\*NOTE:**
The above photographed home may have been modified by the homeowner. Please refer to floor plan and/or drawn elevation shown for actual blueprint details.

**TO ORDER THIS BLUEPRINT, CALL TOLL-FREE 1-800-547-5570**     **Plan E-2004**     **PRICES AND DETAILS ON PAGES 12-15**

# Colonial Design Alive with Solar Energy

This gracious colonial home combines traditional design with contemporary passive solar efficiency. Southern exposure at the rear provides maximum sunshine in the kitchen, dinette, family room, and cheerful sun room. Heat energy, accumulated in the insulated thermal flooring, is later released for night-time comfort. An air-lock vestibule, which minimizes heat loss, adds the elegance we associate with a center-hall colonial.

Upstairs, there are four comfortable bedrooms and two luxury baths — one accented by a whirlpool tub. Also, there is an electrically operated skylight that aids in natural cooling.

Total living area of the first floor, excluding sun room, comes to 1,030 sq. ft.; second floor adds 1,003 sq. ft. Garage, mud room, etc. are 500 sq. ft., and optional basement is 633 sq. ft.

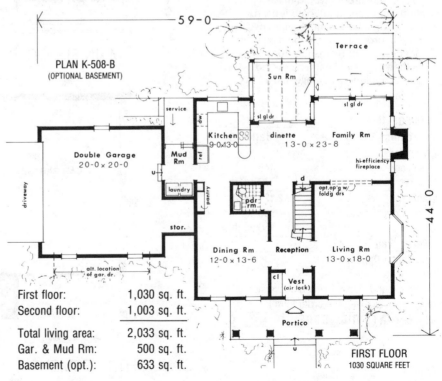

PLAN K-508-B
(OPTIONAL BASEMENT)

First floor: 1,030 sq. ft.
Second floor: 1,003 sq. ft.

Total living area: 2,033 sq. ft.
Gar. & Mud Rm: 500 sq. ft.
Basement (opt.): 633 sq. ft.

SECOND FLOOR
1003 SQUARE FEET

FIRST FLOOR
1030 SQUARE FEET

Blueprint Price Code C

# Plan K-508-B

PRICES AND DETAILS ON PAGES 12-15

# Grand Indoor/ Outdoor Living

- This attractive home is planned around a central Grand Room, which boasts a vaulted ceiling, an adjoining dining area, a serving bar and sliding glass doors to a lovely screened porch.
- The U-shaped kitchen boasts a handy pass-through to an attached dining deck. Volume ceilings enhance all of the rooms on the main floor.
- The owner (master) suite offers a walk-in closet, a private bath and access to a secluded deck.
- A second bedroom would make a great guest room, and a full bath is nearby.
- The daylight basement provides two more bedrooms, which could be used for guests or for recreation. Also included are a full bath, a covered patio, a tuck-under garage and a large storage area.

## Plan EOF-45

| Bedrooms: 3+ | Baths: 3 |
|---|---|
| **Living Area:** | |
| Main floor | 1,448 sq. ft. |
| Daylight basement | 673 sq. ft. |
| **Total Living Area:** | **2,121 sq. ft.** |
| Tuck-under garage | 550 sq. ft. |
| Storage | 150 sq. ft. |
| **Exterior Wall Framing:** | 2x4 |

**Foundation Options:**

Daylight basement
(Typical foundation & framing conversion diagram available—see order form.)

| **BLUEPRINT PRICE CODE:** | C |
|---|---|

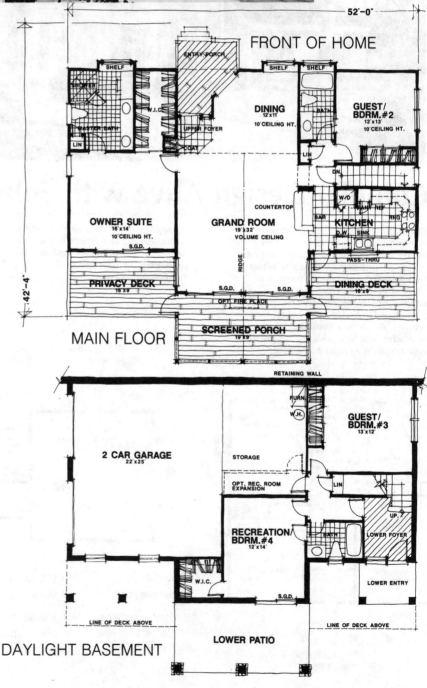

MAIN FLOOR

DAYLIGHT BASEMENT

*TO ORDER THIS BLUEPRINT, CALL TOLL-FREE 1-800-547-5570*

Plan EOF-45

*PRICES AND DETAILS ON PAGES 12-15*

# Colonial with a Contemporary Touch

- Open, flowing rooms highlighted by a two-story round-top window combine to give this colonial design a contemporary, today touch.
- To the left of the elegant, two-story foyer lies the living room, which flows into the rear-facing family room with fireplace.
- The centrally located kitchen serves both the formal dining room and the dinette, with a view of the family room beyond.
- All four bedrooms are located upstairs. The master suite includes a walk-in closet and private bath with double vanities, separate shower and whirlpool tub under skylights.

**Plan AHP-9020**

| Bedrooms: 4 | Baths: 2 ½ |
|---|---|
| **Space:** | |
| Upper floor | 1,021 sq. ft. |
| Main floor | 1,125 sq. ft. |
| **Total Living Area** | **2,146 sq. ft.** |
| Basement | 1,032 sq. ft. |
| Garage | 480 sq. ft. |
| **Exterior Wall Framing** | **2x6** |
| **Foundation options:** | |
| Standard Basement | |
| Slab | |
| (Foundation & framing conversion diagram available—see order form.) | |
| **Blueprint Price Code** | **C** |

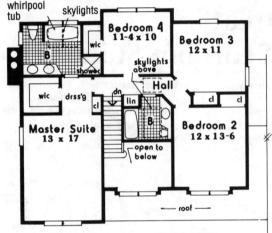

UPPER FLOOR

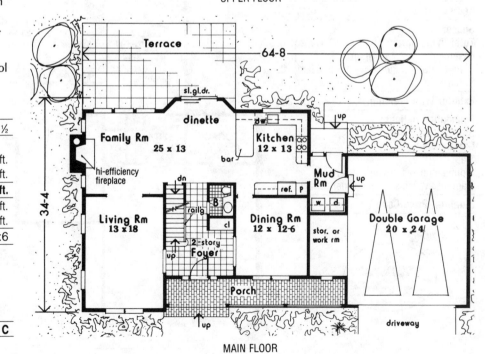

MAIN FLOOR

*Photo courtesy of Breland & Farmer Designers, Inc.*

# "Adult Retreat" in Master Bedroom Suite

- Exciting living room is virtually open on three sides.
- Wet bar lies between living area and large kitchen, which offers an eating bar and island cooktop.
- Elegant master suite features sitting area and attached bath with romantic angled tub covered with skylight and flanked by his 'n hers vanities.

**Plan E-2106**

| Bedrooms: 3 | Baths: 2 |
|---|---|

**Space:**

| | |
|---|---|
| Total living area: | 2,177 sq. ft. |
| Basement: | approx. 2,177 sq. ft. |
| Garage and storage: | 570 sq. ft. |
| Porches: | 211 sq. ft. |

| Exterior Wall Framing: | 2x4 |
|---|---|

**Foundation options:**
Standard basement.
Crawlspace.
Slab.
(Foundation & framing conversion diagram available — see order form.)

| Blueprint Price Code: | C |
|---|---|

**\*\*NOTE:**
The above photographed home may have been modified by the homeowner. Please refer to floor plan and/or drawn elevation shown for actual blueprint details.

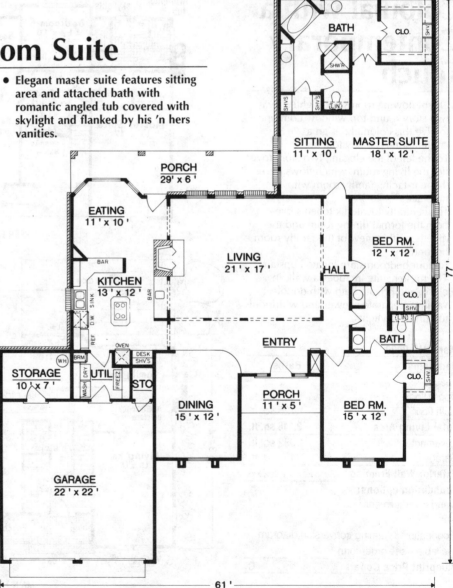

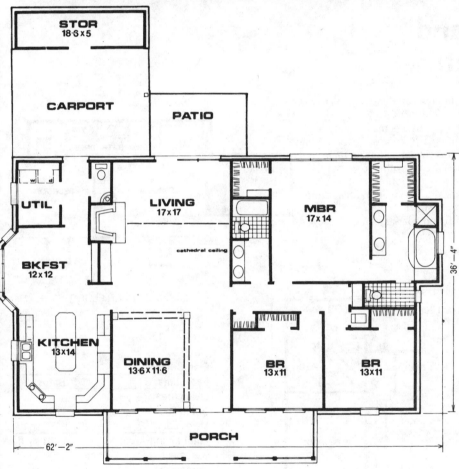

**MAIN FLOOR**

# Southern Country

- This home is distinctly Southern Country in style, from its wide front porch to its multi-paned and shuttered windows.
- The living room boasts a 12' cathedral ceiling, a fireplace and French doors to the rear patio.
- The dining room is open, but defined by three columns with overhead beams.
- The delightful kitchen/nook area is spacious and well-planned for both efficiency and pleasant kitchen working conditions.
- A handy utility room and half-bath are on either side of a short hallway leading to the carport.
- The master suite offers walk-in closets and an incredible bath that incorporates a plant shelf above the garden tub.

**Plan J-86140**

| Bedrooms: 3 | Baths: 2½ |
|---|---|
| **Living Area:** | |
| Main floor | 2,177 sq. ft. |
| **Total Living Area:** | **2,177 sq. ft.** |
| Standard basement | 2,177 sq. ft. |
| Carport | 440 sq. ft. |
| Storage | 120 sq. ft. |
| **Exterior Wall Framing** | 2x4 |
| **Ceiling Heights** | 9' |

**Foundation Options:**
Standard basement
Crawlspace
Slab
(Typical foundation & framing conversion diagram available—see order form.)

| **BLUEPRINT PRICE CODE** | C |
|---|---|

# Country Kitchen and Deluxe Master Bath

- Front porch, dormers and shutters give this home a decidedly country look on the outside, which is complemented by an informal modern interior.
- The roomy country kitchen connects with a sunny breakfast nook and utility area on one hand and a formal dining room on the other.
- The central portion of the home consists of a large family room with

a fireplace and easy access to a rear deck.
- The downstairs master suite is particularly impressive for a home of this size, a features a majestic master bath with two walk-in closets and double vanities.
- Upstairs, you will find two more ample-sized bedrooms, a double bath and a large storage area.

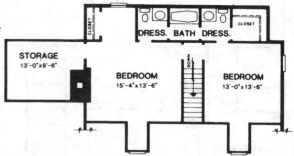

UPPER FLOOR

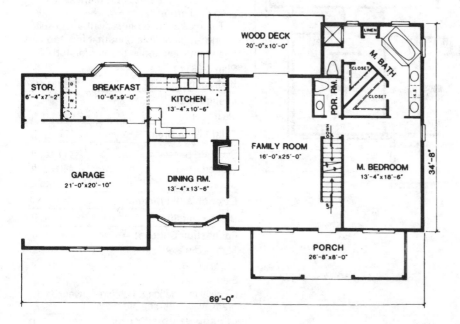

MAIN FLOOR

**Plan C-8645**

| Bedrooms: 3 | Baths: 2 ½ |
|---|---|
| **Living Area:** | |
| Upper floor | 704 sq. ft. |
| Main floor | 1,477 sq. ft. |
| **Total Living Area:** | **2,181 sq. ft.** |
| Basement | Approx. 1,400 sq. ft. |
| Garage | 438 sq. ft. |
| Storage | 123 sq. ft. |
| **Exterior Wall Framing:** | 2x4 |

**Foundation Options:**
Standard basement
Crawlspace
Slab
(Typical foundation & framing conversion diagram available — see order form.)

| **BLUEPRINT PRICE CODE:** | C |
|---|---|

# Distinctive One-Level Sunshine Special

- With its solarium and window walls across the rear, this home offers a real treat for sun lovers.
- In winter, the solar features capture and distribute free heat. In summer, overhangs and clerestory windows provide shade, circulation and heat venting.
- Besides its technical features, this home offers a dramatic floor plan. The kitchen/nook/family room is big and open, and the living and dining rooms flow together to create a huge space.
- The master suite includes a private bath and a large walk-in closet, in addition to easy access to a private deck or terrace.
- Three other bedrooms share another full bath and the entire bedroom wing is insulated from the more active areas.

### Plan K-502-J

| Bedrooms: 4 | Baths: 2½ |
|---|---|
| **Space:** | |
| Main floor | 2,052 sq. ft. |
| Sun room (approx) | 144 sq. ft. |
| **Total Living Area** | **2,196 sq. ft.** |
| Basement | 1,264 sq. ft. |
| Garage | 426 sq. ft. |
| **Exterior Wall Framing** | 2x4 or 2x6 |

**Foundation options:**
Standard Basement
Slab
(Foundation & framing conversion diagram available—see order form.)

| **Blueprint Price Code** | **C** |
|---|---|

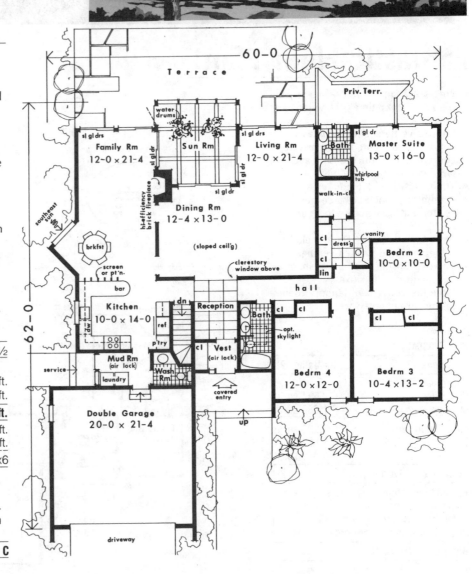

Photo by Mark Englund

# Fantastic Floor Plan!

- This is the famous house shown on the PBS "Hometime" television series.
- Impressive floor plan includes a deluxe master suite with a private courtyard, magnificent bath and large closet.
- The large island kitchen/nook combination includes a corner pantry and easy access to a rear deck.
- The spacious family room includes a fireplace and vaulted ceiling.
- The two upstairs bedrooms share a bath with double sinks.
- Note the convenient laundry room in the garage entry area.

**Plan B-88015**

| Bedrooms: 3 | Baths: 2½ |
|---|---|
| **Space:** | |
| Upper floor: | 534 sq. ft. |
| Main floor: | 1,689 sq. ft. |
| **Total living area:** | **2,223 sq. ft.** |
| Basement: | approx. 1,689 sq. ft. |
| Garage: | 455 sq. ft. |
| **Exterior Wall Framing:** | 2x4 |

**Foundation options:**
Standard basement only.
(Foundation & framing conversion diagram available — see order form.)

| **Blueprint Price Code:** | C |
|---|---|

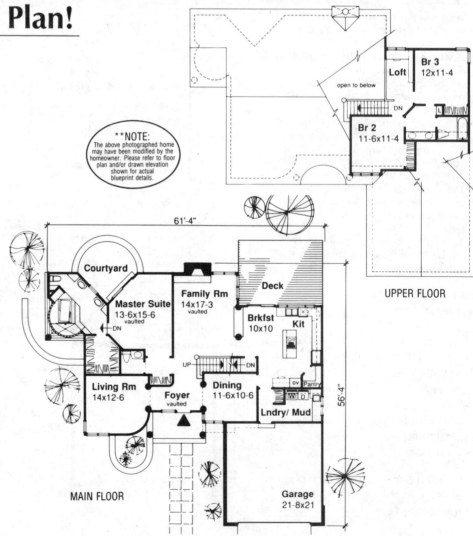

**NOTE:**
The above photographed home may have been modified by the homeowner. Please refer to floor plan and/or drawn elevation shown for actual blueprint details.

UPPER FLOOR

Br 3
12x11-4

Loft

open to below

DN

Br 2
11-6x11-4

61'-4"

Courtyard

Master Suite
13-6x15-6
vaulted

Family Rm
14x17-3
vaulted

Deck

Brkfst
10x10

Kit

DN

56'-4"

UP

DN

Living Rm
14x12-6

Foyer
vaulted

Dining
11-6x10-6

Pantry

Lndry/ Mud

MAIN FLOOR

Garage
21-8x21

*TO ORDER THIS BLUEPRINT, CALL TOLL-FREE 1-800-547-5570*

Plan B-88015

*PRICES AND DETAILS ON PAGES 12-15*

Photo by Gil Ford

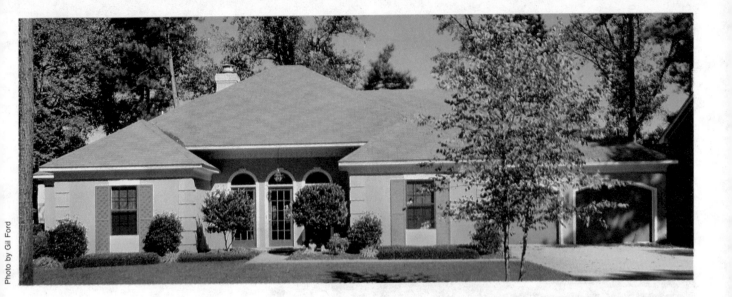

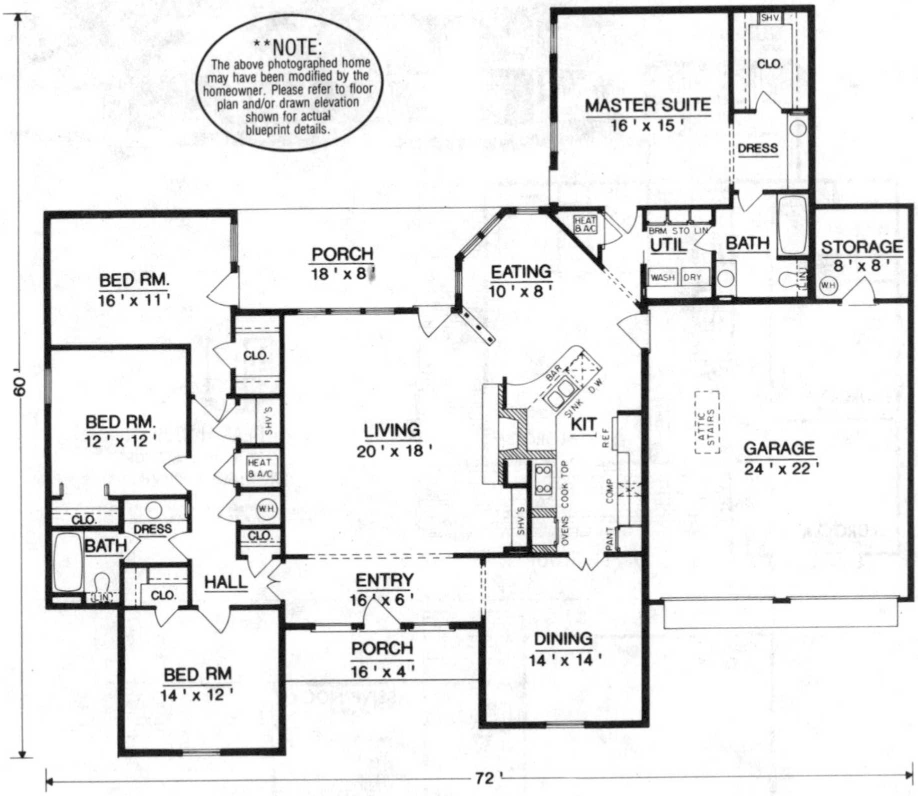

**NOTE:
The above photographed home may have been modified by the homeowner. Please refer to floor plan and/or drawn elevation shown for actual blueprint details.
MASTER SUITE
16' x 15'
CLO.
SHV
DRESS
HEAT & A/C
BRM STO LIN
UTIL
WASH DRY
BATH
STORAGE
8' x 8'
WH
PORCH
18' x 8'
EATING
10' x 8'
BED RM.
16' x 11'
CLO.
BED RM.
12' x 12'
LIVING
20' x 18'
BAR
SINK
D.W.
KIT
REF
ATTIC STAIRS
GARAGE
24' x 22'
SHV'S
HEAT & A/C
W.H.
CLO.
CLO.
DRESS
BATH
LIN
CLO.
HALL
ENTRY
16' x 6'
COOK TOP
OVENS
COMP
PANT
PORCH
16' x 4'
DINING
14' x 14'
BED RM
14' x 12'
60'
72'


# Luxury Living on One Level

- Exterior presents a classic air of quality and distinction in design.
- Spacious one-story interior provides space for family life and entertaining.
- The large central living room boasts a 13′ ceiling and large hearth.
- A roomy formal dining room adjoins the foyer.
- The gorgeous kitchen/nook combination provides a sunny eating area along with an efficient and attractive kitchen with eating bar and abundant counter space.
- The master suite is isolated from the other bedrooms for more privacy, and includes a luxurious bath and dressing area.
- Three additional bedrooms make up the left side of the plan, and share a second bath.
- The garage is off the kitchen for maximum convenience in carrying in groceries; also note the storage space off the garage.

**Plan E-2208**

| | |
|---|---|
| **Bedrooms:** 4 | **Baths:** 2 |
| **Total living area:** | 2,252 sq. ft. |
| Garage: | 528 sq. ft. |
| Storage: | 64 sq. ft. |
| **Exterior Wall Framing:** | 2x6 |
| **Typical Ceiling Heights:** 8′ unless otherwise noted. | |

**Foundation options:**
Standard basement.
Crawlspace.
Slab.
(Foundation & framing conversion diagram available — see order form.)

| | |
|---|---|
| **Blueprint Price Code:** | C |

FRONT VIEW

# Something Old, Something New

"Something old, something new" aptly describes the flavor and sentiment of this replica of earlier times.

Beveled oval plate glass with heavy oak surrounds and appropriate hand-carved wreaths and borders make entering the home the delightful experience it was meant to be. Inside one finds the huge central entry hall with the magnificent open staircase with turned balusters and shapely handrails.

With all bedrooms being on the second floor, the main level is entirely devoted to daily living in a generous atmosphere. The 14' x 23' living room and 14' x 13' dining room give one an idea of the spaciousness of this home.

Notice the 80 cubic foot pantry closet and the adjacent storage closet with an equal amount of space. A two-thirds bath and well equipped laundry room complete the mechanical area of the home.

Certainly the most provocative room on the main floor is the beautiful glass-enclosed morning or breakfast room. Huge skylight panels augment the bank of windows and sliding doors to create a delightful passive solar room suitable for many uses while contributing greatly to the heating efficiency of the entire building.

Upstairs two good-sized bedrooms with adjoining bathroom serve the junior members of the family while the parents enjoy the spacious master suite with walk-in wardrobes and private bath.

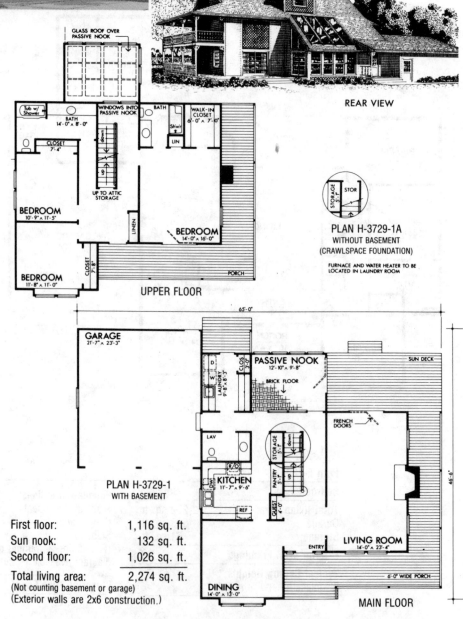

REAR VIEW

PLAN H-3729-1A
WITHOUT BASEMENT
(CRAWLSPACE FOUNDATION)

FURNACE AND WATER HEATER TO BE
LOCATED IN LAUNDRY ROOM

UPPER FLOOR

PLAN H-3729-1
WITH BASEMENT

| First floor: | 1,116 sq. ft. |
| Sun nook: | 132 sq. ft. |
| Second floor: | 1,026 sq. ft. |
| Total living area: | 2,274 sq. ft. |

(Not counting basement or garage)
(Exterior walls are 2x6 construction.)

MAIN FLOOR

Blueprint Price Code C

TO ORDER THIS BLUEPRINT, CALL TOLL-FREE 1-800-547-5570

## Plans H-3729-1 & H-3729-1A

PRICES AND DETAILS
ON PAGES 12-15

# Gracious Traditional

- This traditional-style ranch is perfect for a corner building lot. Long windows and dormers add distinctive elegance.
- The floor plan has a popular "split-bedroom" design. The master bedroom is secluded away from the other bedrooms.
- The large Great Room has a vaulted ceiling and stairs leading up to a loft.
- The upstairs loft is perfect for a recreation area, and has a full bath.

- The master bedroom bath has a large corner tub and his and hers vanities. A large walk-in closet provides plenty of storage space.
- The two other bedrooms have large walk-in closets, desks, and a shared bath.
- The kitchen and private breakfast nook are located conveniently near the utility/garage area.

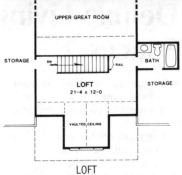

LOFT

MAIN FLOOR

| Plan C-8920 | |
|---|---|
| **Bedrooms:** 3 | **Baths:** 3 |
| **Living Area:** | |
| Upper floor | 305 sq. ft. |
| Main floor | 1,996 sq. ft. |
| **Total Living Area:** | **2,301 sq. ft.** |
| Basement | 1,996 sq. ft. |
| Garage | 469 sq. ft. |
| **Exterior Wall Framing:** | 2x4 |
| **Foundation Options:** | |
| Daylight basement | |
| Standard basement | |
| Crawlspace | |
| (Typical foundation & framing conversion diagram available — see order form.) | |
| **BLUEPRINT PRICE CODE:** | C |

**NOTE:**
The above photographed home may have been modified by the homeowner. Please refer to floor plan and/or drawn elevation shown for actual blueprint details.

**Plans P-7710-3A & P-7710-3D**

| Bedrooms: 2-3 | Baths: 2½ |
|---|---|

| **Space:** | |
|---|---|
| Main floor: | 2,392 sq. ft. |
| Garage: | 678 sq. ft. |
| Basement: | 2,392 sq. ft. |

| **Exterior Wall Framing:** | 2x6 |
|---|---|

**Foundation options:**
Daylight basement, Plan P-7710-3D.
Crawlspace, Plan P-7710-3A.
(Foundation & framing conversion diagram available — see order form.)

| **Blueprint Price Code:** | C |
|---|---|

MAIN FLOOR
PLAN P-7710-3A
WITHOUT BASEMENT

PLAN P-7710-3D
WITH DAYLIGHT BASEMENT

BASEMENT

# Deluxe Living Spaces

- Visitors approaching the front entry are welcomed by a courtyard with a wrought-iron fence and brick columns.
- The front door opens to a large entry magnified by a vaulted ceiling and skylight.
- The large, sunken living/dining area is great for formal entertaining.
- A huge kitchen/nook combination includes an island eating bar which adjoins the spacious, vaulted family room.
- The magnificent master suite includes an incredible bath with spa tub, separate shower and a large walk-in wardrobe closet.
- Daylight basement version doubles the space.

*TO ORDER THIS BLUEPRINT, CALL TOLL-FREE 1-800-547-5570*  Plans P-7710-3A &-3D  **PRICES AND DETAILS ON PAGES 12-15**

# High Luxury in One Story

- Beautiful arched windows lend a luxurious feeling to the exterior of this one-story home.
- Twelve-foot-high ceilings add volume to both the wide entry area and the central living room, which boasts a large fireplace and access to a covered porch and the patio beyond.
- Double doors separate the formal dining room from the corridor-style kitchen. Features of the kitchen include a pantry, a trash compactor, garage access and an angled eating bar with double sinks and a dishwasher. The sunny, bayed eating area is perfect for casual family meals.
- The plush master suite has amazing amenities: patio access, a walk-in closet, a skylighted, angled whirlpool tub, a separate shower, and private access to the laundry/utility room.
- Three bedrooms and a full bath are situated on the opposite side of the home.

## Plan E-2302

| Bedrooms: 4 | Baths: 2 |
|---|---|
| **Living Area:** | |
| Main floor | 2,396 sq. ft. |
| **Total Living Area:** | **2,396 sq. ft.** |
| Standard basement | 2,396 sq. ft. |
| Garage | 484 sq. ft. |
| **Exterior Wall Framing:** | 2x6 |

**Foundation Options:**
Standard basement
Crawlspace
Slab
(Typical foundation & framing conversion diagram available—see order form.)

**BLUEPRINT PRICE CODE:** C

**NOTE:**
The above photographed home may have been modified by the homeowner. Please refer to floor plan and/or drawn elevation shown for actual blueprint details.

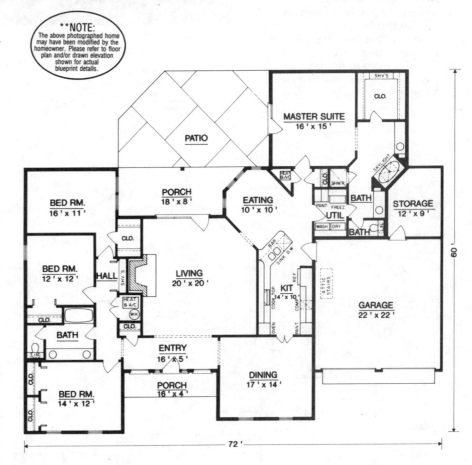

MAIN FLOOR

TO ORDER THIS BLUEPRINT,
CALL TOLL-FREE 1-800-547-5570

Plan E-2302

PRICES AND DETAILS
ON PAGES 12-15

143

# Dramatic Interior Makes a Best-Seller

- An incredible master suite takes up the entire 705 sq. ft. second floor, and includes deluxe bath, huge closet and skylighted balcony.
- Main floor design utilizes angles and shapes to create dramatic interior.
- Extra-spacious kitchen features large island, sunny windows and plenty of counter space.
- Sunken living room focuses on massive fireplace and stone hearth.
- Impressive two-level foyer is lit by skylights high above.
- Third bedroom or den with an adjacent bathroom makes an ideal home office or hobby room.

Photo by Karlis Grants

**\*\*NOTE:**
The above photographed home may have been modified by the homeowner. Please refer to floor plan and/or drawn elevation shown for actual blueprint details.

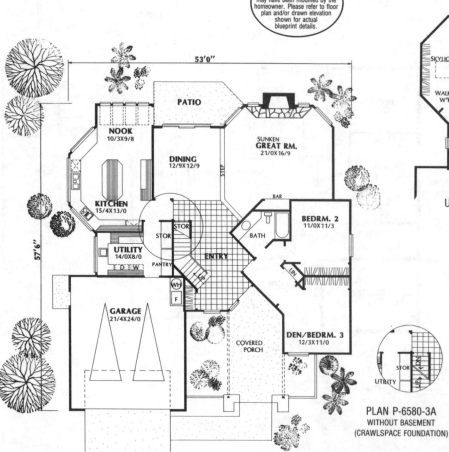

**MAIN FLOOR**

PLAN P-6580-3A
WITHOUT BASEMENT
(CRAWLSPACE FOUNDATION)

**UPPER FLOOR**

## Plans P-6580-3A & -3D

| Bedrooms: 2-3 | Baths: 2 |
|---|---|
| **Space:** | |
| Upper floor: | 705 sq. ft. |
| Main floor: | 1,738 sq. ft. |
| **Total living area:** | 2,443 sq. ft. |
| Basement: | 1,738 sq. ft. |
| Garage: | 512 sq. ft. |
| **Exterior Wall Framing:** | 2x4 |

**Foundation options:**
Daylight basement (Plan P-6580-3D).
Crawlspace (Plan P-6580-3A).
(Foundation & framing conversion diagram available — see order form.)

| **Blueprint Price Code:** | C |
|---|---|

# High-Style Hillside Home

- This beautiful hillside home is loaded with stylish features.
- The inviting foyer leads guests into the vaulted Great Room, with its fabulous fireplace and sweeping views of a wide rear deck and the yard beyond.
- The U-shaped kitchen includes a walk-in pantry, a greenhouse window, an eating bar and an adjoining nook.
- The vaulted master bedroom offers access to a relaxing hot tub on the deck. The skylighted master bath also has a vaulted ceiling, and boasts a whirlpool tub and a separate shower.
- The versatile den could be used as a media room or as a bedroom.
- Two bedrooms downstairs share a full bath. The central bedroom would make a great guest room, with its walk-in closet and private patio.

### Plan S-41892

| Bedrooms: 3-4 | Baths: 3 |
|---|---|

**Living Area:**

| | |
|---|---|
| Main floor | 1,485 sq. ft. |
| Partial daylight basement | 590 sq. ft. |
| **Total Living Area:** | **2,075 sq. ft.** |
| Mechanical room | 30 sq. ft. |
| Garage | 429 sq. ft. |
| **Exterior Wall Framing:** | 2x6 |

**Foundation Options:**

Partial daylight basement

(Typical foundation & framing conversion diagram available—see order form.)

| **BLUEPRINT PRICE CODE:** | **C** |
|---|---|

**MAIN FLOOR**

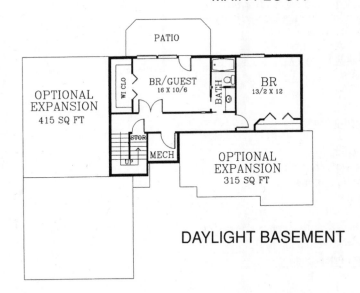

**DAYLIGHT BASEMENT**

# Lavish Ranch

- A spectacular central living room with 11' ceiling, corner fireplace and rear porch lies at the center of this luxurious farmhouse.
- An angled eating bar is the only separation from the adjoining kitchen and bayed nook; a formal dining alternative is located on the opposite end of the kitchen, overlooking the front porch.
- The lavish master suite is separated from the other bedrooms; it boasts a private, bayed sitting area, panoramic rear view, and a bath with dual vanities and walk-in closet.
- A study, two additional bedrooms and a second full bath are located to the right of the foyer.

**Plan VL-2085**

| Bedrooms: 3 | Baths: 2 ½ |
|---|---|
| **Space:** | |
| Main floor | 2,085 sq. ft. |
| **Total Living Area** | **2,085 sq. ft.** |
| Garage | 460 sq. ft. |
| Ceiling height: | 9 ft. |
| **Exterior Wall Framing** | 2x4 |
| **Foundation options:** | |

Crawlspace

Slab

(Foundation & framing conversion diagram available—see order form.)

| **Blueprint Price Code** | C |
|---|---|

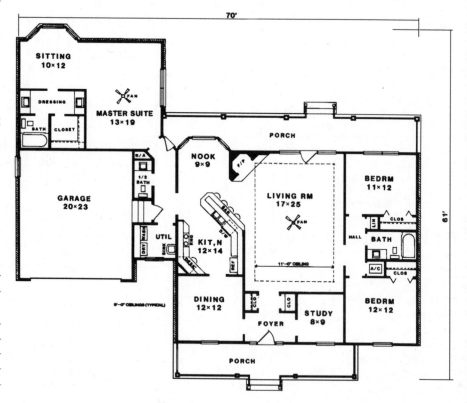

SITTING
10×12

DRESSING

BATH  CLOSET

MASTER SUITE
13×19

GARAGE
20×23

R/A

1/2 BATH

NOOK
9×9

PORCH

LIVING RM
17×25

BEDRM
11×12

CLOS

HALL

BATH

A/C  CLOS

DRY WASH

UTIL

KIT, N
12×14

REF

11'-0" CEILING

DINING
12×12

CLO  CLO

STUDY
8×9

BEDRM
12×12

FOYER

PORCH

9'-0" CEILINGS (TYPICAL)

70'

61'

Plan VL-2085

# Home with High Style

- Sweeping rooflines attract attention to this stylish contemporary home.
- The vaulted entry is enhanced by a clerestory window above.
- Sunlight invades the main floor by way of a window wall in the living room and a sunspace off the patio or deck.
- A main-floor den could serve as a handy guest bedroom.
- The open family room shares a woodstove with the kitchen and nook.
- A formal dining room looks out on the home's natural surroundings.
- Upstairs, a large master bedroom features a private deck, a walk-in closet and a master bath with corner tub, separate shower and dual vanities.

## Plan S-2001

| Bedrooms: 3-4 | Baths: 2½ |
|---|---|
| **Living Area:** | |
| Upper floor | 890 sq. ft. |
| Main floor | 1,249 sq. ft. |
| **Total Living Area:** | **2,139 sq. ft.** |
| Basement | 1,249 sq. ft. |
| Garage | 399 sq. ft. |
| **Exterior Wall Framing:** | 2x6 |

**Foundation Options:**
Daylight basement
Standard basement
Crawlspace
Slab
(Typical foundation & framing conversion diagram available—see order form.)

**BLUEPRINT PRICE CODE:** C

UPPER FLOOR

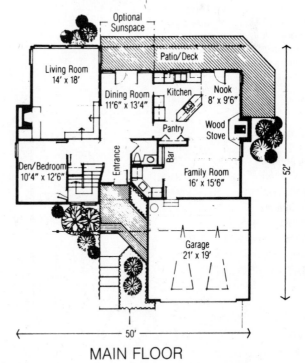

MAIN FLOOR

# Sunny Country-Style Design

- Open, sun-filled rooms that merge with outdoor living spaces make this country-style design a real showstopper.
- The covered front porch runs across the entire width of the home. Inside, a huge Great Room extends from the front porch to the rear deck.
- The sunken Great Room offers a cozy woodstove in one corner and an optional greenhouse. The adjoining kitchen has a long eating bar facing the nook and a boxed-out window overlooking the backyard.
- A formal dining room and a half-bath complete the well-designed first floor.
- The upper floor hosts three large bedrooms and two baths, plus a handy storage room.
- The basement plan includes a spacious recreation room for expanded living.

**Plan LMB-9823-E**

| Bedrooms: 3 | Baths: 2½ |
|---|---|
| **Living Area:** | |
| Upper floor | 1,010 sq. ft. |
| Main floor | 1,136 sq. ft. |
| **Total Living Area:** | **2,146 sq. ft.** |
| Standard basement | 1,136 sq. ft. |
| **Exterior Wall Framing:** | 2x6 |

**Foundation Options:**
Standard basement
(Typical foundation & framing conversion diagram available—see order form.)

**BLUEPRINT PRICE CODE:**     C

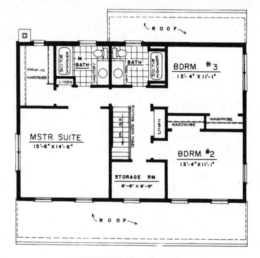

**UPPER FLOOR**

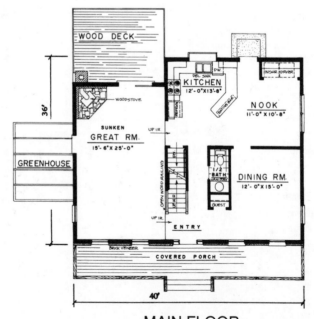

**MAIN FLOOR**

*TO ORDER THIS BLUEPRINT, CALL TOLL-FREE 1-800-547-5570*

Plan LMB-9823-E

*PRICES AND DETAILS ON PAGES 12-15*

# Bold and Beautiful

- This exotic four-bedroom oozes in elegance and durability.
- Arched top windows, volume 10' and 12' ceilings and decorative columns bordering the dining room add a vertical dimension to the sprawling single-level room arrangement.
- The grand foyer reveals elegant living and dining rooms; secluded to the right is the master bedroom with elaborate private bath, featuring a huge walk-in closet and corner step-up tub.
- The spacious kitchen has extra counter space and breakfast nook with sliders for porch dining.
- Plant shelves, a barrel vault ceiling and fireplace add drama to the attached family room.
- Three additional bedrooms share a second full bath.

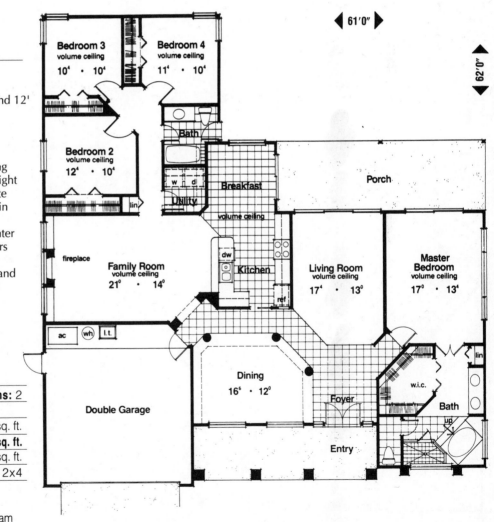

**Plan HDS-90-815**

| Bedrooms: 4 | Baths: 2 |
|---|---|
| **Space:** | |
| Main floor | 2,153 sq. ft. |
| **Total Living Area** | **2,153 sq. ft.** |
| Garage | 434 sq. ft. |
| **Exterior Wall Framing** | 2x4 |

**Foundation options:**

Slab

(Foundation & framing conversion diagram available—see order form.)

| **Blueprint Price Code** | C |
|---|---|

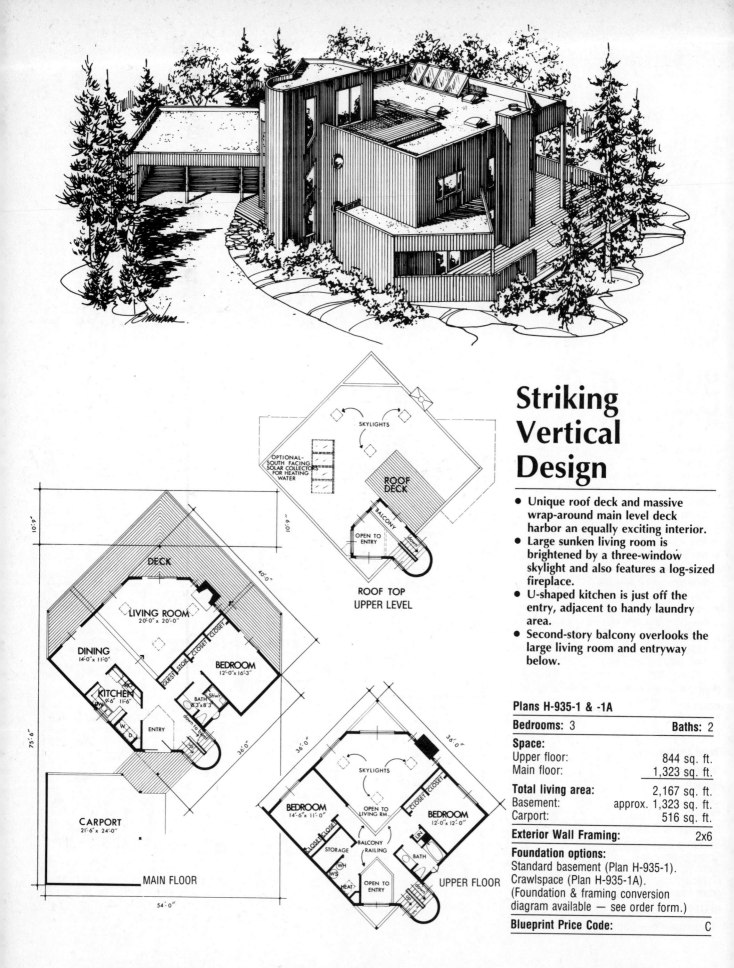

# Striking Vertical Design

- Unique roof deck and massive wrap-around main level deck harbor an equally exciting interior.
- Large sunken living room is brightened by a three-window skylight and also features a log-sized fireplace.
- U-shaped kitchen is just off the entry, adjacent to handy laundry area.
- Second-story balcony overlooks the large living room and entryway below.

**Plans H-935-1 & -1A**

| Bedrooms: 3 | Baths: 2 |
|---|---|

**Space:**

| | |
|---|---|
| Upper floor: | 844 sq. ft. |
| Main floor: | 1,323 sq. ft. |

| Total living area: | 2,167 sq. ft. |
|---|---|
| Basement: | approx. 1,323 sq. ft. |
| Carport: | 516 sq. ft. |

| Exterior Wall Framing: | 2x6 |
|---|---|

**Foundation options:**
Standard basement (Plan H-935-1).
Crawlspace (Plan H-935-1A).
(Foundation & framing conversion diagram available — see order form.)

| Blueprint Price Code: | C |
|---|---|

ROOF TOP
UPPER LEVEL

SKYLIGHTS

OPTIONAL-
SOUTH FACING
SOLAR COLLECTORS
FOR HEATING
WATER

ROOF DECK

BALCONY

OPEN TO ENTRY

DECK

LIVING ROOM
20'-0" x 20'-0"

DINING
14'-0" x 11'-0"

KITCHEN
9'-6" x 11'-6"

BEDROOM
12'-0" x 16'-3"

BATH
8'-3" x 8'-3"

ENTRY

CARPORT
21'-6" x 24'-0"

MAIN FLOOR

BEDROOM
14'-6" x 11'-0"

BEDROOM
12'-0" x 12'-0"

SKYLIGHTS

OPEN TO
LIVING RM.

BALCONY
RAILING

STORAGE

BATH

OPEN TO
ENTRY

UPPER FLOOR

## Plans H-935-1 & -1A

**PRICES AND DETAILS
ON PAGES 12-15**

# Sunny Indoor or Outdoor Dining

- This cozy country-style home offers an inviting front porch and an interior just as welcoming.
- A spacious living room features a warming fireplace and windows that overlook the porch.
- The living room opens to the dining area, which leads to a rear porch and patio.
- The island kitchen has plenty of counter space, a sink view and an adjoining sun room that could be used as a sunny formal dining area.
- The private master suite is secluded to the rear. Dual walk-in closets, vanities and a large windowed tub are nice features in the master bath.

## Plan J-90014

| Bedrooms: 3 | Baths: 2½ |
|---|---|
| **Living Area:** | |
| Main floor | 2,190 sq. ft. |
| **Total Living Area** | **2,190 sq. ft.** |
| Basement | 2,190 sq. ft. |
| Garage | 465 sq. ft. |
| Storage | 34 sq. ft. |
| **Exterior Wall Framing** | 2x6 |

**Foundation Options:**
Standard Basement
Crawlspace
Slab
(Typical foundation & framing conversion diagram available—see order form.)

| **BLUEPRINT PRICE CODE** | C |
|---|---|

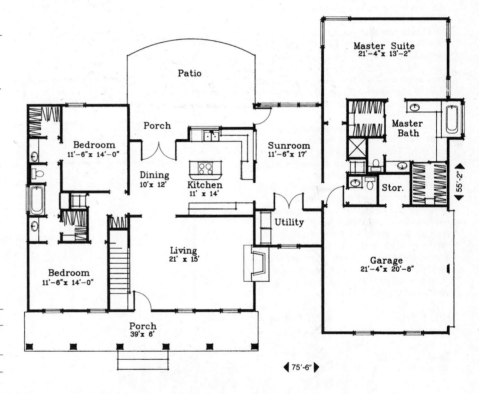

MAIN FLOOR

**TO ORDER THIS BLUEPRINT,**
**CALL TOLL-FREE 1-800-547-5570**

Plan J-90014

**PRICES AND DETAILS**
**ON PAGES 12-15**

151

FRONT VIEW

# Sun Room
# Adds Warmth

At first glance this seems like just another very nice home, with crisp contemporary lines, a carefully conceived traffic flow and generous bedroom and living areas. What sets this home apart from most other houses is its passive sun room, a 13' x 11'6" solarium that collects, stores and distributes solar energy to warm the home, conserving fossil fuel and cutting energy costs. Adding to the energy efficiency of the design are 2x6 stud walls, allowing use of R-19 insulation batts, R-30 insulation in the ceiling, and an air-tight wood stove in the family room.

The passive sun room has glazing on three walls as it juts out from the home, and has a fully glazed ceiling to capture the maximum solar energy. A masonry tile floor stores the collected heat which is distributed to the family and living rooms through sliding glass doors. The wall adjoining the dining area also is glazed. With hanging plants, the sun room can be a visually stunning greenhouse extension of the vaulted-ceilinged living room. A French door from the sun room and sliding glass doors from the family room open onto a wood deck, for outdoor entertaining and relaxing.

| First floor: | 2,034 sq. ft. |
|---|---|
| Sun room: | 159 sq. ft. |
| Total living area: | 2,193 sq. ft. |

(Not counting basement or garage)

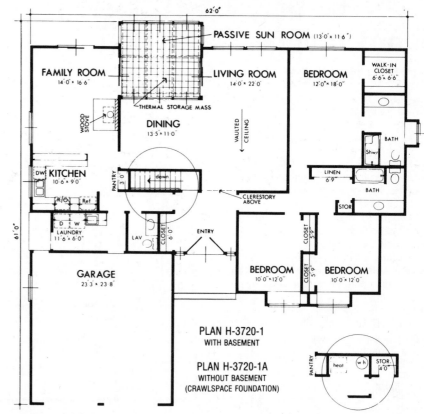

PLAN H-3720-1
WITH BASEMENT

PLAN H-3720-1A
WITHOUT BASEMENT
(CRAWLSPACE FOUNDATION)

REAR VIEW

Blueprint Price Code C

**TO ORDER THIS BLUEPRINT,**
CALL TOLL-FREE 1-800-547-5570

Plans H-3720-1 & -1A

*PRICES AND DETAILS*
ON PAGES 12-15

# Chalet Style for Town or Country

- The exterior features exposed beams, board siding and viewing decks with cut-out railings to give this home the look of a mountain chalet.
- Inside, the design lends itself equally well to year-round family living or part-time recreational enjoyment.
- An expansive Great Room features an impressive fireplace and includes a dining area next to the well-planned kitchen.
- The upstairs offers the possibility of an adult retreat, with a fine master bedroom with private bath and large closets, plus a loft area available for many uses.
- Two secondary bedrooms are on the main floor, and share another bath.
- The daylight basement level includes a garage and a large recreation room with a fireplace and a half-bath.

**Plan P-531-2D**

| Bedrooms: 3 | Baths: 2½ |
|---|---|
| **Living Area:** | |
| Upper floor | 573 sq. ft. |
| Main floor | 1,120 sq. ft. |
| Daylight basement | 532 sq. ft. |
| **Total Living Area:** | **2,225 sq. ft.** |
| Garage | 541 sq. ft. |
| **Exterior Wall Framing:** | 2x6 |

**Foundation Options:**
Daylight basement
(Typical foundation & framing conversion diagram available—see order form.)

**BLUEPRINT PRICE CODE:**      C

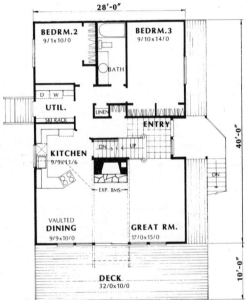

MAIN FLOOR

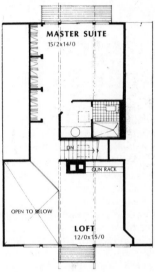

UPPER FLOOR

DAYLIGHT BASEMENT

# Neatly Arranged Family Living

- This distinguished ranch home has a neatly arranged floor plan with a large activity area at the center and a strategically placed master bedroom.
- The double-doored entry opens to the large sunken family room with cathedral ceiling, decorative columned bridge, fireplace and patio view.
- A formal living room and dining room flank the foyer.
- The huge modern kitchen offers a handy snack counter, open to the adjacent family room. The bayed breakfast room has French-door access to the covered patio.
- Secluded to one end of the home is a deluxe master bedroom with a cathedral ceiling, a spacious walk-in closet, a private patio and a personal bath with dual vanities and additional outdoor access.
- Three additional bedrooms and two more baths are located at the opposite end of the home.

### Plan Q-2266-1A

| Bedrooms: 4 | Baths: 3 |
|---|---|
| **Living Area:** | |
| Main floor | 2,266 sq. ft. |
| **Total Living Area:** | **2,266 sq. ft.** |
| Garage | 592 sq. ft. |
| **Exterior Wall Framing:** | 2x4 |

**Foundation Options:**

Slab

(Typical foundation & framing conversion diagram available—see order form.)

**BLUEPRINT PRICE CODE:**       C

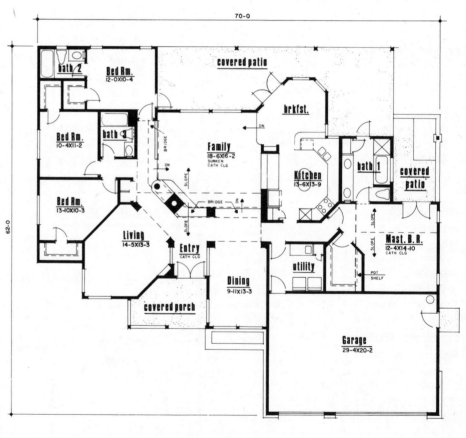

**MAIN FLOOR**

Plan Q-2266-1A

*PRICES AND DETAILS*
*ON PAGES 12-15*

BEDROOM
16'-0" x 13'-4"

BEDROOM
13'-10" x 13'-4"

DRESS. BATH DRESS.

SECOND FLOOR

First floor: 1,535 sq. ft.
Second floor: 765 sq. ft.

Total living area: 2,300 sq. ft.
(Not counting basement or garage)

PLAN C-8535
WITH BASEMENT

# Traditional Touches Dress Up a Country Cottage

**Multipaned windows, shutters and a covered porch embellish the traditional exterior of this country cottage. The floor plan incorporates a central Great Room. A raised-hearth stone fireplace forms part of a wall separating the Great Room from the kitchen.**

**The large country kitchen features an island and abundant counter space. The breakfast room includes a bay window. A large dining room faces the front.**

**First-level master bedroom has its own super bath with separate shower, garden tub, twin vanities and walk-in closets. Two large bedrooms, separate dressing areas and compartment tub occupy the second level.**

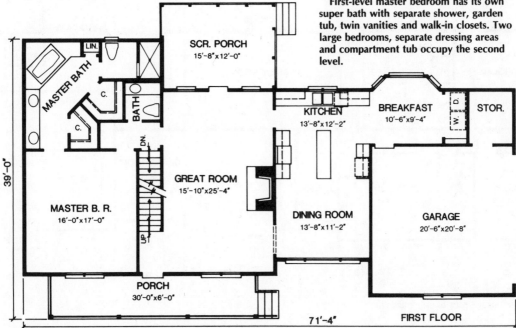

MASTER BATH
LIN.
SCR. PORCH
15'-8" x 12'-0"
KITCHEN
13'-8" x 12'-2"
BREAKFAST
10'-6" x 9'-4"
W. D.
STOR.
BATH
C.
C.
39'-0"
DN.
GREAT ROOM
15'-10" x 25'-4"
UP
MASTER B. R.
16'-0" x 17'-0"
DINING ROOM
13'-8" x 11'-2"
GARAGE
20'-6" x 20'-8"
PORCH
30'-0" x 6'-0"
71'-4"
FIRST FLOOR

Blueprint Price Code C

## Plan C-8535

# Spacious and Inviting

The four-column front porch, picture window, siding, brick, stone and cupola combine for a pleasing exterior for this three-bedroom home.

Extra features include a fireplace, screen porch, deluxe master bath and a large separate breakfast room.

Total living area:     2,306 sq. ft.
(Not counting basement or garage)

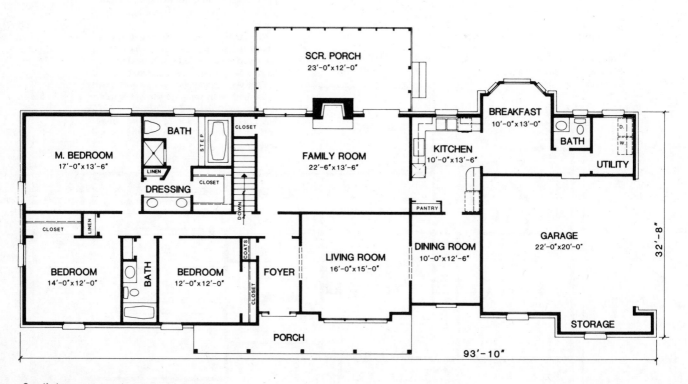

Specify basement, crawlspace or slab foundation.

**TO ORDER THIS BLUEPRINT,**
**CALL TOLL-FREE 1-800-547-5570**

Blueprint Price Code C
## Plan C-8625

**PRICES AND DETAILS**
**ON PAGES 12-15**

# Vertical Sophistication

- This sophisticated two-story demands a second look. The vertical theme of the elegant exterior is also evident in the home's interior.
- Off the two-story-high foyer is a vaulted living room with a patio view and a two-sided fireplace that is shared with the adjoining dining room. Tall columns visually separate the two formal rooms.

- A skylighted sun porch to the rear of the dining room is surrounded in glass.
- A spacious island kitchen and breakfast area combine at the front of the home. A laundry room connects the kitchen to the garage.
- The elegant master suite is privately positioned to the rear. A skylighted sitting area and a private bath with dual sinks are featured.
- Two more bedrooms and another full bath share the upper floor.

**Plan B-92019**

| Bedrooms: 3 | Baths: 2½ |
|---|---|
| **Living Area:** | |
| Upper floor | 767 sq. ft. |
| Main floor | 1,554 sq. ft. |
| **Total Living Area:** | **2,321 sq. ft.** |
| Standard basement | 1,554 sq. ft. |
| Garage | 547 sq. ft. |
| **Exterior Wall Framing:** | 2x4 |

**Foundation Options:**

Standard basement
(Typical foundation & framing conversion diagram available—see order form.)

**BLUEPRINT PRICE CODE:** C

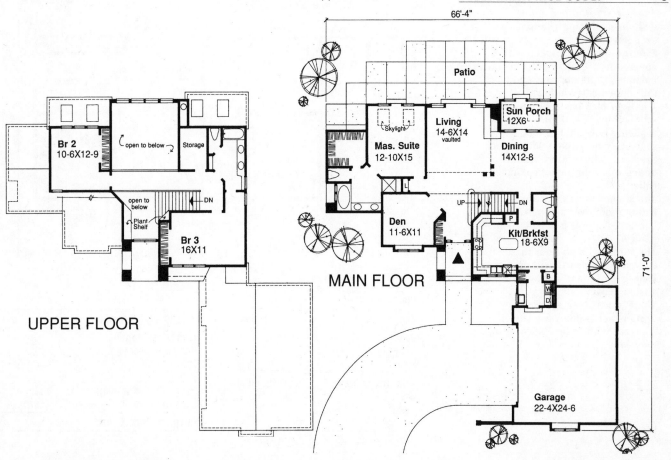

UPPER FLOOR

MAIN FLOOR

# You Asked For It!

- Our most popular plan in recent years, E-3000, has now been downsized for affordability, without sacrificing character or excitement.
- Exterior appeal is created with a covered front porch with decorative columns, triple dormers and rail-topped bay windows.
- The floor plan has combined the separate living and family rooms available in E-3000 into one spacious family room with corner fireplace, which flows into the dining room through a columned gallery.
- The kitchen serves the breakfast eating room over an angled snack bar, and features a huge walk-in pantry.
- The stunning main-floor master suite offers a private sitting area, a walk-in closet and a dramatic, angled master bath.
- There are two large bedrooms upstairs accessible via a curved staircase with bridge balcony.

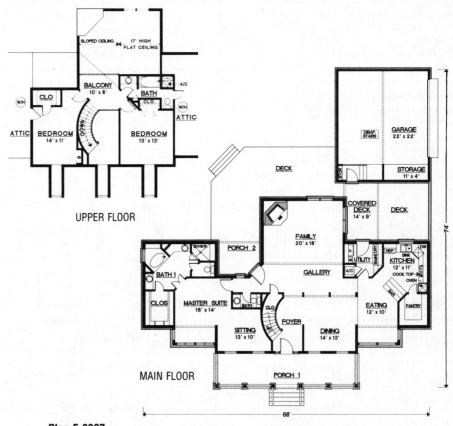

UPPER FLOOR

MAIN FLOOR

**Plan E-2307**

| Bedrooms: 3 | Baths: 2½ |
|---|---|

| Space: | |
|---|---|
| Upper floor: | 595 sq. ft. |
| Main floor: | 1,765 sq. ft. |

| Total living area: | 2,360 sq. ft. |
|---|---|
| Basement: | 1,765 sq. ft. |
| Garage: | 484 sq. ft. |
| Storage area: | 44 sq. ft. |

| Exterior Wall Framing: | 2x6 |
|---|---|

**Foundation options:**
Standard basement.
Crawlspace.
Slab.
(Foundation & framing conversion diagram available — see order form.)

| Blueprint Price Code: | C |
|---|---|

**Plan E-2307**

**PRICES AND DETAILS ON PAGES 12-15**

# Great Room for Entertaining

- The focal point of this stylish contemporary home is its central sunken Great Room with luxurious features. Guests are easily served at a handy wet bar or at an angled counter by the kitchen and breakfast area. Open beams above and a woodstove to the left add a rustic ambience. A rear window wall gives sweeping views of the outdoors.
- A wraparound deck or patio expands the entertaining area.
- The main-floor master suite boasts a raised tub, a separate shower, a walk-in closet and outdoor access. A sunspace may be added if desired.
- Two bedrooms and a bath are located upstairs.

### Plan LRD-22884

| Bedrooms: 3 | Baths: 2½ |
|---|---|
| **Living Area:** | |
| Upper floor | 674 sq. ft. |
| Main floor | 1,686 sq. ft. |
| **Total Living Area:** | **2,360 sq. ft.** |
| Standard basement | 1,686 sq. ft. |
| Garage | 450 sq. ft. |
| **Exterior Wall Framing:** | 2x6 |

**Foundation Options:**
Standard basement
Crawlspace
Slab
(Typical foundation & framing conversion diagram available—see order form.)

**BLUEPRINT PRICE CODE:**         C

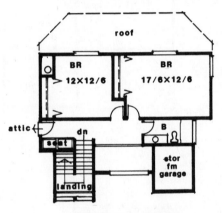

UPPER FLOOR

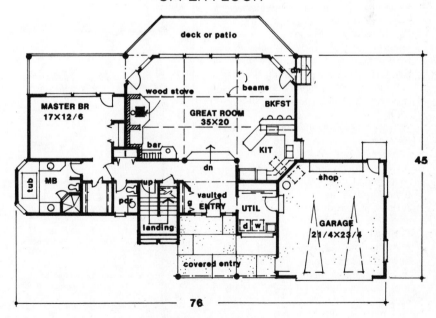

MAIN FLOOR

*TO ORDER THIS BLUEPRINT,*
*CALL TOLL-FREE 1-800-547-5570*

Plan LRD-22884

*PRICES AND DETAILS*
*ON PAGES 12-15*

159

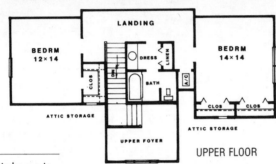

LANDING

BEDRM 12×14

DRESS
LINEN
BATH
CLOS
A/C

BEDRM 14×14

CLOS
CLOS

ATTIC STORAGE

ATTIC STORAGE

UPPER FOYER

**UPPER FLOOR**

# Simply Beautiful

- The beautiful symmetry of this home is marked by the double-door entry with overhead dormer windows and the full-width porch with columns and railings. The clean-cut lines of the design belie the home's 2,360 sq. ft. of luxurious living space.

- Guests are greeted by a two-story-high foyer that is flooded with light from the elegant, half-round dormer window above. Abundant closet space and a half-bath are just ahead.

- The home's spaciousness is enhanced by 9-ft. ceilings throughout the first floor. The large living room features a centrally located fireplace that can also be enjoyed from the adjoining dining room.

- Storage space is again well accounted for in the kitchen. An island cooktop counter is convenient to the full-glass nook. A French door in the nook opens to a covered porch for outdoor entertaining.

- An oversized utility room has plenty of space for a freezer, plus a clothes-folding table with extra storage below.

- The first-floor master suite is an appreciated feature, with an enticing master bath that includes a whirlpool tub, shower, dual vanities and a walk-in closet.

- The two spacious bedrooms upstairs share a compartmentalized bath.

**Plan VL-2360**

| **Bedrooms:** 3 | **Baths:** 2 ½ |
|---|---|
| **Space:** | |
| Upper floor | 683 sq. ft. |
| Main floor | 1,677 sq. ft. |
| **Total Living Area** | **2,360 sq. ft.** |
| Garage | 458 sq. ft. |
| **Exterior Wall Framing** | **2x4** |

**Foundation options:**
Crawlspace
Slab
(Foundation & framing conversion diagram available—see order form.)

| **Blueprint Price Code** | **C** |
|---|---|

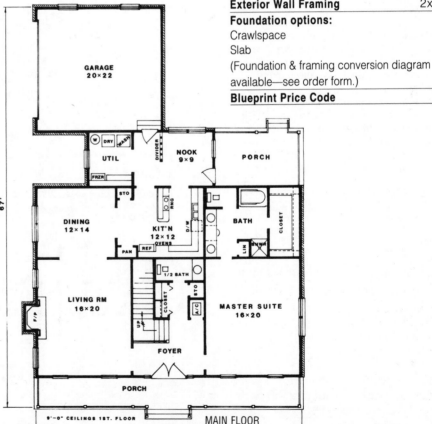

GARAGE 20×22

UTIL
W DRY WASH
DIVIDER
FRZR
STO

NOOK 9×9

PORCH

DINING 12×14

KIT'N 12×12
OVENS
PAN REF

BATH
CLOSET
LIN

LIVING RM 16×20

1/2 BATH
CLOSET
STO
A/C

MASTER SUITE 16×20

F/P

FOYER

PORCH

67'

9'-0" CEILINGS 1ST. FLOOR

46'

**MAIN FLOOR**

# Drama Inside and Out

- Dramatic arched top windows, a brick chimney and rear lanai accent the exterior of this stylish transitional one-story.
- Vaulted living and dining areas flank the spacious foyer.
- Off the open kitchen and breakfast area is the central family room with 10' sloped ceiling, fireplace and built-in entertainment center.
- The secluded master suite offers a coffered ceiling, angled wall with access to the lanai, and private bath with separate closets, vanities and tub and shower.
- Three additional bedrooms share a second full bath at the opposite end of the home.

| Plan DW-2403 | |
|---|---|
| **Bedrooms:** 4 | **Baths:** 2 ½ |
| **Space:** | |
| Main floor | 2,403 sq. ft. |
| **Total Living Area** | **2,403 sq. ft.** |
| Basement | 2,403 sq. ft. |
| Garage | 380 sq. ft. |
| **Exterior Wall Framing** | 2x4 |
| **Foundation options:** | |
| Standard Basement | |
| Crawlspace | |
| Slab | |
| (Foundation & framing conversion diagram available—see order form.) | |
| **Blueprint Price Code** | C |

# Rise Above It All!

- This plan offers "reverse living," with the main rooms located on the upper level to take advantage of the view.
- The vaulted Great Room is dynamite, with its walls of windows and a fireplace with built-in wood storage.
- A roomy area for a dining room table lies between the Great Room and the kitchen, which is defined by a dropped ceiling. A large cooktop island/eating bar, a built-in desk and a pantry add to the kitchen's versatility and function.
- The vaulted master suite overlooks the rear deck, which is also accessible from the utility area. Another deck presides above the front door.
- The lower level includes two bedrooms, a large rec room and a full bath. Sliding doors open to the ground-level patio.

### Plan LRD-9492

| Bedrooms: 3 | Baths: 2½ |
|---|---|
| **Living Area:** | |
| Main floor | 1,373 sq. ft. |
| Lower floor | 1,057 sq. ft. |
| **Total Living Area:** | **2,430 sq. ft.** |
| Standard basement | 1,057 sq. ft. |
| Garage | 468 sq. ft. |
| **Exterior Wall Framing:** | 2x6 |

**Foundation Options:**

Standard basement
Crawlspace
Slab

(Typical foundation & framing conversion diagram available—see order form.)

**BLUEPRINT PRICE CODE:**      C

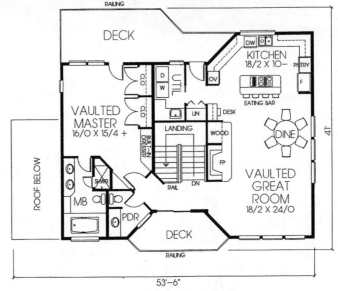

**MAIN FLOOR**

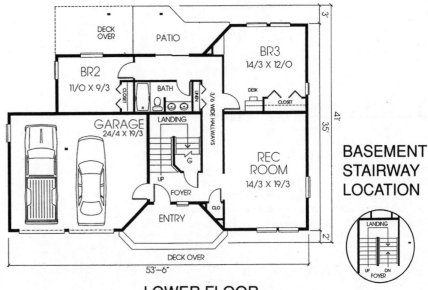

**LOWER FLOOR**

**BASEMENT STAIRWAY LOCATION**

## Plan LRD-9492

**PRICES AND DETAILS ON PAGES 12-15**

# Old-Fashioned Charm

- A trio of dormers add old-fashioned charm to this modern design.
- Both the living room and the dining room offer vaulted ceilings, and the two rooms flow together to create a sense of even more spaciousness.
- The open kitchen, nook and family room combination features a sunny alcove, a walk-in pantry and an inviting wood stove.
- A first-floor den and a walk-through utility room are other big bonuses.
- Upstairs, the master suite includes a walk-in closet and a deluxe bath with a spa tub and a separate shower and water closet.
- Two more bedrooms, each with a window seat, and a bonus room complete this stylish design.

**Plan CDG-2004**

| Bedrooms: 4 | Baths: 2½ |
|---|---|
| **Living Area:** | |
| Upper floor | 928 sq. ft. |
| Main floor | 1,317 sq. ft. |
| Bonus room | 192 sq. ft. |
| **Total Living Area:** | **2,437 sq. ft.** |
| Partial daylight basement | 780 sq. ft. |
| Garage | 537 sq. ft. |
| **Exterior Wall Framing:** | 2x6 |

**Foundation Options:**

Partial daylight basement

Crawlspace

(Typical foundation & framing conversion diagram available—see order form.)

| **BLUEPRINT PRICE CODE:** | C |
|---|---|

**UPPER FLOOR**

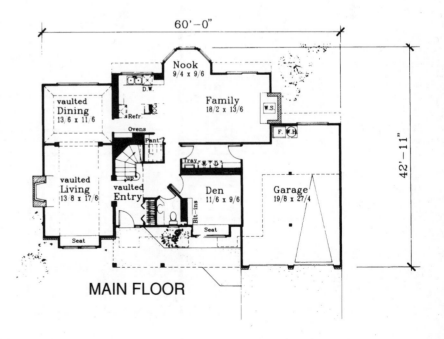

**MAIN FLOOR**

# Rear of Home As Attractive As Front

The rear of this rustic/contemporary home features a massive stone fireplace and a full-length deck which make it ideal for mountain, golf course, lake or other locations where both the front and rear offer scenic views.

Sliding glass doors in the family room and breakfast nook open onto the deck. The modified A-Frame design combines a 20'6" cathedral ceiling over the sunken family room with a large studio over the two front bedrooms. An isolated master suite features a walk-in closet and compartmentalized bath with double vanity and linen closet. The front bedrooms include ample closet space and share a unique bath-and-a-half arrangement.

On one side of the U-shaped kitchen and breakfast nook is the formal dining room which opens onto the foyer. On the other side is a utility room which can be entered from either the kitchen or garage.

The exterior features a massive stone fireplace, large glass areas and a combination of vertical wood siding and stone.

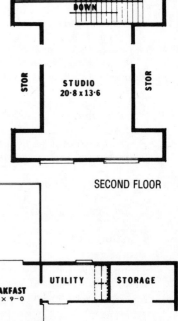

**SECOND FLOOR**

**FIRST FLOOR**

SPECIFY BASEMENT, CRAWLSPACE OR SLAB FOUNDATION WHEN ORDERING

First floor: 2,192 sq. ft.

Second floor: 248 sq. ft.

Total living area: 2,440 sq. ft.
(Not counting basement or garage)

Blueprint Price Code C
## Plan C-7710

**PRICES AND DETAILS ON PAGES 12-15**

# Elegant Post-Modern Design

- Here's a design that is highly fashionable today and that will undoubtedly stay in style for decades.
- A wagon roof porch with paired columns lends sophistication to an elegant design.
- Half-round transom windows and gable vents unify the facade.
- Inside, a diagonal stairway forms the keystone of an exciting, angular design.
- The foyer leads visitors past the den into the sunken living room with vaulted ceiling and fireplace.
- Square columned arcades separate the living room from the dining room.
- A sunny bay window defines the breakfast area, which includes a sliding glass door to the deck.
- The thoroughly modern kitchen includes an islet cooktop and pantry.
- The generously sized family room also sports a vaulted ceiling and offers easy access to the outdoor deck.
- Upstairs, a stylish master suite features a private bath and large closet.

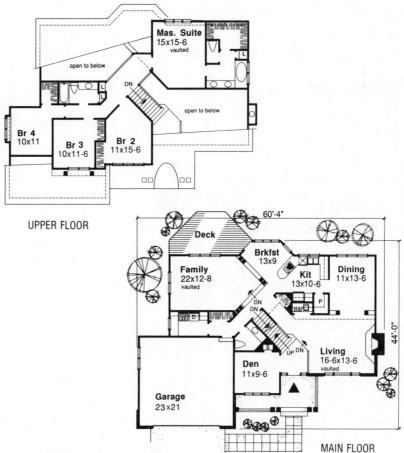

UPPER FLOOR

MAIN FLOOR

**Plan B-89005**

| Bedrooms: 4 | Baths: 2½ |
|---|---|

**Space:**

| | |
|---|---|
| Upper floor: | 1,083 sq. ft. |
| Main floor: | 1,380 sq. ft. |
| **Total living area:** | **2,463 sq. ft.** |
| Basement: | 1,380 sq. ft. |
| Garage: | 483 sq. ft. |

**Exterior Wall Framing:** 2x4

**Foundation options:**
Standard basement only.
(Foundation & framing conversion diagram available — see order form.)

**Blueprint Price Code:** C

# Full of Surprises

- While dignified and reserved on the outside, this plan presents delightful surprises throughout the interior.
- Interesting angles, vaulted ceilings, surprising spaces and bright windows abound everywhere you look in this home.
- The elegant, vaulted living room is off the expansive foyer, and includes an imposing fireplace and large windows areas.
- The delightful kitchen includes a handy island and large corner windows in front of the sink.
- The nook is brightened not only by large windows, but also by a skylight.
- The vaulted family room includes a corner wood stove area plus easy access to the outdoors.
- A superb master suite includes an exquisite bath with a skylighted dressing area and large walk-in closet.
- Three secondary bedrooms share another full bath, and the large laundry room is conveniently positioned near the bedrooms.

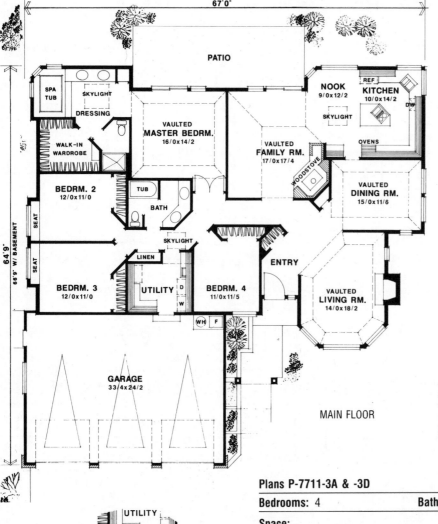

MAIN FLOOR

GARAGE
PLAN P-7711-3D
WITH DAYLIGHT BASEMENT

### Plans P-7711-3A & -3D

| Bedrooms: 4 | Baths: 2 |
|---|---|

**Space:**

| | |
|---|---|
| Main floor (non-basement version): | 2,510 sq. ft. |
| Main floor (basement version): | 2,580 sq. ft. |
| Basement: | 2,635 sq. ft. |
| Garage: | 806 sq. ft. |

| **Exterior Wall Framing:** | 2x6 |
|---|---|

**Foundation options:**
Daylight basement (Plan P-7711-3D).
Crawlspace (Plan P-7711-3A).
(Foundation & framing conversion diagram available — see order form.)

| **Blueprint Price Code:** | D |
|---|---|

*TO ORDER THIS BLUEPRINT, CALL TOLL-FREE 1-800-547-5570*

## Plans P-7711-3A & -3D

*PRICES AND DETAILS ON PAGES 12-15*

# Extraordinary Estate Living

- Extraordinary estate living is at its best in this palatial beauty.
- The double-doored entry opens to a large central living room that overlooks a covered patio with a vaulted ceiling. Volume 14-ft. ceilings are found in the living room, in the formal dining room and in the den or study, which may serve as a fourth bedroom.
- The gourmet chef will enjoy the spacious kitchen, which flaunts a cooktop island, a walk-in pantry and a

peninsula snack counter shared with the breakfast room and family room.
- This trio of informal living spaces also shares a panorama of glass and a corner fireplace centered between TV and media niches.
- Isolated at the opposite end of the home is the spacious master suite, which offers private patio access. Dual walk-in closets define the entrance to the adjoining master bath, complete with a garden Jacuzzi and separate dressing areas.
- The hall bath also opens to the outdoors for use as a pool bath.

**Plan HDS-99-177**

| | |
|---|---|
| **Bedrooms:** 3-4 | **Baths:** 3 |

| **Living Area:** | |
|---|---|
| Main floor | 2,597 sq. ft. |

| **Total Living Area:** | **2,597 sq. ft.** |
|---|---|
| Garage | 761 sq. ft. |

| **Exterior Wall Framing:** | 2x4 |
|---|---|

**Foundation Options:**

Slab

(Typical foundation & framing conversion diagram available—see order form.)

| **BLUEPRINT PRICE CODE:** | D |
|---|---|

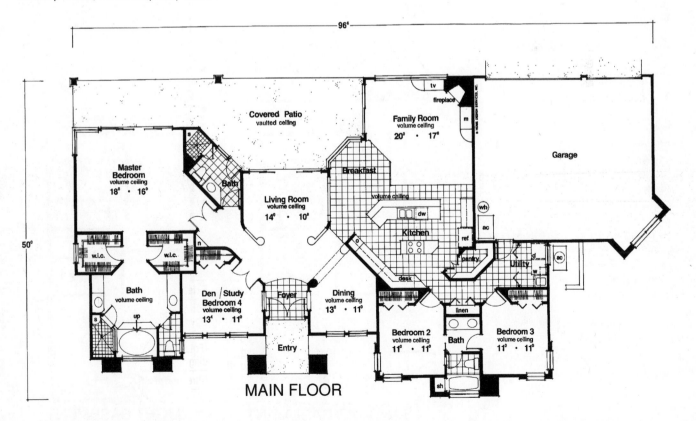

**MAIN FLOOR**

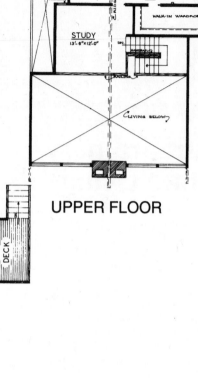

**UPPER FLOOR**

# Scenic Splendor

- This great-looking rustic design is well-suited to a scenic or narrow lot.
- Guests enter the home from a lovely side deck and enjoy picturesque views through the floor-to-ceiling windows in the vaulted living room. The living room also boasts a fireplace and access to a large wraparound deck.
- The dining room is open to the living room, and is easily serviced by the walk-through kitchen with breakfast bar.
- Two main-floor bedrooms share a compartmentalized bath.
- Upstairs, the master suite boasts a walk-in closet and a compartmentalized bath.
- The study/loft overlooks the living room and offers outdoor views and access to attic storage space.
- The standard basement features a large activity room with a second fireplace, while the daylight basement has a tuck-under garage, a game room and a guest room. Both basement options include a third full bath.

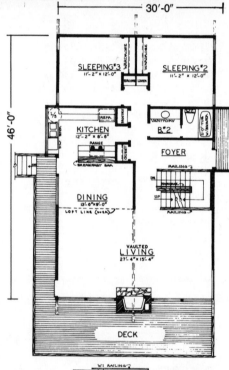

**MAIN FLOOR**

**Plan LMB-3683**

| Bedrooms: 3-4 | Baths: 3 |
|---|---|
| **Living Area:** | |
| Upper floor | 598 sq. ft. |
| Main floor | 1,306 sq. ft. |
| Standard basement (finished) | 700 sq. ft. |
| Daylight basement (finished) | 742 sq. ft. |
| **Total Living Area:** | **2,604/2,646 sq. ft.** |
| Standard basement (unfinished) | 588 sq. ft. |
| Garage (in daylight basement) | 546 sq. ft. |
| **Exterior Wall Framing:** | 2x4 |

**Foundation Options:**
Daylight basement
Standard basement
(Typical foundation & framing conversion diagram available—see order form.)

| **BLUEPRINT PRICE CODE:** | D |
|---|---|

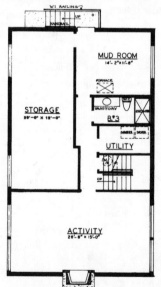

**STANDARD BASEMENT**

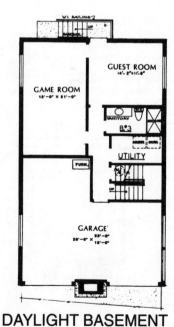

**DAYLIGHT BASEMENT**

**Plan LMB-3683**

**PRICES AND DETAILS ON PAGES 12-15**

# Deck Wraps Home with Plenty of Views

- A full deck and an abundance of windows surround this exciting two-level contemporary.
- Skywalls are found in the kitchen and dining room; the kitchen also features an island kitchen.
- The brilliant living room boasts a huge fireplace and cathedral ceiling, besides the stunning window wall.
- The master bedroom offers private access to the deck and an attached bath with dual vanities, large tub and a walk-in closet.
- A generous-sized family room and two extra bedrooms share the lower level with a two-car garage and storage area.

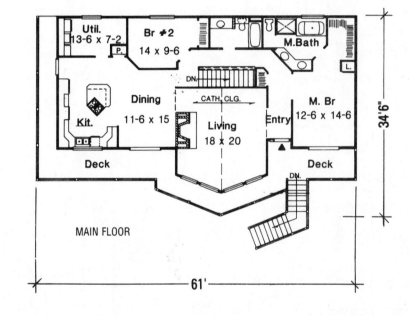

MAIN FLOOR

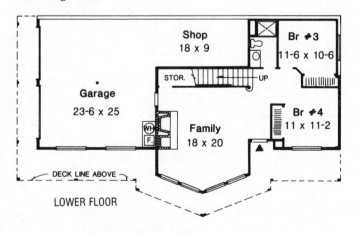

LOWER FLOOR

**Plan NW-579**

| Bedrooms: 2-4 | Baths: 2-3 |
|---|---|
| **Space:** | |
| Main/upper floor: | 1,707 sq. ft. |
| Lower floor: | 901 sq. ft. |
| **Total living area:** | 2,608 sq. ft. |
| Shop: | 162 sq. ft. |
| Garage: | 588 sq. ft. |
| **Exterior Wall Framing:** | 2x6 |

**Foundation options:**
Daylight basement.
(Foundation & framing conversion diagram available — see order form.)

| **Blueprint Price Code:** | D |
|---|---|

# Privacy and Luxury

- This home's large roof planes and privacy fences enclose a thoroughly modern, open floor plan.
- A beautiful courtyard greets guests on their way to the secluded entrance. Inside, a vaulted entry area leads directly into the living and dining rooms, which also boast a vaulted ceiling, plus floor-to-ceiling windows, a fireplace and a wall-length stone hearth.
- A sun room next to the spacious, angular kitchen offers passive solar heating and natural brightness.
- The vaulted family room features access to a rear patio through sliding glass doors.
- The main-floor master bedroom boasts sliders to a secluded portion of the front courtyard. The vaulted master bath includes a walk-in closet, a raised tub, a separate shower and access to a private sun deck with a hot tub.
- Upstairs, two bedrooms are separated by a bridge hallway that overlooks the rooms below.

### Plans P-7663-3A & -3D

| Bedrooms: 3+ | Baths: 3 |
|---|---|
| **Living Area:** | |
| Upper floor | 569 sq. ft. |
| Main floor | 2,039 sq. ft. |
| **Total Living Area:** | **2,608 sq. ft.** |
| Daylight basement | 2,039 sq. ft. |
| Garage | 799 sq. ft. |
| **Exterior Wall Framing:** | 2x4 |
| **Foundation Options:** | **Plan #** |
| Daylight basement | P-7663-3D |
| Crawlspace | P-7663-3A |
| (Typical foundation & framing conversion diagram available—see order form.) | |
| **BLUEPRINT PRICE CODE:** | D |

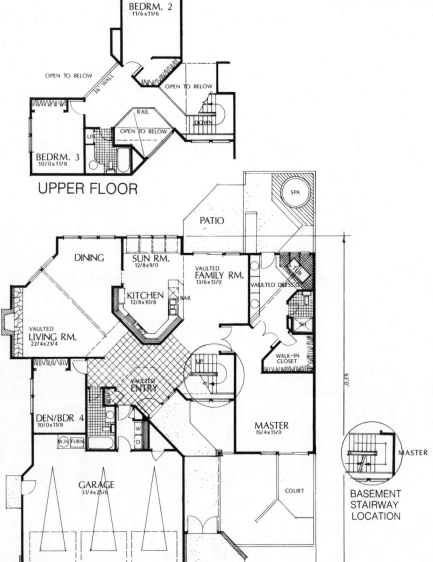

UPPER FLOOR

MAIN FLOOR

Plans P-7663-3A & -3D

**PRICES AND DETAILS ON PAGES 12-15**

# Well-Planned Walkout

- A dramatic double-back stair atrium descending from the Great Room to the bonus family room below ties the main floor design to the walkout lower level.
- A traditional exterior leads into a dramatic, open-feeling interior.
- The vaulted Great Room and dining room are separated by stylish columns.
- A see-thru fireplace is shared by the Great Room and the exciting kitchen with octagonal breakfast bay.
- A double-doored den/guest room opens off the Great Room.
- The spacious main floor master suite includes a huge walk-in closet and lavish master bath.

### Plan AG-9105

| Bedrooms: 3-4 | Baths: 2½ |
|---|---|
| **Space:** | |
| Main floor: | 1,838 sq. ft. |
| Daylight basement: | 800 sq. ft. |
| **Total living area:** | **2,638 sq. ft.** |
| Unfinished basement area: | 1,038 sq. ft. |
| Garage: | 462 sq. ft. |
| **Exterior Wall Framing:** | 2x6 |

**Foundation options:**
Daylight basement.
(Foundation & framing conversion diagram available — see order form.)

| **Blueprint Price Code:** | D |
|---|---|

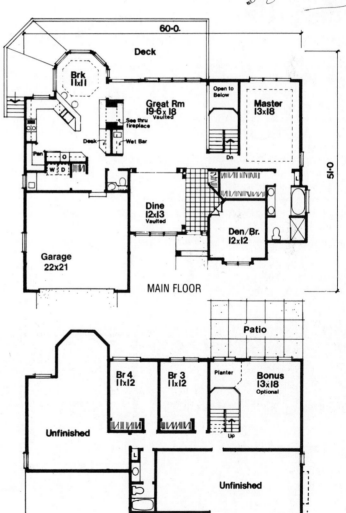

MAIN FLOOR

BASEMENT

# Bordered in Brick

- Decorative brick borders, front columns and arched windows give a classy look to this two-story palace.
- The entry is flanked by formal dining and living rooms, both with dramatic front windows.
- A fireplace warms the massive family room that stretches to the morning room and the kitchen at the rear of the home. The bayed morning room offers access to an attached deck; the kitchen has an island worktop.
- A unique sun room also overlooks the deck.
- Windows also surround the master bedroom, which has a large bath.
- Three nice-sized bedrooms share a second full bath on the upper level.

### Plan DD-2689

| Bedrooms: 4 | Baths: 2 ½ |
|---|---|
| **Space:** | |
| Upper floor | 755 sq. ft. |
| Main floor | 1,934 sq. ft. |
| **Total Living Area** | **2,689 sq. ft.** |
| Basement | 1,934 sq. ft. |
| Garage | 436 sq. ft. |
| **Exterior Wall Framing** | 2x4 |

**Foundation options:**

Standard Basement

Crawlspace

Slab

(Foundation & framing conversion diagram available—see order form.)

| **Blueprint Price Code** | D |
|---|---|

UPPER FLOOR

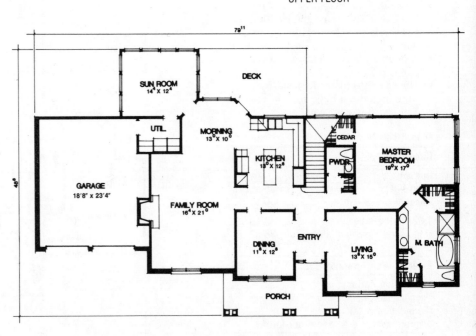

MAIN FLOOR

*TO ORDER THIS BLUEPRINT, CALL TOLL-FREE 1-800-547-5570*

Plan DD-2689

*PRICES AND DETAILS ON PAGES 12-15*

# Dramatic Contemporary Takes Advantage of Slope

- Popular plan puts problem building site to work by taking advantage of the slope to create a dramatic and pleasant home.
- Spacious vaulted living/dining area is bathed in natural light from cathedral windows facing the front and clerestory windows at the peak.
- Big kitchen includes pantry and abundant counter space.
- Three main-level bedrooms are isolated for more peace and quiet.
- Lower level includes large recreation room, a fourth bedroom, third bath, laundry area and extra space for a multitude of other uses.

Photo by Kevin Robinson

**NOTE:**
The above photographed home may have been modified by the homeowner. Please refer to floor plan and/or drawn elevation shown for actual blueprint details.

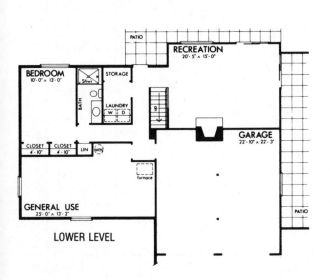

LOWER LEVEL

MAIN FLOOR

## Plan H-2045-5

| Bedrooms: 4 | Baths: 3 |
|---|---|

**Space:**

| | |
|---|---|
| Main floor: | 1,602 sq. ft. |
| Lower floor: | 1,133 sq. ft. |
| **Total living area:** | 2,735 sq. ft. |
| Garage: | 508 sq. ft. |

| **Exterior Wall Framing:** | 2x4 |
|---|---|

**Foundation options:**
Daylight basement only.
(Foundation & framing conversion diagram available — see order form.)

| **Blueprint Price Code:** | D |
|---|---|

FRONT VIEW

# Luxury on a Compact Foundation

Sky-lighted sloped ceilings, an intriguing stairway and overhead bridge and a carefully planned first floor arrangement combine to delight the senses as one explores this spacious 2737 sq. ft. home. A major element of the design is the luxurious master suite that is reached via the stairway and bridge. An abundance of closet space and an oversized bath are welcome features here.

Two bedrooms, generous bath facilities and a large family room provide lots of growing room for the younger members of the household.

All these features are available within a mere 36' width which allows the house to be built on a 50' wide lot — a real bonus these days.

| | |
|---|---|
| Main floor: | 1,044 sq. ft. |
| Upper level: | 649 sq. ft. |
| Lower level: | 1,044 sq. ft. |
| Total living area:<br>(Not counting garage) | 2,737 sq. ft. |

(Exterior walls are 2x6 construction)

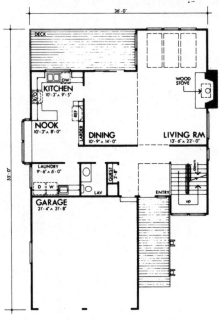

MAIN FLOOR
1044 SQUARE FEET

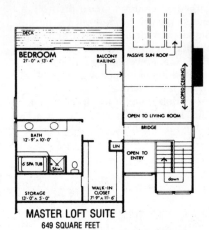

MASTER LOFT SUITE
649 SQUARE FEET

LOWER LEVEL
1044 SQUARE FEET

REAR VIEW

Blueprint Price Code D

## Plan H-2110-1B

# An Ever-Popular Floor Plan

The basic concept of this plan is to provide a simple straight-forward design for an uphill site. The plan is available with either a family room or dining room adjacent to the kitchen. Other features include a convenient laundry room, three bedrooms and two full baths. The living room features a fireplace and the wrap-around deck has access through the kitchen and laundry room. Total main floor area is 1,664 sq. ft.

| | |
|---|---|
| Main floor: | 1,664 sq. ft. |
| Lower level: | 1,090 sq. ft. |
| Total living area: | 2,754 sq. ft. |
| Garage: | 573 sq. ft. |

(Exterior walls are 2x6 construction)

### PLAN H-2029-4
MAIN FLOOR
(DINING ROOM VERSION)
1664 SQUARE FEET

### PLAN H-2029-5
MAIN FLOOR
(FAMILY ROOM VERSION)
1664 SQUARE FEET

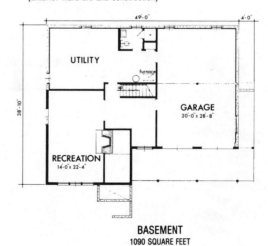

### BASEMENT
1090 SQUARE FEET

Blueprint Price Code D

# Better than Ever Before

- This Victorian proves that today's homes are better than ever before.
- Beyond the traditional exterior styling that makes the Victorian so appealing, this home offers a fantastic floor plan that will make your dreams come true.
- The fabulous foyer, true to the turrets of years gone by, offers a vaulted ceiling and an arched window. French doors open to the octagonal living room – styled after the old-fashioned parlor but much brighter and more inviting.
- The spacious dining room overlooks the turn-of-the century porch, but opens to a thoroughly modern kitchen. Both the sunny dinette and the partially vaulted family room have access to a deck.
- Upstairs, the master suite is simply a delight, with its boxed-out window and luxurious bath. Two more bedrooms, a full bath and a convenient laundry complete the upper floor.

**Plan PM-690**

| Bedrooms: 3 | Baths: 2½ |
|---|---|
| **Living Area:** | |
| Upper floor | 1,172 sq. ft. |
| Main floor | 1,612 sq. ft. |
| **Total Living Area:** | **2,784 sq. ft.** |
| Standard basement | 1,612 sq. ft. |
| Garage | 672 sq. ft. |
| **Exterior Wall Framing:** | 2x6 |

**Foundation Options:**

Standard basement

(Typical foundation & framing conversion diagram available—see order form.)

| **BLUEPRINT PRICE CODE:** | D |
|---|---|

UPPER FLOOR

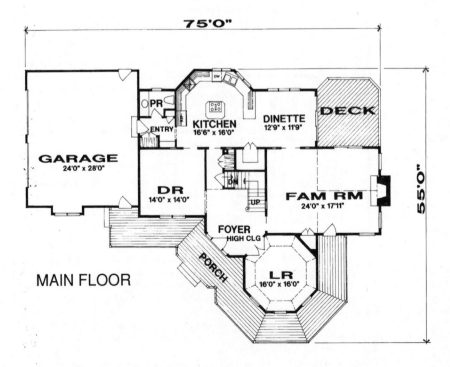

MAIN FLOOR

# Vintage Victorian

- Appreciators of the Victorian era will love the exterior of this dazzling house.
- A fantastic foyer launches a stunning staircase. The bright living room, the oversized, bayed dining room and a handy powder room are nearby.
- The kitchen boasts an angled eating bar and a large breakfast area that opens to a delightful double-tiered rear porch.

- The fireplace in the gorgeous Great Room gives guests a feeling of warmth as they look out over a nice deck through a window wall. French doors access the front and rear porches.
- Above, an unequaled master suite offers a private porch, two walk-in closets, a whirlpool bath and a separate shower.
- The two remaining bedrooms feature walk-in closets and a shared bath.
- Dramatic 10-ft. ceilings are found throughout the main floor, while the upper floor has 9-ft. ceilings.

| Plan V-2798 | |
|---|---|
| **Bedrooms:** 3 | **Baths:** 2½ |
| **Living Area:** | |
| Upper floor | 1,358 sq. ft. |
| Main floor | 1,440 sq. ft. |
| **Total Living Area:** | **2,798 sq. ft.** |
| Standard basement | 1,440 sq. ft. |
| **Exterior Wall Framing:** | 2x6 |
| **Foundation Options:** | |
| Standard basement | |
| (Typical foundation & framing conversion diagram available—see order form.) | |
| **BLUEPRINT PRICE CODE:** | D |

**UPPER FLOOR**

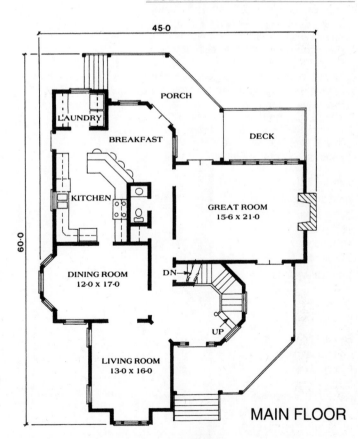

**MAIN FLOOR**

# Sunlit Elegance

- This elegant contemporary design offers just about all the amenities today's families expect in a home.
- The formal dining room is large enough for a good-sized dinner party.
- The living room is sunken and vaulted and includes a handsome fireplace.
- The spacious kitchen includes a large island and a pantry, and is open to the vaulted family room.
- Upstairs, the master bedroom is impressive, with a private master bath, large closets and easy access to a private deck. (If the greenhouse is built, stairs go from the master bath down to the hot tub.)
- The second floor also includes a roomy library and a bonus room or extra bedroom.
- The plan also offers an optional solar greenhouse, which may contain a hot tub or simply offer a great space for green plants and sunbathing.

### Plan S-8217

| Bedrooms: 3-4 | Baths: 2 |
|---|---|
| **Living Area:** | |
| Upper floor | 789 sq. ft. |
| Main floor | 1,709 sq. ft. |
| Bonus room | 336 sq. ft. |
| **Total Living Area:** | **2,834 sq. ft.** |
| Partial basement | 1,242 sq. ft. |
| Garage | 441 sq. ft. |
| **Exterior Wall Framing:** | 2x6 |

**Foundation Options:**
Partial basement
Crawlspace
Slab
(Typical foundation & framing conversion diagram available—see order form.)

**BLUEPRINT PRICE CODE:** D

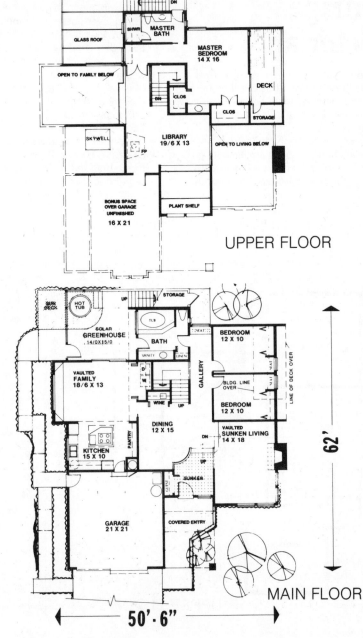

UPPER FLOOR

MAIN FLOOR

50'-6"

62'

*TO ORDER THIS BLUEPRINT, CALL TOLL-FREE 1-800-547-5570*

Plan S-8217

*PRICES AND DETAILS ON PAGES 12-15*

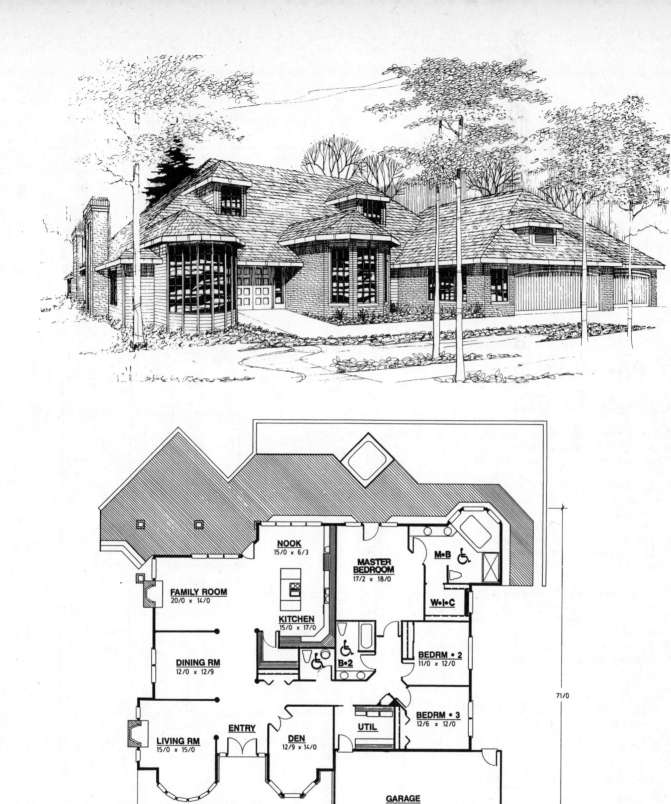

FAMILY ROOM
20/0 x 14/0

NOOK
15/0 x 6/3

MASTER BEDROOM
17/2 x 18/0

M•B

W•I•C

DINING RM
12/0 x 12/9

KITCHEN
15/0 x 17/0

B•2

BEDRM • 2
11/0 x 12/0

LIVING RM
15/0 x 15/0

ENTRY

DEN
12/9 x 14/0

UTIL

BEDRM • 3
12/6 x 12/0

GARAGE
32/9 x 24/3

PLAN I-2844-M
WITHOUT BASEMENT

Specify crawlspace or slab foundation.

Total living area:      2,844 sq. ft.
(Not counting garage)

71/0

72/6

Blueprint Price Code D
Plan I-2844-M

**TO ORDER THIS BLUEPRINT,**
**CALL TOLL-FREE 1-800-547-5570**

*PRICES AND DETAILS*
*ON PAGES 12-15*      **179**

# Two-Story Great Room

- A large two-story Great Room, with a fireplace and sliding glass doors to a backyard deck, is the highlight of this distinguished brick home.
- The front dining room and study both feature bay windows; the study can be used as an extra bedroom or guest room.
- A second stairway off the breakfast room accesses a home office or bonus space; an optional bath could also be built in.
- The main-floor master suite offers his and hers walk-in closets, a splashy master bath, and private access to the rear deck.
- Three secondary bedrooms are located off the second-floor balcony that overlooks the Great Room and the foyer.

### Plan C-9010

| Bedrooms: 4-5 | Baths: 2½-3½ |
|---|---|
| **Living Area:** | |
| Upper floor | 761 sq. ft. |
| Main floor | 1,637 sq. ft. |
| Bonus room | 347 sq. ft. |
| Optional bath and closet | 106 sq. ft. |
| **Total Living Area:** | **2,851 sq. ft.** |
| Standard basement | 1,637 sq. ft. |
| Garage | 572 sq. ft. |
| **Exterior Wall Framing:** | 2x4 |

**Foundation Options:**

Standard basement

Crawlspace

(Typical foundation & framing conversion diagram available—see order form.)

| **BLUEPRINT PRICE CODE:** | D |
|---|---|

UPPER FLOOR

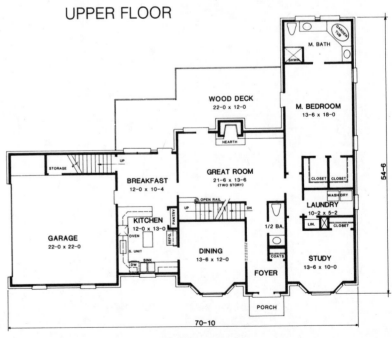

MAIN FLOOR

# Gables Galore

- This traditional beauty features brick trim, transom windows and plenty of eye-catching gables.
- The two-story entry with a plant shelf above is flanked by the vaulted living room and the formal dining room.
- The corner den could serve as a guest room, with a handy half-bath nearby.
- Central to the plan is the vaulted family room, which boasts a warm fireplace.
- The skylighted sun room offers a wet bar for entertaining or gardening use.
- The large island kitchen has a step-in pantry and a sunny breakfast area with patio access. Adjacent to the kitchen is a convenient main-floor laundry room.
- Upstairs, the master suite is a romantic retreat, with its see-through fireplace, bright sitting room and private whirlpool bath.
- Two additional bedrooms share a compartmentalized bath.

### Plan AG-2801

| | |
|---|---|
| **Bedrooms:** 3-4 | **Baths:** 2½ |
| **Living Area:** | |
| Upper floor | 1,080 sq. ft. |
| Main floor | 1,777 sq. ft. |
| **Total Living Area:** | **2,857 sq. ft.** |
| Standard basement | 1,640 sq. ft. |
| Garage | 693 sq. ft. |
| **Exterior Wall Framing:** | 2x6 |

**Foundation Options:**

Standard basement

(Typical foundation & framing conversion diagram available—see order form.)

| **BLUEPRINT PRICE CODE:** | D |
|---|---|

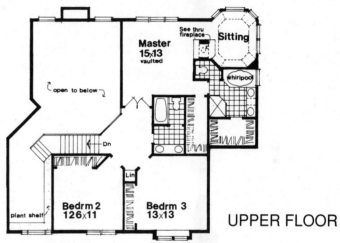

**UPPER FLOOR**

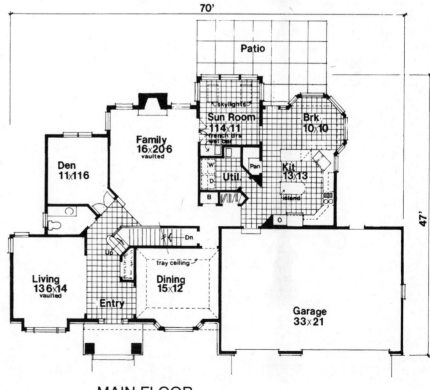

**MAIN FLOOR**

***TO ORDER THIS BLUEPRINT,***
***CALL TOLL-FREE 1-800-547-5570***

Plan AG-2801

***PRICES AND DETAILS***
***ON PAGES 12-15***

181

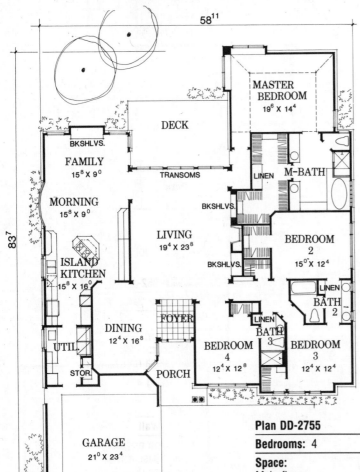

58<sup>11</sup>

83<sup>7</sup>

**MASTER BEDROOM** 19⁸ X 14⁴

**DECK**

**BKSHLVS.**

**FAMILY** 15⁸ X 9⁰

TRANSOMS

**M-BATH**

**MORNING** 15⁸ X 9⁰

LINEN

BKSHLVS.

**LIVING** 19⁴ X 23⁸

**BEDROOM 2** 15⁰ X 12⁴

**ISLAND KITCHEN** 15⁸ X 16⁰

BKSHLVS.

LINEN

**BATH 2**

**FOYER**

**DINING** 12⁴ X 16⁸

LINEN

**UTIL**

**BATH 3**

STOR.

**PORCH**

**BEDROOM 4** 12⁴ X 12⁸

**BEDROOM 3** 12⁴ X 12⁴

**GARAGE** 21⁰ X 23⁴

# Central Living Room Overlooks Deck

- This stylish, updated home offers an open floor plan that revolves around a spacious living room; an attached deck is visible through a spectacular rear window wall. A fireplace flanked by bookshelves and a high ceiling add more drama to this attention center.
- An island kitchen, morning room with bay window and family room combine for convenient family dining or entertaining.
- A formal dining room on the other side is also handy for meal serving.
- The sleeping wing includes three bedrooms, two baths and an elegant master suite; a beautiful cornered bay window and gambrel ceiling in the bedroom and dual vanities and closets and a 6' tub in the private bath are highlights.

**Plan DD-2755**

| | |
|---|---|
| **Bedrooms:** 4 | **Baths:** 3 |

**Space:**

| | |
|---|---|
| Main floor: | 2,868 sq. ft. |
| **Total living area:** | 2,868 sq. ft. |
| Basement: | (approx.) 2,800 sq. ft. |
| Garage: | 496 sq. ft. |

**Exterior Wall Framing:** 2x4

**Foundation options:**
Basement.
Crawlspace.
Slab.
(Foundation & framing conversion diagram available — see order form.)

**Blueprint Price Code:** D

**TO ORDER THIS BLUEPRINT, CALL TOLL-FREE 1-800-547-5570**

Plan DD-2755

**PRICES AND DETAILS ON PAGES 12-15**

**FRONT VIEW**

**REAR VIEW**

# Popular Plan for Any Setting

- City, country, or casual living is possible in this versatile two-story design.
- A spa room and sunning area lie between the master suite and Great Room, all encased in an extended eating and viewing deck.
- U-shaped kitchen, nook, and dining area fulfill your entertaining and dining needs.
- Two additional bedrooms and a balcony hall are located on the second level.
- Daylight basement option provides a fourth bedroom, shop, and recreation area.

BASEMENT

MAIN FLOOR

UPPER FLOOR

### Plans H-952-1A &-1B

| Bedrooms: 3-4 | Baths: 2-3 |
|---|---|

**Space:**

| | |
|---|---|
| Upper floor: | 470 sq. ft. |
| Main floor: | 1,207 sq. ft. |
| Passive spa room: | 102 sq. ft. |
| **Total living area:** | **1,779 sq. ft.** |
| Basement: | 1,105 sq. ft. |
| Garage: | 496 sq. ft. |

| **Exterior Wall Framing:** | 2x6 |
|---|---|

**Foundation options:**
Daylight Basement (Plan H-952-1B).
Crawlspace (Plan H-952-1A).
(Foundation & framing conversion diagram available — see order form.)

**Blueprint Price Code:**

| H-952-1A: | B |
|---|---|
| H-952-1B: | D |

FRONT VIEW

# Dramatic Western Contemporary

- Dramatic and functional building features contribute to the comfort and desire of this family home.
- Master suite offers a spacious private bath and luxurious hydro spa.
- Open, efficient kitchen accommodates modern appliances, a large pantry, and a snack bar.
- Skylights shed light on the entryway, open staircase, and balcony.
- Upper level balcony area has private covered deck, and may be used as a guest room or den.

REAR VIEW

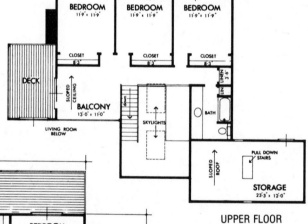

UPPER FLOOR

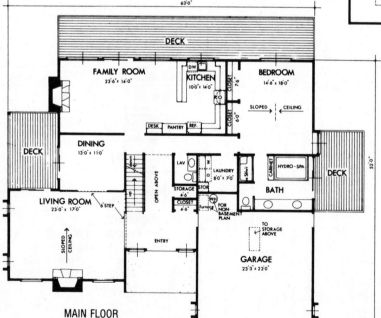

MAIN FLOOR

**Plans H-3708-1 & -1A**

| Bedrooms: 4 | Baths: 2½ |
|---|---|

**Space:**

| Upper floor: | 893 sq. ft. |
|---|---|
| Main floor: | 2,006 sq. ft. |

| **Total living area:** | **2,899 sq. ft.** |
|---|---|
| Basement: | approx. 2,006 sq. ft. |
| Garage: | 512 sq. ft. |

| **Exterior Wall Framing:** | 2x6 |
|---|---|

**Foundation options:**
Daylight basement (Plan H-3708-1).
Crawlspace (Plan H-3708-1A).
(Foundation & framing conversion diagram available — see order form.)

| **Blueprint Price Code:** | D |
|---|---|

**TO ORDER THIS BLUEPRINT, CALL TOLL-FREE 1-800-547-5570**

## Plans H-3708-1 & -1A

**PRICES AND DETAILS ON PAGES 12-15**

# Designed with the Master in Mind

- This elegant stucco home is designed with the master of the home in mind.
- Over 600 sq. ft. has been reserved for the master bedroom with an angled sitting area and patio access and a private bath with a large Jacuzzi, a private toilet room, dual dressing areas and an elegant double-doored entry.
- The formal living areas extend from the foyer. The central living room features a vaulted ceiling and a spectacular window wall overlooking the adjoining covered patio with a summer kitchen.
- The large gourmet kitchen merges with a breakfast area and a spacious family room. The breakfast area boasts a fascinating curved glass wall and opens to the patio. A handy snack bar serves refreshments to guests in the family room, which features a volume ceiling and a warming fireplace.
- Two secondary bedrooms, a den or guest room, and a hall or pool bath complete this unique floor plan.

### Plan HDS-99-178

| Bedrooms: 3-4 | Baths: 3 |
|---|---|

**Living Area:**

| Main floor | 2,931 sq. ft. |
|---|---|
| **Total Living Area:** | **2,931 sq. ft.** |
| Garage | 703 sq. ft. |

**Exterior Wall Framing:** 8-in. concrete block

**Foundation Options:**

Slab

(Typical foundation & framing conversion diagram available—see order form.)

**BLUEPRINT PRICE CODE:** D

MAIN FLOOR

# Nostalgic but New

- Triple dormers, a covered front porch and half-round windows lend a nostalgic country feel to this exciting two-story home.
- A dramatic two-story foyer makes an elegant introduction, leading into the vaulted living room with a fireplace, a window seat and round-top windows.
- The formal dining room, which features a tray ceiling, opens to the living room through an arch supported by stylish columns.
- The island kitchen has an open view into the breakfast nook and the family room with rear patio beyond.
- Upstairs, there are three bedrooms, plus a large bonus room that could be used as a fourth bedroom or as a playroom.
- The master suite dazzles with double doors, a sitting bay, a huge walk-in closet and an angled bath with a corner spa tub beneath windows.

**UPPER FLOOR**

Master 16/6 x 15/4
Blt-in
Spa
Arch
Walk-in Wardrobe
Br.3 15/0 X 11/4
dn.
Lin.
Open to Below
Br.2 10/10 x 11/8
Linen
Bonus 12/6 x 17/10
Seat
Seat

**MAIN FLOOR**

72'-0"
43'-11"
Patio
Nook 9/6 x 10/0
D.W.
vaulted Dining 15/8 x 11/4
Refr.
Ovens
Pan.
Family 20/2 x 13/4
W.S.
F.
W.H.
vaulted Living 15/8 x 17/8
Arch
vaulted Foyer
up
Arch
Garage 29/8 x 27/4
Den 11/10 x 9/8
Blt-in
Seat
Seat
Porch

### Plan CDG-2031

| Bedrooms: 3-5 | Baths: 2½ |
|---|---|
| **Living Area:** | |
| Upper floor | 1,203 sq. ft. |
| Main floor | 1,495 sq. ft. |
| Bonus room | 238 sq. ft. |
| **Total Living Area:** | **2,936 sq. ft.** |
| Garage | 811 sq. ft. |
| **Exterior Wall Framing:** | 2x6 |

**Foundation Options:**

Crawlspace
(Typical foundation & framing conversion diagram available—see order form.)

| **BLUEPRINT PRICE CODE:** | D |
|---|---|

**TO ORDER THIS BLUEPRINT, CALL TOLL-FREE 1-800-547-5570**

## Plan CDG-2031

*PRICES AND DETAILS ON PAGES 12-15*

REAR VIEW

# Solar Flair

- Full window walls and a sun room with glass roof act as passive energy collectors in this popular floor plan.
- Expansive living room features wood stove and vaulted ceilings.
- Dining room shares a breakfast counter with the merging kitchen.
- Convenient laundry room is positioned near kitchen and garage entrance.
- Second level is devoted entirely to the private master suite, featuring vaulted ceiling and a balcony view to the living room below.

## Plans H-877-5A & -5B

| Bedrooms: 3+ | Baths: 2-3 |
|---|---|
| **Living Area:** | |
| Upper floor | 382 sq. ft. |
| Main floor | 1,200 sq. ft. |
| Sun room | 162 sq. ft. |
| Daylight basement | 1,200 sq. ft. |
| **Total Living Area:** | **1,744/2,944 sq. ft.** |
| Garage | 457 sq. ft. |
| **Exterior Wall Framing:** | **2x6** |

**Foundation options:**
Daylight basement (Plan H-877-5B).
Crawlspace (Plan H-877-5A).
(Foundation & framing conversion diagram available — see order form.)

**Blueprint Price Code:**
Without basement: B
With basement: D

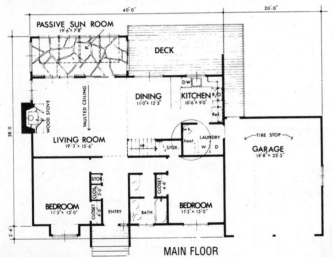

MAIN FLOOR

PLAN H-877-5B
WITH BASEMENT

UPPER FLOOR

BASEMENT

FRONT VIEW

**TO ORDER THIS BLUEPRINT,**
**CALL TOLL-FREE 1-800-547-5570**

## Plans H-877-5A & -5B

**PRICES AND DETAILS**
**ON PAGES 12-15**

**187**

# Spacious and Stately

- Covered porches front and rear.
- Downstairs master suite with spectacular bath.
- Family/living/dining areas combine for entertaining large groups.
- Classic Creole/plantation exterior.

## Plan E-3000

| | |
|---|---|
| **Bedrooms:** 4 | **Baths:** 3½ |

**Space:**

| | |
|---|---|
| Upper floor: | 1,027 sq. ft. |
| Main floor: | 2,008 sq. ft. |
| **Total living area:** | 3,035 sq. ft. |
| Porches: | 429 sq. ft. |
| Basement: | 2,008 sq. ft. |
| Garage: | 484 sq. ft. |
| Storage: | 96 sq. ft. |
| **Exterior Wall Framing:** | 2x6 |

**Typical Ceiling Heights:**

| | |
|---|---|
| Upper floor: | 8' |
| Main floor: | 9' |

**Foundation options:**
Standard basement.
Crawlspace.
Slab.
(Foundation & framing conversion diagram available — see order form.)

**Blueprint Price Code:**       E

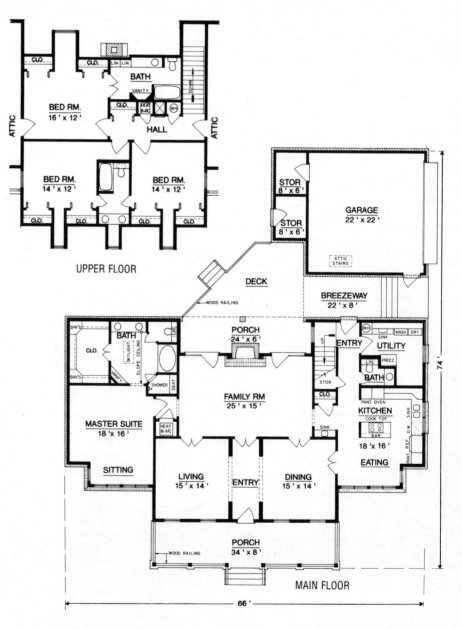

UPPER FLOOR

MAIN FLOOR

## Plan E-3000

*PRICES AND DETAILS*
*ON PAGES 12-15*

# Stunning Master Bedroom with Bay Window

- A lovely front porch offers a friendly welcome to this bold two-story.

- Inside, a handful of main-level living areas revolve around the central kitchen and dinette, complete with island worktop, desk/work area and attached rear deck.

- A raised hearth fireplace, French doors, and a cathedral ceiling highlight the casual setting of the family room.

- A formal dining and living room combination ends with a large front-facing bay window that overlooks the porch; a den or fifth bedroom lies across the formal foyer.

- The stunning master bedroom upstairs is entered through double doors; a sitting area may be set in the bay window. The attached private bath features a spa tub, dual vanities and his and hers walk-in closets.

- Three large additional bedrooms share a full bath designed for multiple users.

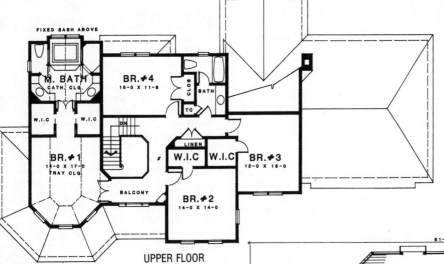

UPPER FLOOR

**Plan A-538-R**

| Bedrooms: 4-5 | Baths: 2½ |
|---|---|

**Space:**

| | |
|---|---|
| Upper floor: | 1,325 sq. ft. |
| Main floor: | 1,728 sq. ft. |

| **Total living area:** | **3,053 sq. ft.** |
|---|---|
| Garage: | 576 sq. ft. |
| Basement: | 1,728 sq. ft. |

| **Exterior Wall Framing:** | 2x4 |
|---|---|

**Foundation options:**
Standard basement.
(Foundation & framing conversion diagram available — see order form.)

| **Blueprint Price Code:** | E |
|---|---|

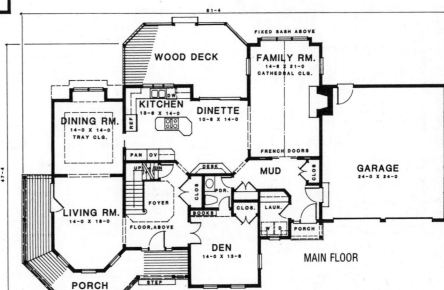

MAIN FLOOR

*TO ORDER THIS BLUEPRINT,*
*CALL TOLL-FREE 1-800-547-5570*

Plan A-538-R

*PRICES AND DETAILS*
*ON PAGES 12-15*

189

BEDROOM
12'-0"x17'-6"

DRESS

BATH

CLOSET

28'-6"

DN

BEDROOM
13'-0"x11'-10"

CLOSET

BEDROOM
12'-8"x11'-10"

CLOSET

RAIL

SITTING
8'-0"x10'-8"

DN

STORAGE
18'-0"x10'-4"

STOR

65'-6"

**UPPER FLOOR**

# Bay Windows Enhance a Country Home

A large master bedroom suite includes a deluxe bath with separate shower, garden tub, twin vanities and two large walk-in closets. Kitchen has direct access to both the breakfast nook and the dining room, which features a large bay window. Three bedrooms, a sitting area and storage or bonus room combine to form the second level.

First floor: 2,005 sq. ft.
Second floor: 1,063 sq. ft.

Total living area: 3,068 sq. ft.
(Not counting basement or garage)

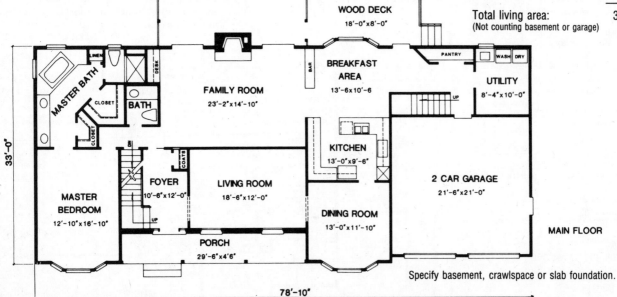

SCREENED PORCH
23'-10"x16'-0"

WOOD DECK
18'-0"x8'-0"

LINEN

MASTER BATH

DESK

CLOSET

BATH

FAMILY ROOM
23'-2"x14'-10"

BAR

PANTRY

WASH DRY

BREAKFAST AREA
13'-6"x10'-6"

UTILITY
8'-4"x10'-0"

CLOSET

33'-0"

COATS

FOYER
10'-6"x12'-0"

LIVING ROOM
18'-6"x12'-0"

UP

KITCHEN
13'-0"x9'-6"

UP

2 CAR GARAGE
21'-6"x21'-0"

MASTER BEDROOM
12'-10"x16'-10"

UP

DINING ROOM
13'-0"x11'-10"

**MAIN FLOOR**

PORCH
29'-6"x4'-6"

78'-10"

Specify basement, crawlspace or slab foundation.

Blueprint Price Code E

## Plan C-8409

# Solar Design that Shines

- A passive-solar sun room, an energy-efficient woodstove and a panorama of windows make this design really shine.
- The open living/dining room features a vaulted ceiling, walls filled with glass and access to the dramatic decking. A balcony above gives the huge living/dining area definition while offering spectacular views.
- The streamlined kitchen has a convenient serving bar that connects it to the living/dining area.
- The main-floor bedroom features dual closets and easy access to a full bath. The laundry room, located just off the garage, doubles as a mudroom and includes a handy coat closet.
- The balcony hallway upstairs is bathed in natural light. The two nice-sized bedrooms are separated by a second full bath.

### Plans H-855-3A & -3B

| Bedrooms: 3 | Baths: 2-3 |
|---|---|
| **Living Area:** | |
| Upper floor | 586 sq. ft. |
| Main floor | 1,192 sq. ft. |
| Sun room | 132 sq. ft. |
| Daylight basement | 1,192 sq. ft. |
| **Total Living Area:** | **1,910/3,102 sq. ft.** |
| Garage | 520 sq. ft. |
| **Exterior Wall Framing:** | **2x6** |
| **Foundation Options:** | **Plan #** |
| Daylight basement | H-855-3B |
| Crawlspace | H-855-3A |
| **BLUEPRINT PRICE CODE:** | **B/E** |

UPPER FLOOR

DAYLIGHT BASEMENT

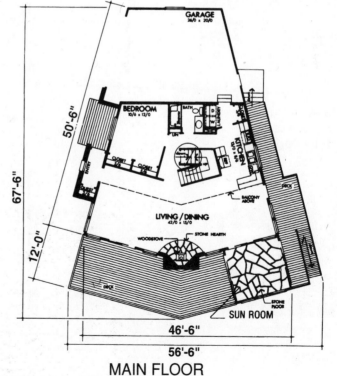

MAIN FLOOR

STAIRWAY AREA IN CRAWLSPACE VERSION

# Extravagant Arches

- The extravagant porch and window arches, an elegant upper balcony and a tiled roof give this home a striking Mediterranean look.
- Inside, formal living areas flank the long foyer, each adorned with entry columns and arched window treatments.
- The central family room offers a warm fireplace and a spectacular view of the patio and the optional pool.
- A large island kitchen is equipped with a walk-in pantry and generous counter space. A snack counter separates the kitchen from the bayed morning room, which also overlooks the patio.
- At the opposite end of the home is the spacious master suite, which features a bayed sitting area, a private bath, two walk-in closets and an exercise room.
- Upstairs are three more bedrooms, each with a private dressing area or bath. An exciting game room is also included!

## Plan DD-3045

| Bedrooms: 4 | Baths: 3½ |
|---|---|
| **Living Area:** | |
| Upper floor | 1,202 sq. ft. |
| Main floor | 1,952 sq. ft. |
| **Total Living Area:** | **3,154 sq. ft.** |
| Standard basement | 1,728 sq. ft. |
| Garage | 480 sq. ft. |
| **Exterior Wall Framing:** | 2x4 |

**Foundation Options:**
Standard basement
Crawlspace
Slab
(Typical foundation & framing conversion diagram available—see order form.)

**BLUEPRINT PRICE CODE:** E

FRONT VIEW

UPPER FLOOR

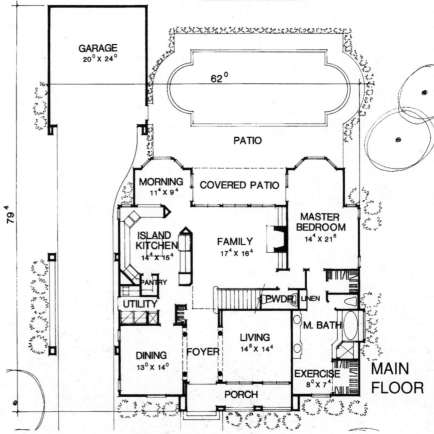

MAIN FLOOR

REAR VIEW

**TO ORDER THIS BLUEPRINT, CALL TOLL-FREE 1-800-547-5570**

Plan DD-3045

**PRICES AND DETAILS ON PAGES 12-15**

# Creative Spaces

- Here's a home that is not only large, but extremely creative in its use of indoor space.
- A huge area is created by the combination of the vaulted living and dining rooms, which flow together visually but are separated by a railing.
- Another expansive space results from the kitchen/nook/family room arrangement, and their easy access to deck and patio.
- Upstairs, the master suite includes a lavish bath and generous closets.
- Three large secondary bedrooms share another full bath, and each has its own unique design feature.

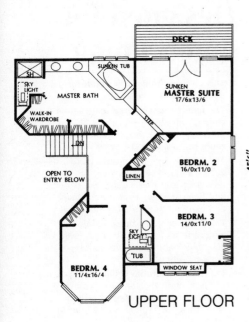

UPPER FLOOR

BASEMENT STAIRWAY
LOCATION

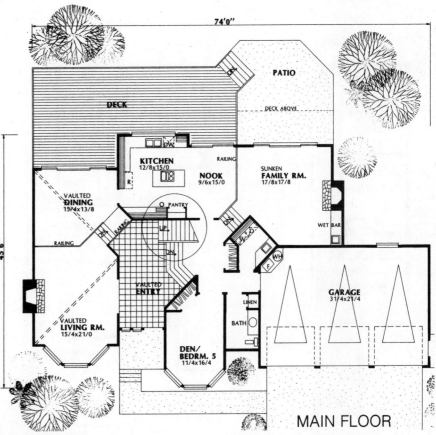

MAIN FLOOR

**Plans P-7664-4A & -4D**

| Bedrooms: 4-5 | Baths: 2½ |
|---|---|
| **Living Area:** | |
| Upper floor | 1,254 sq. ft. |
| Main floor | 1,824 sq. ft. |
| **Total Living Area:** | **3,078 sq. ft.** |
| Daylight basement | 1,486 sq. ft. |
| Garage | 668 sq. ft. |

| Exterior Wall Framing: | 2x4 |
|---|---|
| **Foundation Options:** | **Plan #** |
| Daylight basement | P-7664-4D |
| Crawlspace | P-7664-4A |
| (Typical foundation & framing conversion diagram available—see order form.) | |
| **BLUEPRINT PRICE CODE:** | E |

*TO ORDER THIS BLUEPRINT,*
CALL TOLL-FREE 1-800-547-5570

Plans P-7664-4A & -4D

*PRICES AND DETAILS
ON PAGES 12-15*

193

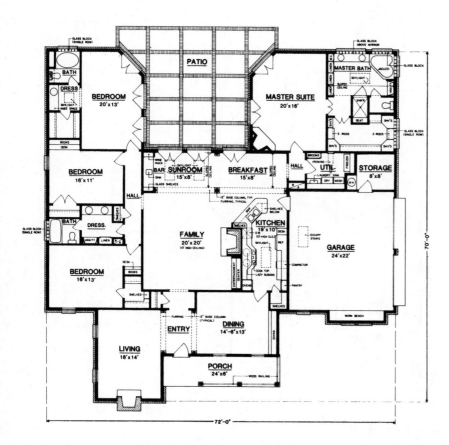

PLAN E-3102
WITHOUT BASEMENT

Exterior walls are 2x6 construction.
Specify crawlspace or slab foundation.

# Ranch-Style Designed for Entertaining

- This all-brick home offers both formal living and dining rooms.
- The family room is large scale with 13′ ceilings, formal fireplace and an entertainment center. An adjoining sun room reveals a tucked away wet bar.
- The master suite has private patio access and its own fireplace. An adjoining bath offers abundant closet and linen storage, a separate shower and garden tub with glass block walls.
- The home contains three additional bedrooms and two baths. Each bath has glass block above the tubs and separate dressing rooms.
- The master bedroom ceiling is sloped to 14′ high. Both the sun room and the breakfast room have sloped ceilings with skylights. Typical ceiling heights are 9′.
- The home is energy efficient.

| | |
|---|---|
| Heated area: | 3,158 sq. ft. |
| Unheated area: | 767 sq. ft. |
| Total area: | 3,925 sq. ft. |

TO ORDER THIS BLUEPRINT,
CALL TOLL-FREE 1-800-547-5570

PRICES AND DETAILS
ON PAGES 12-15

Blueprint Price Code E
Plan E-3102

# An Instant Hit

- Clean lines, a covered front porch and spectacular spaces for indoor/outdoor living make this home an instant hit.
- The vaulted, skylighted foyer leads past the open stairway, straight ahead to the sunken Great Room. A vaulted ceiling, a fireplace with built-in shelves, and access to the expansive rear deck make this the perfect all-purpose room.
- The bayed dining area also opens to the deck, and a possible three-season porch adds more potiential for sunny living space. The galley-style kitchen features an island eating counter, a large pantry closet and easy access to the oversized laundry room.
- The vaulted master bedroom suite includes a wonderful bath with a whirlpool tub. Three more bedrooms and a large family room are quietly located on the the lower level.
- The upper-level loft offers stunning views of the Great Room, plus extra storage space.

### Plan PI-86-527

| Bedrooms: 4 | Baths: 3 |
|---|---|
| **Living Area:** | |
| Upper floor | 400 sq. ft. |
| Main floor (without future porch) | 1,600 sq. ft. |
| Daylight basement (finished) | 1,200 sq. ft. |
| **Total Living Area:** | **3,200 sq. ft.** |
| Future porch | 196 sq. ft. |
| Daylight basement (unfinished) | 400 sq. ft. |
| Garage | 832 sq. ft. |
| **Exterior Wall Framing:** | 2x6 |

**Foundation Options:**

Daylight basement

(Typical foundation & framing conversion diagram available—see order form.)

**BLUEPRINT PRICE CODE:** E

UPPER FLOOR

MAIN FLOOR

DAYLIGHT BASEMENT

# Flexible Swing Suite

- This charming traditional home is greatly enhanced with the flexibility of a swing suite.
- Perfect as an in-law apartment or as a private shelter for a child returning to the nest, the swing suite is an added feature of this design.
- The spacious kitchen is the focal point of family activities. A long, angled counter nicely serves the breakfast room, dining room and family room.
- The bayed breakfast room has its own snack bar that doubles as a wet bar for guests in the family room. To the rear is an exciting, skylighted sun room that opens to a backyard patio.
- A unique corner fireplace at the center of the floor plan faces the family room and the breakfast room.
- A vaulted master suite with a private garden bath, plus three more bedrooms and two other full baths, occupies the upper floor.

**Plan B-92034**

| Bedrooms: 4-5 | Baths: 4½ |
|---|---|
| **Living Area:** | |
| Upper floor | 1,351 sq. ft. |
| Main floor | 1,882 sq. ft. |
| **Total Living Area:** | **3,233 sq. ft.** |
| Standard basement | 1,734 sq. ft. |
| Garage | 450 sq. ft. |
| **Exterior Wall Framing:** | 2x4 |

**Foundation Options:**

Standard basement

(Typical foundation & framing conversion diagram available—see order form.)

| **BLUEPRINT PRICE CODE:** | E |
|---|---|

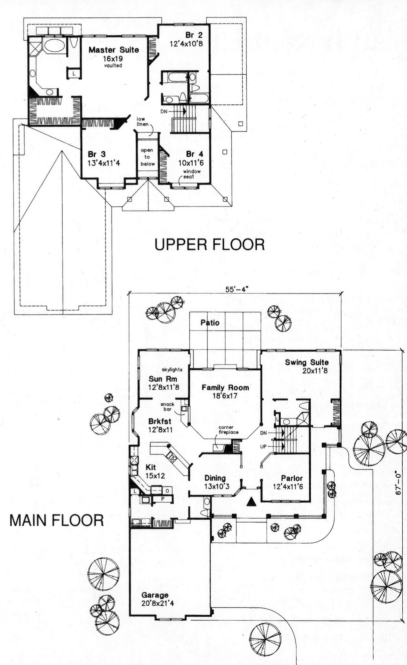

**UPPER FLOOR**

**MAIN FLOOR**

FRONT VIEW

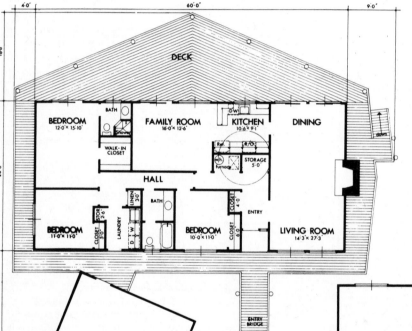

MAIN FLOOR

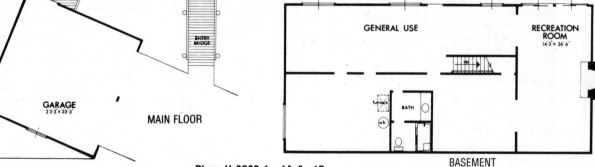

BASEMENT

# Gracious Indoor/ Outdoor Living

- A clean design makes this plan adaptable to almost any climate or setting.
- Perfect for a scenic, hillside lot, the structure and wrap-around deck offers a spanning view.
- Kitchen is flanked by family and dining rooms, allowing easy entrance from both.
- Foundation options include a daylight basement on concrete slab (H-2083-1), a wood-framed lower level (H-2083-1B), and a crawlspace (H-2083-1A).

**PLAN H-2083-1**
WITH DAYLIGHT BASEMENT
(ON CONCRETE SLAB)

**PLAN H-2083-1B**
(WITH WOOD-FRAMED LOWER LEVEL)

**Plans H-2083-1, -1A & -1B**

| Bedrooms: 3 | Baths: 2-3 |
|---|---|

**Space:**

| | |
|---|---|
| Main floor: | 1,660 sq. ft. |
| Basement: | 1,660 sq. ft. |

**Total living area:**
| with basement: | 3,320 sq. ft. |
|---|---|
| Garage: | 541 sq. ft. |

**Exterior Wall Framing:** 2x4

**Foundation options:**
Daylight basement (Plan H-2083-1 or -1B).
Crawlspace (Plan H-2083-1A).
(Foundation & framing conversion diagram available — see order form.)

**Blueprint Price Code:**
| Without basement: | B |
|---|---|
| With basement: | E |

*TO ORDER THIS BLUEPRINT,*
*CALL TOLL-FREE 1-800-547-5570*

Plans H-2083-1, -1A & -1B

*PRICES AND DETAILS*
*ON PAGES 12-15*

**197**

# Spectacular Sweeping Views

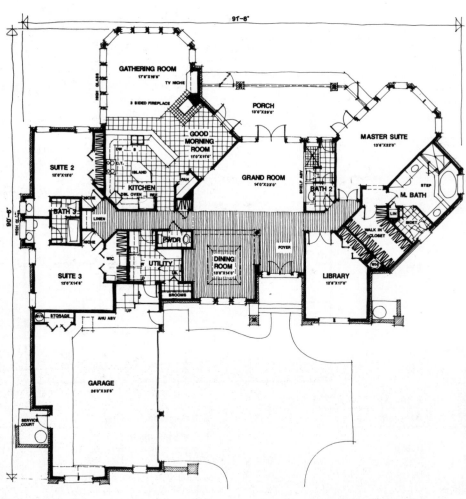

- The elegant brick facade of this exciting home conceals a highly contemporary interior.
- The foyer opens to a huge Grand Room that further opens to a delightful rear porch, also accessed through the morning room, pool bath and master suite.
- Completely surrounded in windows and high fixed glass is a spacious gathering room, also featuring a three-sided fireplace and built-in entertainment center.
- The spectacular master suite is secluded to the rear of the home, but wrapped in windows and offering its own fantastic bath with luxury tub and bidet.
- Two additional sleeping suites found at the other end of the home share a bath with private vanities.

| Plan EOF-8 | |
|---|---|
| **Bedrooms:** 3-4 | **Baths:** 3 ½ |
| **Space:** | |
| Main floor | 3,392 sq. ft. |
| **Total Living Area** | **3,392 sq. ft.** |
| Garage | 871 sq. ft. |
| **Exterior Wall Framing** | 2x6 |
| **Foundation options:** | |
| Slab | |
| (Foundation & framing conversion diagram available—see order form.) | |
| **Blueprint Price Code** | E |

# Living Areas Have Lofty View

- This design raises elegant living to new heights. The living areas are on the upper floor, providing a lofty view for homes on lake, golf-course or other scenic lots.
- The expansive living/dining room features a fireplace, a rear wall lined with windows and a French door that opens to the covered deck.
- The sunny breakfast room is open to the island kitchen, which boasts a spectacular barrel-vaulted ceiling with a large arched window above the sink. The adjacent study/dining room offers flexible living space.
- One whole wing of the home is devoted to the luxurious master suite, with its built-in entertainment center, sitting area and access to the deck. The master bath has a barrel-vaulted ceiling, a spa tub and a deluxe wardrobe.
- The first floor hosts three bedrooms, two baths and a large family room, plus a utility/sewing room with a handy dumbwaiter to the second floor.

### Plan KY-3399

| Bedrooms: 4 | Baths: 3½ |
|---|---|
| **Living Area:** | |
| Main floor | 1,841 sq. ft. |
| Lower floor | 1,558 sq. ft. |
| **Total Living Area:** | **3,399 sq. ft.** |
| Garage | 506 sq. ft. |
| **Exterior Wall Framing:** | 2x4 |

**Foundation Options:**

Slab

(Typical foundation & framing conversion diagram available—see order form.)

| **BLUEPRINT PRICE CODE:** | E |
|---|---|

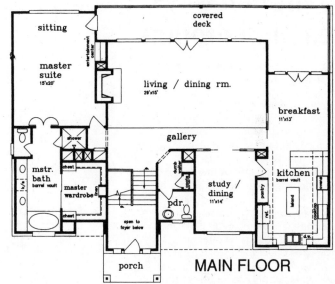

MAIN FLOOR

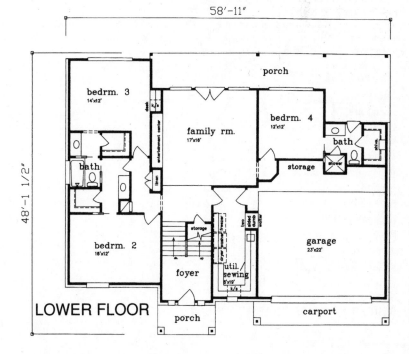

LOWER FLOOR

58'-11"

48'-1 1/2"

# Dual Stairways Reach Bedrooms

- This spacious traditional home is available with an exterior of siding or stucco.
- The four-bedroom upper level is conveniently accessed from stairways in the foyer and the family room.
- To the left of the foyer are the formal areas, which provide a spacious entertaining expanse. A fireplace sits on the side and bay windows adorn either end.
- The large gourmet kitchen and sunny breakfast area combine at the rear of the home. The kitchen offers an oversized cooktop island, a pantry closet and sliders to the backyard deck.
- The sunken family room is seen through an open railing and boasts a warm fireplace and a wet bar.
- An exciting bayed sun room connects with the family room, for a warm, informal extension of family activities.

## Plan CH-255-A

| Bedrooms: 4 | Baths: 3½ |
|---|---|
| **Living Area:** | |
| Upper floor | 1,589 sq. ft. |
| Main floor | 1,919 sq. ft. |
| **Total Living Area:** | **3,508 sq. ft.** |
| Basement | 1,919 sq. ft. |
| Garage | 662 sq. ft. |
| **Exterior Wall Framing:** | 2x4 |

**Foundation Options:**

Daylight basement

Standard basement

Crawlspace

(Typical foundation & framing conversion diagram available—see order form.)

**BLUEPRINT PRICE CODE:** F

**UPPER FLOOR**

**MAIN FLOOR**

*TO ORDER THIS BLUEPRINT, CALL TOLL-FREE 1-800-547-5570*

Plan CH-255-A

*PRICES AND DETAILS ON PAGES 12-15*

# Elegant Estate

- The columned, covered entry of this home combines with wonderful window treatments and dramatic dormers to create a fantastic facade.
- Once inside, the two-story entry with its wide, split stairway is reminiscent of a grand Southern estate.
- The formal living areas lie on either side of the foyer, and feature built-in units.
- The huge kitchen with a central island cooktop boasts a handy pantry and a large wet bar. An adjacent screen porch and sunny breakfast room both provide access to an expansive rear deck.
- The fabulous family room features a fireplace along with two window seats and built-in shelving. French doors give way to a deluxe drawing room with a cathedral ceiling and lots of glass.
- The master suite upstairs is large and lavish. A sitting area, a whirlpool bath surrounded by glass and a separate shower are just a few of its features.
- Two secondary bedrooms share a bath, while the fourth bedroom has its own.

### Plan UDG-92005

| Bedrooms: 4 | Baths: 3½ |
|---|---|
| **Living Area:** | |
| Upper floor | 1,707 sq. ft. |
| Main floor | 1,803 sq. ft. |
| **Total Living Area:** | **3,510 sq. ft.** |
| Screen porch | 163 sq. ft. |
| Standard basement | 1,803 sq. ft. |
| Garage | 848 sq. ft. |
| **Exterior Wall Framing:** | 2x4 |

**Foundation Options:**

Standard basement

(Typical foundation & framing conversion diagram available—see order form.)

| **BLUEPRINT PRICE CODE:** | F |
|---|---|

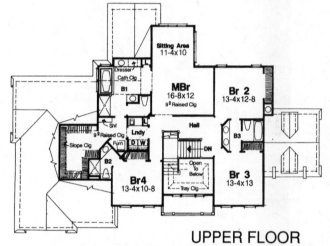

**UPPER FLOOR**

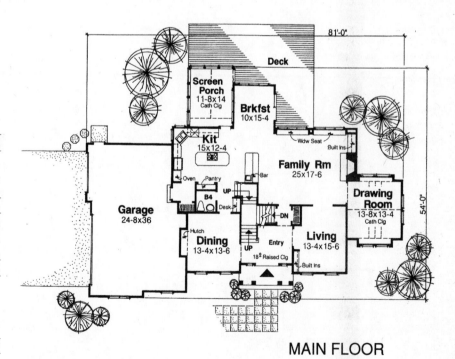

**MAIN FLOOR**

*TO ORDER THIS BLUEPRINT,*
*CALL TOLL-FREE 1-800-547-5570*

Plan UDG-92005

*PRICES AND DETAILS*
*ON PAGES 12-15*

**201**

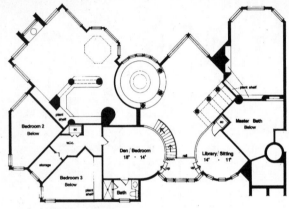

**UPPER FLOOR**

# Modern, Refined Design

- Light years ahead of its time, this exquisite home has an exterior that reflects a European villa and an interior that incorporates the refined features of the '90s.
- Curved walls, high ceilings and uniquely shaped living spaces are some of the home's distinguishing characteristics. At the center are a circular dining room and media room.
- The kitchen, breakfast nook and family room adjoin at the rear, all with views of the fireplace and the huge rear patio and pool area.
- The luxurious master bedroom has a fireplace and a huge private bath with garden tub, circular shower, back-to-back vanities and separate toilet room.
- A sitting room and a den or extra bedroom occupy the upper floor.

**MAIN FLOOR**

| Plan HDS-99-139 | |
|---|---|
| **Bedrooms:** 3-4 | **Baths:** 4½ |
| **Living Area:** | |
| Upper floor | 494 sq. ft. |
| Main floor | 3,236 sq. ft. |
| **Total Living Area:** | **3,730 sq. ft.** |
| Garage | 572 sq. ft. |
| **Exterior Wall Framing:** | |
| 2x4 and 8" concrete block | |
| **Foundation Options:** | |
| Slab | |
| (Typical foundation & framing conversion diagram available—see order form.) | |
| **BLUEPRINT PRICE CODE:** | F |

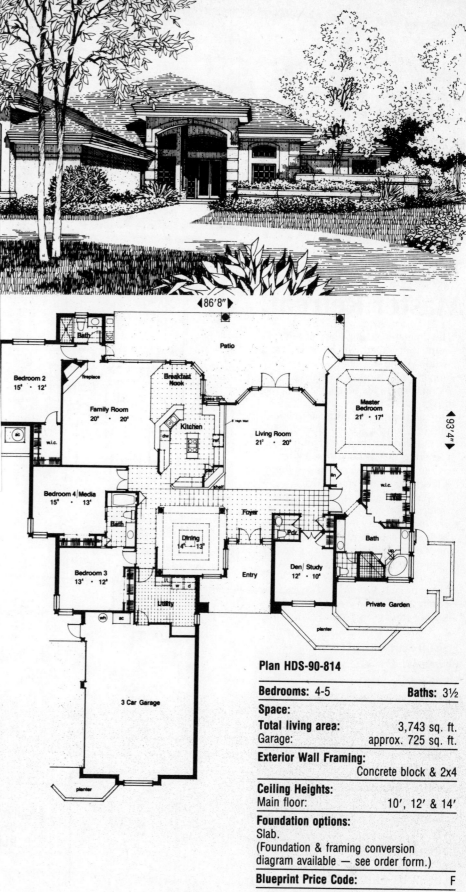

# Sun-Drenched Home

- Sweeping hip rooflines, stucco siding with interesting quoins and banding, and interesting arched transom windows give this exciting sunbelt design a special flair.
- From an important 1½ story covered entry leading into the foyer, guests are greeted with a stunning view. A bay-window-wall opens the living room, straight ahead, to the covered patio, rear yard, and possible pool. To the left is an open-feeling formal dining room with columns and spectacular receding tray ceiling.
- The island kitchen overlooks the large family room with corner fireplace and breakfast bay.
- The master wing, well separated from the secondary bedrooms, features a coffered ceiling, sitting area with patio access, massive walk-in closet, and sun-drenched garden bath.

**Plan HDS-90-814**

| Bedrooms: 4-5 | Baths: 3½ |
|---|---|

**Space:**

| | |
|---|---|
| Total living area: | 3,743 sq. ft. |
| Garage: | approx. 725 sq. ft. |

**Exterior Wall Framing:**
Concrete block & 2x4

**Ceiling Heights:**
Main floor: 10', 12' & 14'

**Foundation options:**
Slab.
(Foundation & framing conversion diagram available — see order form.)

**Blueprint Price Code:** F

**TO ORDER THIS BLUEPRINT, CALL TOLL-FREE 1-800-547-5570**

Plan HDS-90-814

# Two-Story Master Retreat!

- The dramatic soaring entry of this brick home is accented with attractive arched windows and staggered rooflines.
- Sloped ceilings open the foyer and the living room to the balcony area at the top of the stairs.
- Oriented to the rear and incorporated into one large space are the morning room, island kitchen and family gathering area. A central snack bar adjoining the cooktop island in the kitchen serves the entire area. A fireplace and generous views of the outdoors are also offered.
- The extraordinary main-floor master bedroom features a bayed reading area, deck access and a private stairway to a unique second-floor retreat with a romantic fireplace.
- Three more bedrooms and an exciting family activity center with a handy kitchenette are also found on this floor.

### Plan DD-3894

| Bedrooms: 4 | Baths: 3½ |
|---|---|
| **Living Area:** | |
| Upper floor | 1,621 sq. ft. |
| Main floor | 2,273 sq. ft. |
| **Total Living Area:** | **3,894 sq. ft.** |
| Partial basement | 1,307 sq. ft. |
| Garage | 467 sq. ft. |
| **Exterior Wall Framing:** | 2x4 |

**Foundation Options:**

Partial basement
Crawlspace
Slab
(Typical foundation & framing conversion diagram available—see order form.)

**BLUEPRINT PRICE CODE:** F

UPPER FLOOR

MAIN FLOOR

*TO ORDER THIS BLUEPRINT, CALL TOLL-FREE 1-800-547-5570*

Plan DD-3894

*PRICES AND DETAILS ON PAGES 12-15*

# Exciting Angles and Amenities

- The interior of this elegant stucco design oozes in luxury, with an exciting assortment of angles and glass.
- Beyond the 14-ft.-high foyer and gallery is a huge parlour with an angled stand-behind ale bar and an adjoining patio accessed through two sets of glass doors.
- The diamond-shaped kitchen offers a sit-down island, a spacious walk-in pantry and a pass-through window to a summer kitchen.
- Opposite the kitchen is an octagonal morning room surrounded in glass and a spacious, angled gathering room with a fireplace and a TV niche.
- The luxurious master suite features a glassed lounge area and a spectacular two-sided fireplace, and is separated from the three secondary bedroom suites. The stunning master bath boasts a central linen island and an assortment of amenities designed for two.
- The library could serve as a fifth bedroom or guest room; the bath across the hall could serve as a pool bath.
- An alternate brick elevation is included in the blueprints.

## Plan EOF-59

| Bedrooms: 4-5 | Baths: 4 |
|---|---|
| **Living Area:** | |
| Main floor | 4,021 sq. ft. |
| **Total Living Area:** | **4,021 sq. ft.** |
| Garage | 737 sq. ft. |
| **Exterior Wall Framing:** | 2x6 |

**Foundation Options:**

Slab

(Typical foundation & framing conversion diagram available—see order form.)

| **BLUEPRINT PRICE CODE:** | **G** |
|---|---|

MAIN FLOOR

# Private Suites

- Stucco and stacked stone accent the exterior of this luxurious four-bedroom European traditional.
- Dramatic ceilings throughout the interior complement the many built-ins, such as the entertainment center, cabinets, desks and dressers.
- The focal point of the floor plan is a spectacular Grand Room with a fireplace and a view of the rear deck.
- A functional snack counter connects the Grand Room to a spacious wraparound kitchen. A vegetable sink is included in the work island at the kitchen's center, and a breakfast room and sun room adjoin to the rear.
- A see-through fireplace and an exciting rear window wall are enjoyed in both the breakfast room and the sun room.
- The luxurious master suite features a private whirlpool bath and a personal study that opens to the outdoors.
- The upper floor can be accessed from the foyer or from a second stairway off the Grand Room. Three more bedrooms, each with a tray ceiling and a private bath, are located on this level.

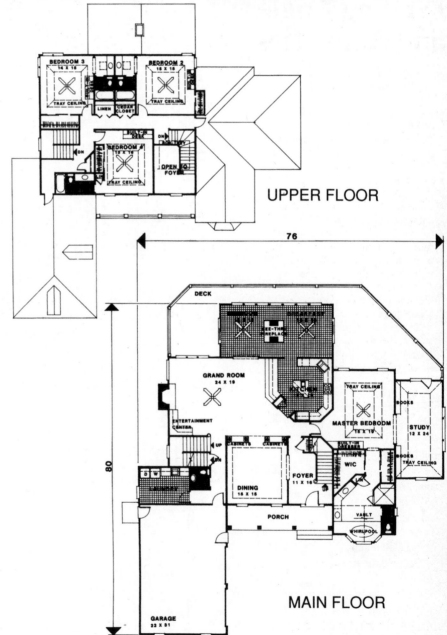

**UPPER FLOOR**

**MAIN FLOOR**

### Plan APS-3601

| Bedrooms: 4 | Baths: 4½ |
|---|---|
| **Living Area:** | |
| Upper floor | 1,239 sq. ft. |
| Main floor | 2,791 sq. ft. |
| **Total Living Area:** | **4,030 sq. ft.** |
| Standard basement | 2,149 sq. ft. |
| Garage | 682 sq. ft. |
| **Exterior Wall Framing:** | 2x4 |

**Foundation Options:**

Standard basement

(Typical foundation & framing conversion diagram available—see order form.)

| **BLUEPRINT PRICE CODE:** | **G** |
|---|---|

*TO ORDER THIS BLUEPRINT, CALL TOLL-FREE 1-800-547-5570*

Plan APS-3601

*PRICES AND DETAILS ON PAGES 12-15*

# Elegance & Grace Perfected

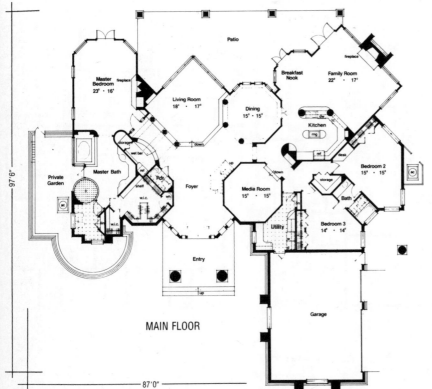

UPPER FLOOR

MAIN FLOOR

Plan HDS-90-819

- The grand style, both inside and out, of this luxurious residence combines elegance and grace to perfection.
- The gothic contemporary architecture exudes an aura of grandeur, drawing the eye to a stately 2½ story entry portico.
- The interior is equally stunning with open high flowing spaces featuring coffered ceilings with columns defining room changes.
- The formal zone impresses with the vast foyer overlooking the sunken living room under corner window walls. The octagonal dining room, loft overlook, and curved wet bar complete the formal area.
- The informal zone of island kitchen, breakfast nook, family room, and octagonal media room make the most of precious family time together.
- The master suite continues the elegance, with a fireplace, endless walk-in closet, and garden bath which brings the outdoors in.

### Plan HDS-90-819

| Bedrooms: 4 + | Baths: 3½ |
|---|---|
| **Space:** | |
| Upper floor: | 765 sq. ft. |
| Main floor: | 3,770 sq. ft. |
| **Total living area:** | 4,535 sq. ft. |
| Garage: | approx. 750 sq. ft. |
| **Exterior Wall Framing:** | 2x4 |
| **Ceiling Heights:** | |
| Upper floor: | 9' |
| Main floor: | 9' |
| **Foundation options:** Slab. (Foundation & framing conversion diagram available — see order form.) | |
| **Blueprint Price Code:** | G |

# Living in Symmetry

- This symmetrical Plantation-style home offers tremendous room for relaxation.
- Large formal areas that overlook the dramatic columned porch flank the big foyer.
- At the center of the home is a spacious Great Room with an inviting fireplace and lots of space for family gatherings.
- Nestled between the Great Room and the Keeping Room, which also offers a fireplace, is a wet bar. The adjoining

kitchen features a modern island worktop.
- The spectacular master suite has his 'n hers baths, two walk-in closets and a spiral staircase access to the study on the upper level.
- A versatile sitting room rests at the center of the upper floor, surrounded by three bedrooms, two baths and a study or optional fifth bedroom. Generous closet space is found throughout.

| Plan V-4566 | |
|---|---|
| **Bedrooms:** 4-5 | **Baths:** 4½ |
| **Space:** | |
| Upper floor | 1,847 sq. ft. |
| Main floor | 2,719 sq. ft. |
| **Total Living Area** | **4,566 sq. ft.** |
| **Exterior Wall Framing** | 2x6 |
| **Foundation options:** | |
| Crawlspace | |
| (Foundation & framing conversion diagram available—see order form.) | |
| **Blueprint Price Code** | **G** |

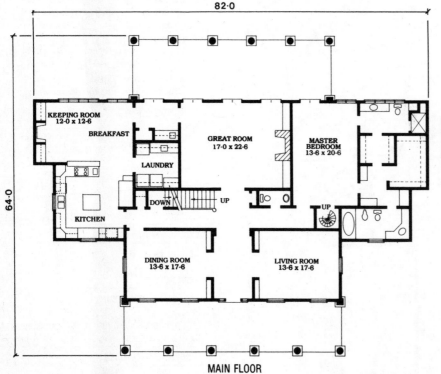

**MAIN FLOOR**

KEEPING ROOM
12-0 x 12-6

BREAKFAST

LAUNDRY

KITCHEN

GREAT ROOM
17-0 x 22-6

MASTER BEDROOM
13-6 x 20-6

DOWN

UP

UP

DINING ROOM
13-6 x 17-6

LIVING ROOM
13-6 x 17-6

82·0

64·0

**UPPER FLOOR**

BEDROOM
17-0 x 22-6

STUDY
9-6 x 13-0

SITTING ROOM
14-0 x 15-6

DOWN

DOWN

BEDROOM
13-6 x 17-6

BEDROOM
13-6 x 17-6

**TO ORDER THIS BLUEPRINT, CALL TOLL-FREE 1-800-547-5570**

Plan V-4566

**PRICES AND DETAILS ON PAGES 12-15**

# Panoramic Porch

- A gracious, ornate rounded front porch and a two-story turreted bay lend a Victorian charm to this home.
- A two-story foyer with round-top transom windows and plant ledge above greets guests at the entry.
- The living room enjoys a panoramic view overlooking the front porch and yard.
- The formal dining room and den each feature a bay window for added style.
- The kitchen/breakfast room incorporates an angled island cooktop, from which the sunken family room with corner fireplace can be enjoyed.
- The three bedrooms and two full baths upstairs are highlighted by a stunning master suite. The master bath offers a quaint octagonal sitting area within the turret bay.

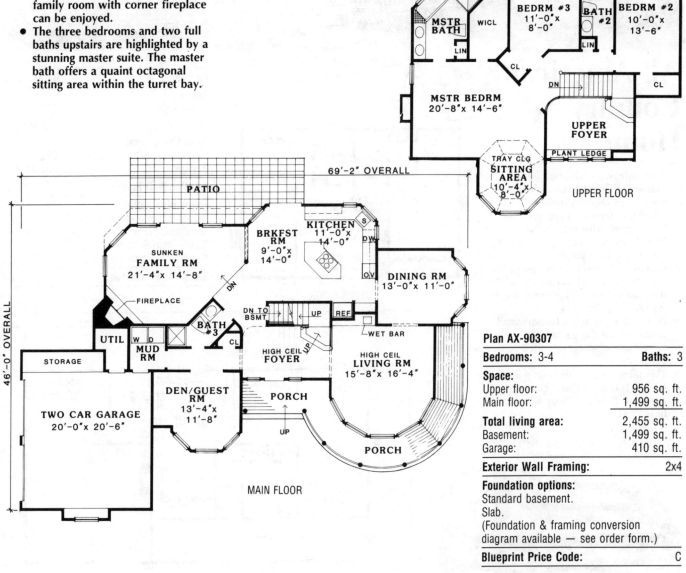

**UPPER FLOOR**

**MAIN FLOOR**

## Plan AX-90307

| Bedrooms: 3-4 | Baths: 3 |
|---|---|

| Space: | |
|---|---|
| Upper floor: | 956 sq. ft. |
| Main floor: | 1,499 sq. ft. |

| Total living area: | 2,455 sq. ft. |
|---|---|
| Basement: | 1,499 sq. ft. |
| Garage: | 410 sq. ft. |

| Exterior Wall Framing: | 2x4 |
|---|---|

**Foundation options:**
Standard basement.
Slab.
(Foundation & framing conversion diagram available — see order form.)

| Blueprint Price Code: | C |
|---|---|

Photo: Kershner Communications

# All-American Country Home

- Romantic, old-fashioned and spacious living areas combine to create this modern home.
- Off the entryway is the generous living room with fireplace and French doors which open onto the traditional rear porch.
- Country kitchen features an island table for informal occasions, while the adjoining family room is ideal for family gatherings.
- Practically placed, a laundry/mud room lies off the garage for immediate disposal of soiled garments.
- This plan is available with garage (H-3711-1) or without garage (H-3711-2) and with or without basement.

**\*\*NOTE:** The above photographed home may have been modified by the homeowner. Please refer to floor plan and/or drawn elevation shown for actual blueprint details.

PLANS H-3711-1 & H-3711-1A
(WITH GARAGE)

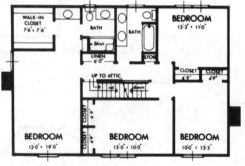

UPPER FLOOR

| Plans H-3711-1/1A & -2/2A | |
|---|---|
| **Bedrooms:** 4 | **Baths:** 2½ |

| **Space:** | |
|---|---|
| Upper floor: | 1,176 sq. ft. |
| Main floor: | 1,288 sq. ft. |

| **Total living area:** | 2,464 sq. ft. |
|---|---|
| Basement: | approx. 1,288 sq. ft. |
| Garage: | 505 sq. ft. |

| **Exterior Wall Framing:** | 2x6 |
|---|---|

**Foundation options:**
Standard basement (Plans H-3711-1 & -2).
Crawlspace (Plans H-3711-1A & -2A).
(Foundation & framing conversion diagram available — see order form.)

| **Blueprint Price Code:** | C |
|---|---|

PLANS H-3711-2 & H-3711-2A
(WITHOUT GARAGE)

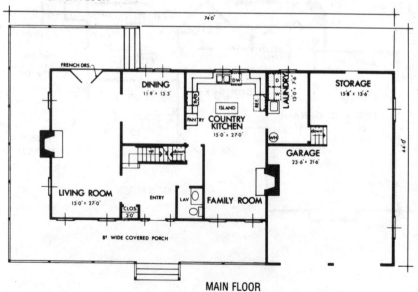

MAIN FLOOR

## Plans H-3711-1/1A & -2/2A

*PRICES AND DETAILS ON PAGES 12-15*

# "Down-Home" Country Flavor

### AREAS

| | |
|---|---|
| Living | 2522 sq. ft. |
| Garage | 484 sq. ft. |
| Porches | 444 sq. ft. |
| Storage Rooms | 90 sq. ft. |
| Total | 3540 sq. ft. |

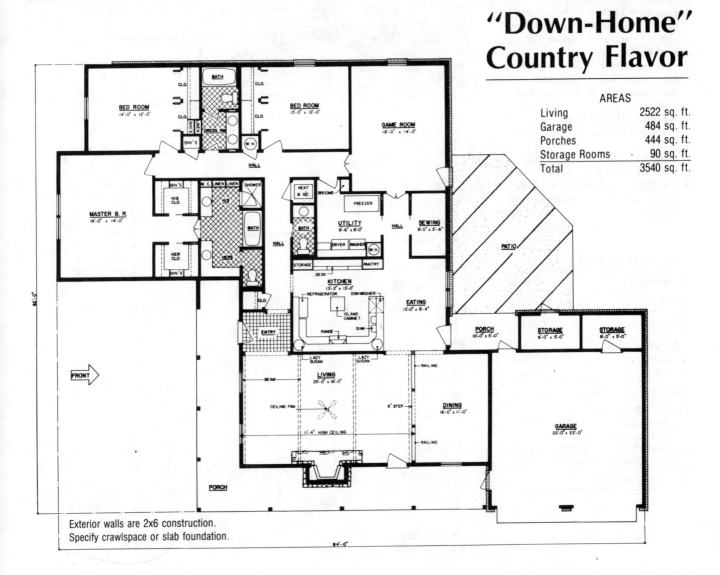

Exterior walls are 2x6 construction.
Specify crawlspace or slab foundation.

**TO ORDER THIS BLUEPRINT,**
**CALL TOLL-FREE 1-800-547-5570**

Blueprint Price Code D
## Plan E-2502

*PRICES AND DETAILS*
*ON PAGES 12-15*

211

# Luxury Home with Outdoor Orientation

- Courtyards, patios and a sun room orient this multi-level home to the outdoors.
- Interior design is carefully zoned for informal family living and formal entertaining.
- Expansive kitchen includes large island and plenty of counter space, and a sunny nook adjoins the kitchen.
- Soaring entry area leads visitors to the vaulted living room with fireplace, or to the more casual family room.
- An optional fourth bedroom off the foyer would make an ideal home office.
- Upstairs master suite includes luxury bath and big walk-in closet.
- Daylight basement version adds nearly 1,500 more square feet of space.

## Plans P-7659-3A & -3D

| Bedrooms: 3-4 | Baths: 3 |
|---|---|

| **Space:** | |
|---|---|
| Upper floor: | 1,050 sq. ft. |
| Main floor: | 1,498 sq. ft. |
| **Total living area:** | 2,548 sq. ft. |
| Basement: | 1,490 sq. ft. |
| Garage: | 583 sq. ft. |

| **Exterior Wall Framing:** | 2x4 |
|---|---|

**Foundation options:**
Daylight basement, Plan P-7659-3D.
Crawlspace, Plan P-7659-3A.
(Foundation & framing conversion diagram available — see order form.)

| **Blueprint Price Code:** | D |
|---|---|

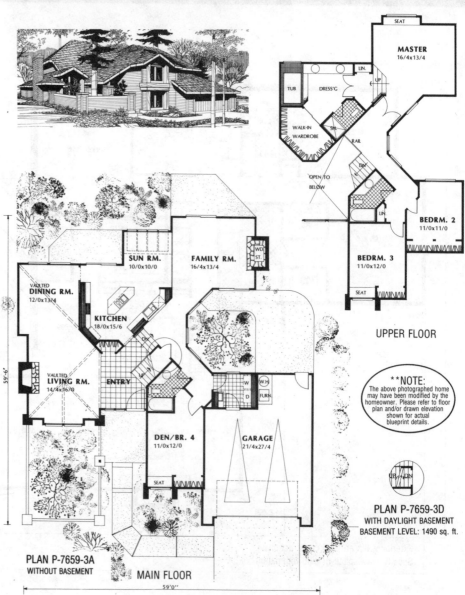

SUN RM.
10/0x10/0

FAMILY RM.
16/4x13/4

VAULTED
DINING RM.
12/0x13/4

KITCHEN
18/0x15/6

VAULTED
LIVING RM.
14/4x16/0

ENTRY

DEN/BR. 4
11/0x12/0

GARAGE
21/4x27/4

SEAT

MASTER
16/4x13/4

TUB   DRESS'G

LIN.

WALK-IN
WARDROBE   SH.

RAIL

OPEN TO
BELOW

BEDRM. 2
11/0x11/0

BEDRM. 3
11/0x12/0

SEAT

UPPER FLOOR

**NOTE:
The above photographed home may have been modified by the homeowner. Please refer to floor plan and/or drawn elevation shown for actual blueprint details.

PLAN P-7659-3D
WITH DAYLIGHT BASEMENT
BASEMENT LEVEL: 1490 sq. ft.

PLAN P-7659-3A
WITHOUT BASEMENT

MAIN FLOOR

59'0"

59'-6"

**TO ORDER THIS BLUEPRINT,
CALL TOLL-FREE 1-800-547-5570**

## Plans P-7659-3A & -3D

**PRICES AND DETAILS
ON PAGES 12-15**

# Gracious Open-Concept Floor Plan

- A striking and luxurious contemporary, this home offers great space and modern styling.
- A covered entry leads to a spacious foyer, which flows into the sunken dining and Great Room area.
- The vaulted Great Room boasts a spectacular two-story-high fireplace, dramatic window walls and access to a rear deck or patio.
- A bright nook adjoins the open kitchen, which includes a corner window above the sink.
- The den, which could be a guest bedroom, features a bay window overlooking the deck.
- The majestic master bedroom on the second floor offers a 10-ft.-high coved ceiling, a splendid bath, a large closet and a private deck.
- Two other upstairs bedrooms share a second bath and a balcony hallway overlooking the Great Room and entry below.

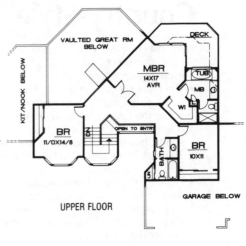

UPPER FLOOR

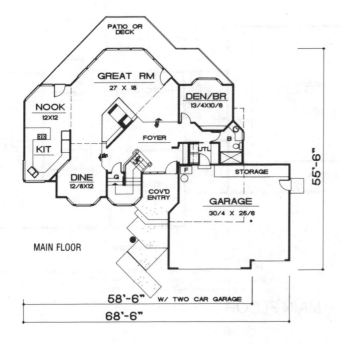

MAIN FLOOR

| Plan S-41587 | |
|---|---|
| **Bedrooms:** 3-4 | **Baths:** 3 |
| **Living Area:** | |
| Upper floor: | 1,001 sq. ft. |
| Main floor | 1,550 sq. ft. |
| **Total Living Area:** | **2,551 sq. ft.** |
| Basement | 1,550 sq. ft. |
| Garage (three-car) | 773 sq. ft. |
| **Exterior Wall Framing:** | 2x6 |

**Foundation Options:**
Daylight basement
Standard basement
Crawlspace
Slab
(Typical foundation & framing conversion diagram available—see order form.)

| **BLUEPRINT PRICE CODE:** | D |
|---|---|

Photo by Felice Photographers

# Classic Country-Style

- Almost completely surrounded by an expansive porch, this classic plan exudes warmth and grace.
- The foyer is liberal in size and leads guests to a formal dining room to the left or the large living room to the right.
- A large country kitchen includes a sunny, bay-windowed breakfast nook.
- The main floor also includes a utility area and full bath.
- Upstairs, the master suite is impressive, with its large sleeping area, big closet and magnificent bath.
- Three secondary bedrooms with ample closets share a full bath with double sinks.
- Also note the stairs leading up to an attic, which is useful for storage space.

**Plan J-86134**

| Bedrooms: 4 | Baths: 3 |
|---|---|
| **Living Area:** | |
| Upper floor | 1,195 sq. ft. |
| Main floor | 1,370 sq. ft. |
| **Total Living Area** | **2,565 sq. ft.** |
| Basement | 1,370 sq. ft. |
| Garage | 576 sq. ft. |
| Storage | 144 sq. ft. |
| **Exterior Wall Framing** | 2x4 |

**Foundation Options:**

Standard basement
Crawlspace
Slab
(Typical foundation & framing conversion diagram available—see order form.)

| **BLUEPRINT PRICE CODE** | D |
|---|---|

**NOTE:**
The above photographed home may have been modified by the homeowner. Please refer to floor plan and/or drawn elevation shown for actual blueprint details.

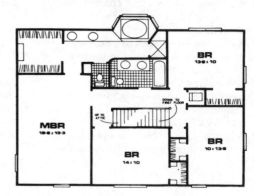

## UPPER FLOOR

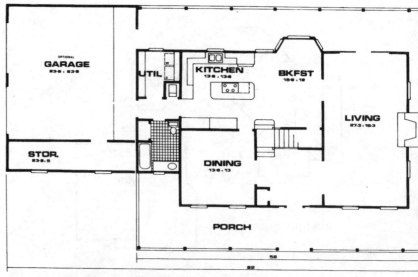

## MAIN FLOOR

***TO ORDER THIS BLUEPRINT,***
***CALL TOLL-FREE 1-800-547-5570***

Plan J-86134

**PRICES AND DETAILS**
**ON PAGES 12-15**

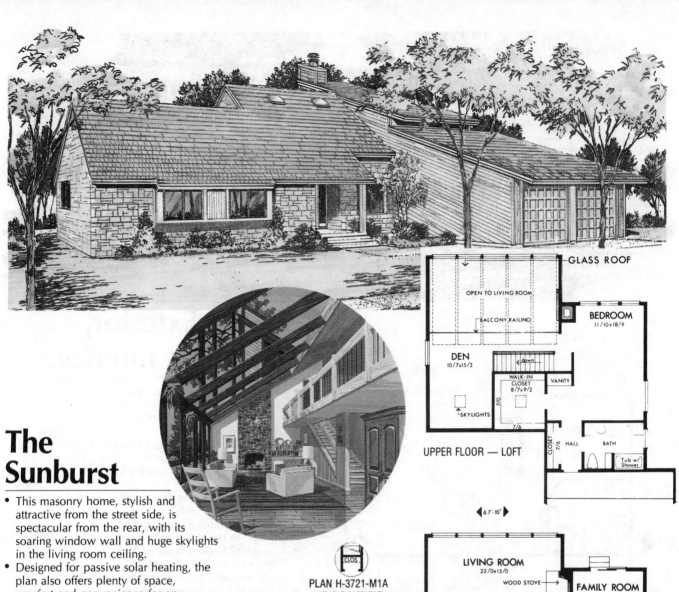

# The Sunburst

- This masonry home, stylish and attractive from the street side, is spectacular from the rear, with its soaring window wall and huge skylights in the living room ceiling.
- Designed for passive solar heating, the plan also offers plenty of space, comfort and convenience for any family.
- Note the master suite, which occupies the entire second floor. Besides a spacious sleeping area, the suite includes a private bath, a dressing area, a huge walk-in closet and a balcony sitting room or den.

### Plans H-3721-M1 & -M1A

| Bedrooms: 4 | Baths: 3½ |
|---|---|
| **Space:** | |
| Upper floor | 757 sq. ft. |
| Main floor | 1,888 sq. ft. |
| **Total Living Area** | **2,645 sq. ft.** |
| Basement | 1,234 sq. ft. |
| Garage | 458 sq. ft. |
| **Exterior Wall Framing** | **2x6** |
| **Foundation options:** | **Plan #** |
| Partial Basement | H-3721-M1 |
| Crawlspace | H-3721-M1A |
| (Foundation & framing conversion diagram available—see order form.) | |
| **Blueprint Price Code** | **D** |

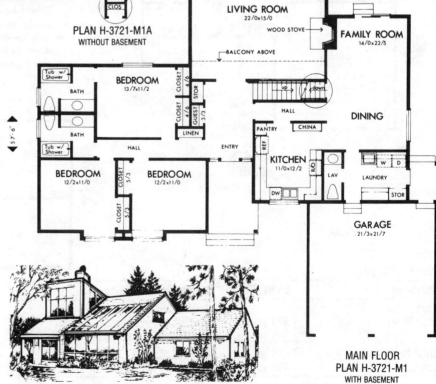

**UPPER FLOOR — LOFT**

GLASS ROOF

OPEN TO LIVING ROOM

BALCONY RAILING

BEDROOM
11/10 x 18/9

DEN
10/7 x 15/3

WALK-IN CLOSET
8/7 x 9/2

VANITY

SKYLIGHTS

CLOSET

HALL

BATH

Tub w/ Shower

◄ 67'-10" ►

PLAN H-3721-M1A
WITHOUT BASEMENT

CLOS

LIVING ROOM
22/0 x 15/0

WOOD STOVE

FAMILY ROOM
14/0 x 22/5

BALCONY ABOVE

Tub w/ Shower
BATH

BEDROOM
13/7 x 11/2

CLOSET

STOR

GUEST

UP

DOWN

HALL

DINING

LINEN

Tub w/ Shower
BATH

HALL

BEDROOM
12/2 x 11/0

CLOSET

BEDROOM
12/2 x 11/0

ENTRY

PANTRY

CHINA

REF

KITCHEN
11/0 x 12/2

LAV

W D

LAUNDRY

DW

R.O.

STOR

57'-6"

GARAGE
21/3 x 21/7

**MAIN FLOOR**
**PLAN H-3721-M1**
WITH BASEMENT

# Simple Exterior, Luxurious Interior

- Modest and unassuming on the exterior, this design provides an elegant and spacious interior.
- Highlight of the home is undoubtedly the vast Great Room/ Dining area, with its vaulted ceiling, massive hearth and big bay windows.
- An exceptionally fine master suite is also included, with a large sleeping area, luxurious bath and big walk-in closet.
- A beautiful kitchen is joined by a bright bay-windowed breakfast nook; also note the large pantry.
- The lower level encompasses two more bedrooms and a generously sized game room and bar.

**MAIN FLOOR**

49'3''

50'8''

RAILING

DECK

HOT TUB

MASTER
19/0x14/0

VAULTED
GREAT RM.
21/6x17/6

VAULTED
DINING
14/4x10/6

PLNTR.

SUNKEN
TUB

DRESSING

WALK IN
WARDROBE

BATH

LIN

RAIL

SKYLIGHT

PANTRY

REF

VAULTED
ENTRY

KITCHEN
13/6x10/6

DW

GARAGE
21/4x21/8

NOOK
10/0x10/0

PATIO

FLOOR LINE ABOVE

BEDRM. 2
12/8x10/8

TUB

WOODSTOVE

BATH

GAME RM.
21/6x17/0

BEDRM. 3
12/0x11/4

LINEN

UTILITY

WH

F

W
D

BAR

**BASEMENT**

## Plan P-6595-3D

| Bedrooms: 3 | Baths: 2½ |
|---|---|

**Space:**

| | |
|---|---|
| Main floor: | 1,530 sq. ft. |
| Lower level: | 1,145 sq. ft. |
| **Total living area:** | **2,675 sq. ft.** |
| Garage: | 462 sq. ft. |

| Exterior Wall Framing: | 2x6 |
|---|---|

**Foundation options:**
Daylight basement only.
(Foundation & framing conversion diagram available — see order form.)

| Blueprint Price Code: | D |
|---|---|

**TO ORDER THIS BLUEPRINT,**
**CALL TOLL-FREE 1-800-547-5570**

## Plan P-6595-3D

*PRICES AND DETAILS*
*ON PAGES 12-15*

**\*\*NOTE:**
The above photographed home may have been modified by the homeowner. Please refer to floor plan and/or drawn elevation shown for actual blueprint details.

69$^{11}$

LANAI

MASTER BEDROOM
14$^6$ X 23$^0$

FAMILY ROOM
17$^4$ X 18$^4$

LIVING ROOM
18$^0$ X 18$^0$

M. BATH

WET BAR

MORNING
12$^0$ X 12$^0$

FOYER

BATH 2

STUDY
11$^4$ X 12$^6$

DINING
12$^0$ X 14$^4$

PANTRY

ISLAND KITCHEN
13$^6$ X 14$^0$

BEDROOM 2
13$^6$ X 12$^4$

BEDROOM 3
12$^4$ X 14$^8$

PORCH

UTILITY

1/2 BATH

81$^5$

GARAGE
24$^0$ X 23$^8$

## Plan DD-2802

| | |
|---|---|
| **Bedrooms:** 3-4 | **Baths:** 2½ |

**Space:**

| | |
|---|---|
| Main floor | 2,899 sq. ft. |
| **Total Living Area** | **2,899 sq. ft.** |
| Basement | 2,899 sq. ft. |
| Garage | 568 sq. ft. |
| **Exterior Wall Framing** | 2x4 |

**Foundation options:**
Basement
Crawlspace
Slab
(Foundation & framing conversion diagram available—see order form.)

| | |
|---|---|
| **Blueprint Price Code** | D |

# Unique Inside and Out

- This plan gives new dimension to one-story living. The exterior features graceful arched windows and a sweeping roofline The interior is marked by unusual angles and curves.
- The living areas are clustered around a large "lanai," or covered porch. French doors in the master bedroom and the family room angle toward the porch.
- Extras include the two-way fireplace, warming both the family room and the living room. The home's expansiveness is enhanced by ceilings that slope up to 10 feet. Columns frame both the living room and the formal dining room, echoing the columns of the porches.
- The island kitchen and the morning room are open to the family room, which features a wet bar. The living room is highlighted by French doors and arched transom windows.
- The formal dining room and the study are stationed near the front of the home, away from the major activity areas.
- The master bedroom includes an irresistible bath with a spa tub, dual vanities, two walk-in closets and a separate shower.
- Two more good-sized bedrooms share another full bath.
- A large utility room and a half-bath are conveniently located between the kitchen and the garage.

*TO ORDER THIS BLUEPRINT,*
*CALL TOLL-FREE 1-800-547-5570*

Plan DD-2802

*PRICES AND DETAILS*
*ON PAGES 12-15*

**217**

# Pure Luxury in a Choice of Styles

- Southwestern colonial or Western contemporary exteriors are available when deciding if this spacious design is for you.
- Elaborate master suite features attached screened spa room, regular and walk-in closets, and luxurious bath with skylight.

- Study, large family and living room with sloped ceilings and rear patio are other points of interest.
- Three additional bedrooms make up the second level.
- The Spanish version (M2A) offers a stucco exterior and slab foundation.

### Plans H-3714-1/1A/1B/M2A

| Bedrooms: 4 | Baths: 3 |
|---|---|
| **Space:** | |
| Upper floor: | 740 sq. ft. |
| Main floor: | 2,190 sq. ft. |
| **Total living area:** | **2,930 sq. ft.** |
| Basement: | 1,153 sq. ft. |
| Garage: | 576 sq. ft. |
| **Exterior Wall Framing:** | 2x6 |

**Foundation options:**
Daylight basement (Plan H-3714-1B).
Standard basement (Plan H-3714-1).
Crawlspace (Plan H-3714-1A).
Slab (Plan H-3714-M2A).
(Foundation & framing conversion diagram available — see order form.)

**Blueprint Price Code:** D

UPPER FLOOR

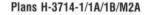

MAIN FLOOR

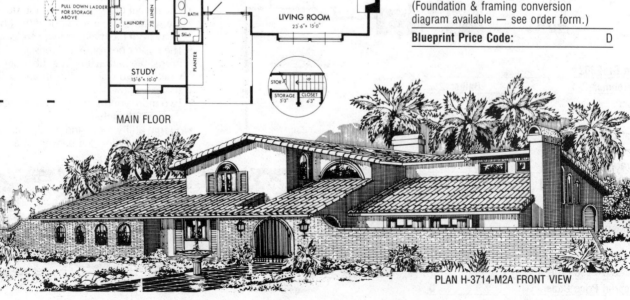

PLAN H-3714-M2A FRONT VIEW

**TO ORDER THIS BLUEPRINT,**
**CALL TOLL-FREE 1-800-547-5570**

# Plans H-3714-1/1A/1B/M2A

**PRICES AND DETAILS**
**ON PAGES 12-15**

FRONT VIEW

Photos by Mark Englund

# Magnificent Courtyard

- This gorgeous home's unusual parking court creates the feeling of driving through the front gates of a magnificent country estate.
- A tall, covered porch gives guests an impressive welcome. Transoms beautify the exterior and brighten the interior.
- Interior columns give the entry a regal flair and define the formal dining room, which boasts a 13-ft. coffered ceiling.
- The parlor could serve as a sitting room, living room or den. It boasts a fireplace, bookshelves and a 10½-ft. ceiling.
- The island kitchen, eating area and vaulted family room offer a fireplace and French doors to a secluded deck.
- The master suite leaves nothing out, with its coffered ceiling, large walk-in closet, Jacuzzi tub and separate shower.
- A roomy bath is featured in the children's wing. A fourth bedroom gives space for hobbies and exercise.
- Ceiling heights are at least 9 ft. throughout the home, enhancing the spacious feeling.

REAR VIEW

**NOTE:**
The above photographed home may have been modified by the homeowner. Please refer to floor plan and/or drawn elevation shown for actual blueprint details.

### Plan NW-464

| Bedrooms: 4 | Baths: 3 |
|---|---|
| **Living Area:** | |
| Main floor | 2,671 sq. ft. |
| **Total Living Area:** | **2,671 sq. ft.** |
| Attached garage | 525 sq. ft. |
| Detached garage | 435 sq. ft. |
| **Exterior Wall Framing:** | 2x6 |

**Foundation Options:**
Crawlspace
(Typical foundation & framing conversion diagram available—see order form.)

| **BLUEPRINT PRICE CODE:** | D |
|---|---|

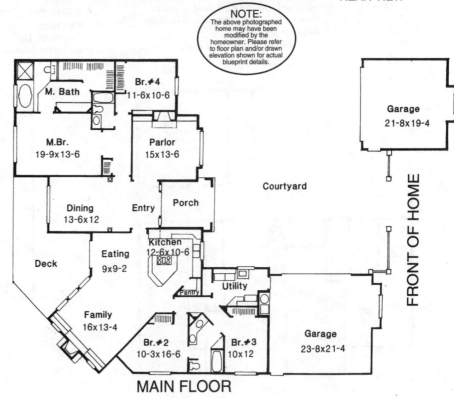

MAIN FLOOR

# Wrap-around Porch Accents Victorian Farmhouse

- Fish-scale shingles and horizontal siding team with the detailed front porch to create this look of yesterday. The sides and rear are brick.
- The main level features a center section

of informal family room and formal living and dining rooms. They can all be connected via French doors.

- A separate workshop is located on the main level and connected to the main house by a covered breezeway.
- The master bath ceiling is sloped and has built-in skylights. The kitchen and eating area have high sloped ceilings also. Typical ceiling heights are 8' on the basement and upper level and 10' on the main level.
- This home is energy efficient.
- This home is designed on a full daylight basement. The two-car garage is located under the workshop.

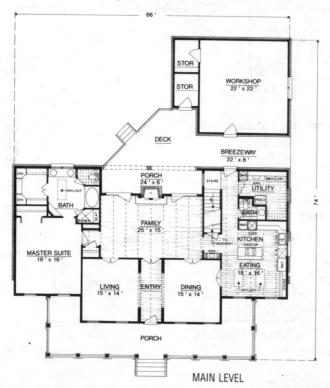

MAIN LEVEL

UPPER LEVEL
PLAN E-3103
WITH DAYLIGHT BASEMENT

Exterior walls are 2x6 construction.

Heated area:          3,153 sq. ft.
Unheated area         2,066 sq. ft.

Total area:           5,219 sq. ft.
(Not counting basement)

Blueprint Price Code E
## Plan E-3103

**PRICES AND DETAILS ON PAGES 12-15**

# Striking Octagonal Solarium

- The center of attraction in this dramatic design is the sunsoaking passive sun room. This 20' diameter solarium reaches above the roofline to capture the most possible solar energy from any direction.
- For passive cooling, several of the vertical windows in the dome can be opened. The room also includes a "splash pool" to provide humidity in the winter.
- Then rooms surrounding the solarium are equally striking, as well as spacious and convenient, providing plenty of space for casual family living as well as more formal entertaining.
- The master suite includes a bath fit for royalty and a huge walk-in closet. Two secondary bedrooms share a large second bath with separate tub and shower and double sinks.

### Plans H-3719-1 & -1A

| Bedrooms: 3 | Baths: 2½ |
|---|---|

**Space:**

| | |
|---|---|
| **Total living area:** | 3,166 sq. ft. |
| (Includes 324 sq. ft. sun room) | |
| Basement (under bedrooms & family room): | approx. 1,400 sq. ft. |
| Garage: | 850 sq. ft. |
| Storage: | 132 sq. ft. |

| **Exterior Wall Framing:** | 2x6 |
|---|---|

**Foundation options:**
Partial basement (H-3719-1).
Crawlspace (H-3719-1A)
(Foundation & framing conversion diagram available — see order form.)

| **Blueprint Price Code:** | E |
|---|---|

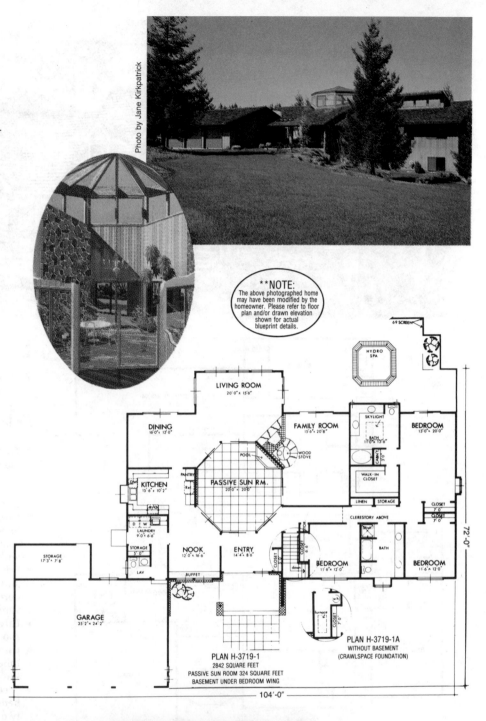

Photo by Jane Kirkpatrick

**\*\*NOTE:**
The above photographed home may have been modified by the homeowner. Please refer to floor plan and/or drawn elevation shown for actual blueprint details.

PLAN H-3719-1
2842 SQUARE FEET
PASSIVE SUN ROOM 324 SQUARE FEET
BASEMENT UNDER BEDROOM WING

PLAN H-3719-1A
WITHOUT BASEMENT
(CRAWLSPACE FOUNDATION)

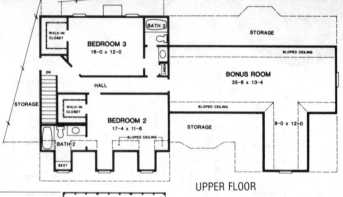

UPPER FLOOR

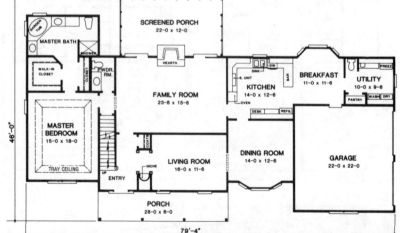

MAIN FLOOR

# Deluxe Main-Floor Master Suite

- Traditional-style exterior with modern floor plan. Dormers and stone add curb appeal to this home.
- Formal entry with staircase leads to formal living or large family room.
- Large kitchen is conveniently located between formal dining room and secluded breakfast nook with bay window.
- Private master suite has tray ceiling and walk-in closet. Master bath has corner tub, shower, and dual vanities.
- Large screened porch off family room is perfect for outdoor living.
- Large utility room with pantry and toilet are conveniently located off the garage.
- Second floor features two large bedrooms with walk-in closets and two full baths.
- Optional bonus room (624 sq. ft.) can be finished as a large game room, bedroom, office, etc.

## Plan C-8915

| Bedrooms: 3 | Baths: 3½ |
|---|---|

**Space:**

| | |
|---|---|
| Upper floor: | 832 sq. ft. |
| Main floor: | 1,927 sq. ft. |
| Bonus area: | 624 sq. ft. |
| **Total living area:** | **3,383 sq. ft.** |
| Basement: | 1,674 sq. ft. |
| Garage: | 484 sq. ft. |

| **Exterior Wall Framing:** | 2x4 |
|---|---|

**Ceiling Heights:**

| | |
|---|---|
| First floor: | 9' |
| Second floor: | 8' |

**Foundation options:**
Daylight basement.
Crawlspace.
(Foundation & framing conversion diagram available — see order form.)

| **Blueprint Price Code:** | E |
|---|---|

PLAN H-2114-1B REAR VIEW

# Designed for Outdoor Living

- Dining room, living room, and spa are oriented toward the full-width deck extending across the rear of the home.
- Floor-to-ceiling windows, vaulted ceilings, and a fireplace are featured in the living room.
- Spa room has tile floor, operable skylights, and private access through connecting master suite.
- Upper level offers two bedrooms, spacious bathroom, and a balcony view of the living room and scenery beyond.

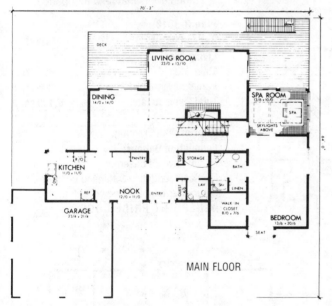

MAIN FLOOR

PLAN H-2114-1A
WITHOUT BASEMENT

PLAN H-2114-1B
WITH DAYLIGHT BASEMENT

UPPER FLOOR

## Plans H-2114-1A & -1B

| Bedrooms: 3-4 | Baths: 2½-3½ |
|---|---|

**Space:**

| | |
|---|---|
| Upper floor: | 732 sq. ft. |
| Main floor: | 1,682 sq. ft. |
| Spa room: | 147 sq. ft. |

| | |
|---|---|
| **Total living area:** | 2,561 sq. ft. |
| Basement: | approx. 1,386 sq. ft. |
| Garage: | 547 sq. ft. |

| **Exterior Wall Framing:** | 2x6 |
|---|---|

**Foundation options:**
Daylight basement (Plan H-2114-1B).
Crawlspace (Plan H-2114-1A).
(Foundation & framing conversion diagram available — see order form.)

**Blueprint Price Code:**

| Without basement: | D |
|---|---|
| With basement: | F |

# Distinguished Design

- This home's distinguished facade boasts stately columns, elegant arched windows and an eye-catching roofline.
- Coved ceilings enhance the formal entry and the sunken living room beyond. Decorative planters flank the steps between these two areas. The living room also offers a fireplace and access to a rear deck.
- The sunken family room has a second fireplace and French doors opening to the deck.
- The island kitchen includes a pantry and a corner window sink. The adjacent breakfast nook features French doors to a secluded deck.
- Double doors introduce the unusual master suite, which features a striking bed alcove framed by a soffit. Deck access, a walk-in closet and a luxurious bath are also included.
- A curved stairway leads to the walk-out basement, highlighted by a generous recreation room with a fireplace and French doors that lead to a patio.

| Plan R-3010 | |
|---|---|
| **Bedrooms:** 4 | **Baths:** 3½ |
| **Living Area:** | |
| Main floor | 3,823 sq. ft. |
| Partial daylight basement | 1,285 sq. ft. |
| **Total Living Area:** | **5,108 sq. ft.** |
| Garage | 811 sq. ft. |
| **Exterior Wall Framing:** | 2x6 |

**Foundation Options:**
Partial daylight basement
(Typical foundation & framing conversion diagram available—see order form.)

| **BLUEPRINT PRICE CODE:** | **G** |
|---|---|

## MAIN FLOOR

112'5"

71'4"

DECK

SUNKEN FAMILY 18/0 X 20/6

NOOK 13/3 X 10/6

MASTER 16/6 X 21/0

SUNKEN LIVING 18/3 X 20/6

KITCHEN 14/6 X 16/6

BR. 2 13/10 X 15/10

GARAGE 33/4 X 24/4

PANTRY

UTIL

DINING 14/0 X 18/0

STUDY 14/0 X 14/0

DN

## DAYLIGHT BASEMENT

PATIO

BR. 3 12/4 X 15/0

REC RM 32/0 X 27/0

BAR

UP

BR. 4 11/10 X 12/0

## Plan R-3010

**PRICES AND DETAILS ON PAGES 12-15**